We Are Family
Sibling relationships in placement
and beyond

Acknowledgements

I should like to thank Sarah Borthwick and Shaila Shah from BAAF for encouraging me to bring together this edited collection, the contributors for making it so rich, Phillida Sawbridge and Sarah Borthwick, the readers of the manuscript, for their support and helpful comments, and Peter Wedge for contributing such an enthusiastic foreword. Above all, to those who have shared their personal experiences, either directly in these pages or indirectly through the research reported here, I extend my warmest appreciation of your courage and honesty. I hope that this book will encourage a wide audience to think deeply and constructively about the experiences of siblings and that policy developments and changes may result.

Note about the Editor

Audrey Mullender is Professor of Social Work at the University of Warwick. She is Editor of the *British Journal of Social Work* and has herself produced over 90 publications in the social work field, including ten books. Two of these were published by BAAF: an edited collection in 1991, '*Open Adoption: The philosophy and the practice*', and, in 1997, '*I'm Here Waiting': Birth relatives' views on Part II of the Adoption Contact Register for England and Wales*, written jointly with Sarah Kearn.

To Lesley, sister and friend

We Are Family
Sibling relationships in placement and beyond

Edited by Audrey Mullender

British
Agencies
for **A**doption
and **F**ostering

Published by
British Agencies for Adoption & Fostering
(BAAF)
Skyline House
200 Union Street
London SE1 0LX

© Audrey Mullender 1999

Charity registration 275689

**British Library Cataloguing in Publication
Data**
A catalogue record for this book is available
from the British Library

ISBN 1 873868 79 0

Designed by Andrew Haig & Associates
Typeset by Avon Dataset Ltd, Bidford on Avon
Printed by Russell Press Ltd. (TU),
Nottingham

Contents

Foreword

Peter Wedge

The critical importance of siblings to one another is still seriously under-recognised. That they can too often be irritants to each other is common knowledge; that they can also be vitally supportive – mutually – at times of stress seems less well understood.

Twenty years ago psychologists had made few systematic studies of sibling interactions. Social workers, magistrates and judges had to rely on their hunches in taking far-reaching decisions about groups of brothers and sisters coming to their notice. They worried about the wisdom or foolishness of causing family groups to be separated, or to be kept together. While such dilemmas remain, a body of knowledge is being constructed and the chapters in this volume – many of them written by social work professionals – make a significant contribution. In other words, the knowledge gap pointed out, notably by Jones and Niblett in their brief article in 1985, is beginning to close. Not that there are, or ever can be, neat and tidy answers in all situations. No one who reads the pages which follow can be in any doubt about that. Family members want to live happily together, of course. When they cannot do so, individuals are left with what amounts to second best, or third best, or worse. Given that human development and human relationships frequently advance in incomprehensible ways, professionals "managing" the second best, or worse, option will sometimes make wrong decisions. If they have heeded the contents of this volume, however, they will be sensitised to sibling concerns, as well as informed by new research into outcomes, service deficiencies, perspectives, children's views and the like.

That so many contributors have sought to address the sibling dimension reflects its past neglect and its continuing importance. They also reflect concerns about information gathering and service delivery which, as Audrey Mullender concludes, often result in the separation of sibling groups 'without intent or on the basis of practice assumptions that are not borne out by research'. The studies here reported also show that contact, as 'the next best thing to a shared placement', remains 'a very hit or miss affair', and that children themselves seem rarely to be consulted.

In our 1991 report (*Sibling Groups and Social Work*), Greg Mantle and I wrote:

> *The importance of siblings to each other is a fact vital to all engaged in child care social work, particularly those involved in reception into care and placement in substitute families. Wherever practicable, in all social work activity with children and families, sibling relationships should be enabled to take their natural course in recognition of the (sometimes closet) importance of brothers and sisters to one another. When siblings must be separated then there remains a powerful case for ensuring that links between them are maintained so that in due course, if they so wish, the individuals can re-unite, and re-locate themselves and their identity in that culture where their social understanding was begun.*

In the light of these conclusions, the papers assembled in this book are particularly apposite and welcome. They draw on a range of more recent examples and perceptions in providing a comprehensive case in support of those earlier conclusions. But beyond that, and crucially, they itemise principles and practices which offer practitioners, managers and policy-makers a way forward to better services for children and their families. In the interests of these service recipients, the book deserves to be widely read and acted upon.

References

Jones M and Niblett R (1985) 'To split or not to split: the placement of siblings', *Adoption & Fostering*, 9:2, pp 26–29.

Wedge P and Mantle G (1991) *Sibling Groups and Social Work*, Aldershot: Avebury.

1   Sketching in the background

Audrey Mullender

In 1964, John Lennon placed an advertisement in a series of newspapers in search of his maternal sister. She had been relinquished for adoption within days of her birth, when John was four, and he had only just learnt of her existence (Harris, 1998). At that time, his sister did not know she was adopted or, obviously therefore, what her original name and connections had been. John did not know his sister's adoptive name and never found her, despite using his wealth and connections to employ private detectives and the extensive reach of the media in his search. When his sister, now known as Ingrid, did find out about her origins in 1966, she decided not to act on the information while her adoptive mother was alive for fear of hurting her feelings (*cf.* Haimes and Timms, 1985). In the event, John died first and Ingrid never knew him.

Only the name of one of the protagonists and the nature of his death makes this story in any way remarkable. All over the UK there are brothers and sisters in similar circumstances and all post-adoption agencies know about and work with numbers of them. Siblings matter to each other, even when they have no shared history. In this volume, first-hand accounts from adults who were separated from brothers and sisters in childhood through adoption or entry to the care system are contained alongside research findings about placements made long ago and placements being made today. Together, they confirm that the issues of sibling placement, sibling contact and sibling separation warrant urgent attention, though we do already know enough to offer some indications for policy and practice.

Background to this book

The source of many of the contributions to this collection was the first BAAF Research Symposium, in 1997, at which there were a number of presentations about siblings, both current and retrospective, and also a groundswell of interest from practitioners and policy makers requesting some clear indications as to how they might confront the dilemmas they face in daily practice. How do you convince managers that there need to be more sibling group placements available? What can we usefully tell the court when it is considered important to keep siblings together – what are the research findings about this? What decision should be made when a child could now be moved to live with a sibling but meanwhile has made new attachments in an interim placement?

It seemed sensible to bring together the best of contemporary wisdom in this field to try and find some answers. To supplement the work introduced at the symposium, other papers were invited through the pages of *Adoption & Fostering*, with a good response from academics, professionals and those with a personal involvement. This has resulted in the book being organised into sections based around current research, first-hand accounts, and the needs of particular groups in placement and beyond.

But, by way of introduction, let us first review the pre-existing knowledge base in law, research and practice.

The policy and research background

Law and policy

There is only relatively recent and brief mention of siblings in child care legislation and accompanying guidance, though the policy direction is clear when it does emerge. The Children Act 1989 gives us section 23(7), and says, in respect of a looked after child who is being accommodated, that 'a local authority shall . . . so far as is reasonably practicable and consistent with his [sic] welfare, secure that . . . (b) where the authority are also providing accommodation for a sibling of his, they are accommodated together'. There are two "let outs" in this section: it may not be deemed practicable to achieve this shared placement and it may not be considered consistent with the child's welfare to make it. This still leaves social workers with some difficult judgements to make and with a problem if there are too few placements available to take sibling groups. There is no guidance available as to how the law might be used creatively in the interests of siblings. For example, in a situation where birth parents are impeding contact with siblings, a young person who is old enough to initiate legal proceedings might seek to apply for a Contact Order under section 8 of the Children Act 1989.

In respect of adoption, the recent Circular, LAC(98)20, *Adoption: Achieving the right balance*, similarly considers that it is not desirable in normal circumstances that siblings should be separated and advises that, where this does happen, there should be detailed and robust plans for maintaining contact between them. So the issue of contact enters the equation as, normally, the next best thing to placing siblings together.

In addition to a paucity of advice from central government, the situation whereby 'there are few references to siblings in local authority policy documents or practice guides' (Department of Health, 1991, p 27) has not changed over the last decade (see chapters by Beckett and Ellison in this volume). This leaves practitioners often struggling to do what they believe is right (see chapters by Jones and Tomlinson).

Nor is there any greater clarity in the UN Convention on the Rights of the Child (United Nations, 1989) where siblings are not specifically mentioned. Two sections which do have some relevance are Article 8, which states that 'parties undertake to respect the rights of the child to preserve his or her identity, including nationality, name and family relations as recognised by law without unlawful interference', and Article 12 on 'the child's right to express an opinion, and to have that opinion taken into account, in any matter or procedure affecting the child'. There is worrying evidence in the chapters which follow that, arguably, neither of these is being fully adhered to in current practice.

Social work research

Patterns and Outcomes in Child Placements (Department of Health, 1991), a research overview, had somewhat more to say, with two-thirds of a chapter on sibling and step-sibling relationships. The research referred to in that publication includes the psychological material from Judy Dunn and others (see next section) as well as academic social work research.

At the time of *Patterns and Outcomes*, between a third and a half of all admissions to care or accommodation were thought to involve sibling groups (see Beckett, this volume, for varying estimates), with the bulk of the children concerned being pre-adolescent and coming into care from a family crisis or for protection – the classic family breakdown scenarios. Older children with behavioural problems were more likely to come in singly, leaving the rest of the family at home (Department of Health, 1991, citing Farmer and Parker, 1991, and Rowe *et al*, 1989).

Sibling group placement

One of the studies summarised (Fratter *et al*, 1991) reported on a sample of 1,165 placements of special needs children made by voluntary agencies in Britain between 1980 and 1984. Fifty per cent more children placed alone experienced disruption than children placed with siblings. Being placed alone emerged as a risk factor even when other variables were held constant. There was no evidence, for example, that the children in question had more severe problems that might have led both to their being placed singly and also to the disruption of their placements – they had actually had fewer moves and a lower prevalence of deprivation and abuse. Despite the added complications that must be entailed in taking on a family group, not one of the placements of three or more siblings together had disrupted by the end of the study (between 18 months and six years after placement). Similarly, in Wedge and Mantle's (1991) study of the same year, for only 15 children (11 per cent of all children placed) did the 'sibling factor' (p 54) appear to have been associated with the placement coming to an end.

These studies built on others with similar conclusions. Berridge and Cleaver (1987) found that foster home breakdowns were more likely where a child was separated from siblings in care than when placed with some or all of them. Thoburn and Rowe (1988) also found that sibling group placement was a protective factor against breakdown (18 per cent breakdown as against 24 per cent for a child placed alone). At worst, other studies since have found a neutral effect (e.g. Staff and Fein, 1992, in an American context). Being rehabilitated to the family may likewise be more successful when it happens with one or more siblings (Farmer and Parker, 1991).

Despite the apparent benefits of maintaining sibling groups, one of Wedge and Mantle's most striking findings was the lack of information on the files about interactions between siblings (noted also by Farmer and Parker, 1991), and that what information there was did not appear to relate to decisions whether to split or maintain sibling groups. Wedge and Mantle (1991, p 36) wryly comment that this might be just as well 'in view of the difficulty of adults entering children's worlds and forming a reliable assessment of the extent to which siblings are "meaningful" to one another'. This stands in stark contrast to the assumed certainties of the 'Sibling Relationship Check List' in *Patterns and Outcomes* (Department of Health, 1991). Wedge and Mantle also cite Timberlake and Hamlin (1982) who point out that, the more siblings share and the closer they are, the harder it is for anyone else to know what is going on in their interactions because they adapt their behaviour and reactions to one another. Wedge and Mantle reiterate (1991, p 75) that:

> ... what the adult observer witnesses might not reflect the actuality of the relationship. At an extreme, this must mean that adults cannot with any expectation of accuracy judge the strength of sibling relationships. Clearly, much fundamental research is needed on this topic before social worker assessments can be expected to represent accurately the strength of feeling between siblings and the importance of a possible splitting of the children concerned.

Wise words.

Most of the children in Wedge and Mantle's research were placed (133 out of 160), and most of these (88 per cent) were kept together in the group in which they had been referred. Voluntary agencies did particularly well at finding placements for sibling groups and this may have been why statutory agencies referred the children to specialist homefinding projects. Those who had been on referral for over six months became more likely to be split and the older age groups were generally harder to place. About one in five placements disrupted but no more so where children had been kept together than where they had been separated. Seven children ended up split after a joint placement disrupted, six moved on together (including four who went home), and five unexpectedly ended up together. This was because, in two cases where the aim had been to seek separate placements, only one of these went well and the children (one pair and one trio) eventually ended up placed together, i.e. both times in phased placements where the children presumably already knew the family. It may be that staggering the dates of placement with a family could be one way to help some sibling groups settle in (Boer and Spiering, 1991; Hegar, 1993; see also Dance and Rushton, this volume).

Older children and those of mixed parentage have been found to be more likely to become separated (Department of Health, 1991), yet may have been given some of the strongest messages about taking responsibility for young siblings (*cf.* Prevatt Goldstein, this volume). Hence such partings might be particularly distressing for them.

Contact

As well as being at risk of losing their new families through an unplanned end to the placement, in the Fratter *et al* (1991) study, children placed alone were likely to have lost their birth siblings for good. Only one in three of those who had been said to need contact with siblings actually had such contact by follow-up. Yet maintaining contact with the birth family emerged as a protective factor against disruption where it did occur.

Of 29 children in 12 groups who were split in Wedge and Mantle's study, only five lost links in the first six months (not all permanently), but most had 'infrequent or tenuous' links (Wedge and Mantle, 1991, p 48) and there must have been a risk that these would wither over time. The authors note the risks this would pose for siblings who might find it difficult to locate one another later on. Several chapters in this volume bear witness to this, including that by Christine Harrison and all those in the final, post-adoption section.

In Bilson and Barker's (1992/3) study, almost half the children with siblings outside the care system saw them only irregularly or not at all. The lack of contact was even higher among those with siblings else-where *within* the care system. As Bilson and Barker point out, this amounts to very large numbers of children separated from their siblings and having lost contact with them when extrapolated across the whole care system. They acknowledge the practical difficulties for busy and under-resourced social workers in maintaining contact between siblings (as is also graphically described by Jones in this volume), so they recommend giving siblings each other's addresses and telephone numbers and helping them to plan visits and outings themselves.

Placement disruptions, they say, should always be reviewed as potential opportunities to reunite siblings and there should be very clear reasons for separation, which should be explained so that children are not left to blame themselves. They draw attention both to the scale of sibling separation and to the complexity of the sibling relationships involved, issues which are fully explored by Kosonen, Neil and others in this volume. Bilson and Barker also suggest that a neglected area of practice may be that of reuniting siblings while still children, which would certainly forestall some of the difficulties experienced by adults searching for each other (see Shobha and Marylin, Pavlovic and Mullender, Hodgkins, Prynn, this volume).

The research summarised thus far offers very important support both for placing siblings together and, where this is not possible, for maintaining contact with siblings and other birth family members. We might have expected to see these findings being routinely carried through into practice by now, but the research reported in this anthology suggests that this is not the case.

Gaining new siblings

One finding that *has* been carried through into a good deal of placement policy relates to the age gap between the child being placed and other children already in the family. Thirty-four per cent of children in Wedge and Mantle's study gained new adoptive siblings, with 21 per cent gaining two or more. This latter group were at higher risk of disruption, particularly among younger children who were not at least three years younger than a child already in the family (see also Berridge and Cleaver, 1987; Fenyo *et al*, 1989; Boer and Spiering, 1991). Younger children placed as substantially the youngest and those with no new "siblings" did best. Being placed where there were "own" children less than three years older increased the chances of disruption, especially for younger children.

One study in this collection suggests, however, that caution may be advisable before assuming that we have all the answers on age differences. Albeit they were looking at a specific group in very special circumstances, Celia Beckett and her colleagues found among Romanian children adopted into this country that some families who took two children quite close in age did very well and that there appeared to be no additional problems.

Of course "cause and effect" research can never firmly predict success or failure in a specific situation. There is considerable material in this volume on successfully creating sibling groups, including from Wilkings, an adoptive mother who has actually made it work, and various of the chapters in the section on special needs groups. Several of these show how children who are not related by blood can nonetheless meet each other's needs while growing up, for example, where one of the children has a learning disability (Selman and Mason) or where they are looked after in residential care together (Horrocks and Milner). Prevatt Goldstein helps us to think about the brother- and sister-like roles that are played out within a generation of the extended family and in the wider society, and which are recognised in the familiar terms of address of many cultural groupings. Both the chapters by Elgar and Head and by Farmer and Pollock explore the converse situation, where children may threaten each other's safety and well-being, but they still come down in favour of not ruling out sibling and wider birth family contact if safe ways can be found to continue it.

Taken together, all the above work suggests that we would do well to think about children in conjunction with their siblings and other peers, and not solely individually or in relation to significant adults.

Sibling separation

Bilson and Barker (1992/3) found the complex patterns of sibling separation that are echoed in this volume, notably by Kosonen and by Neil. In Bilson and Barker's study of six local authorities in England and Scotland, over half the children described by social workers in 1,068 questionnaire returns had siblings not in the care system and half had siblings elsewhere within it. One in ten had a brother or sister who had been adopted. One in 20 had siblings in all three categories. Of siblings who were looked after or accommodated, three-quarters were separated from at least some, and half from all of their siblings. Yet there were only six cases where the social workers mentioned this as a reason for dissatisfaction with the placement.

Children's own views of siblings

Siblings typically value being placed together (Rowe *et al*, 1984; Whitaker *et al*, 1984) and look to one another for support and protection (Whitaker *et al*, 1984) and for the opportunity to talk about their birth family (Rowe *et al*, 1984). This is not surprising given that children in the general population, across all ethnic groups, consider sibling relationships important; while there may be cultural differences of meaning and expectations (resulting from family obligations, for example), brothers and sisters talk affectionately about their relationships with each other as an everyday mixture of fighting or annoyance on the one hand, and mutual trust and support on the other (Borland *et al*, 1998; Morrow, 1998 – from studies conducted respectively in Scotland and England). For many who are separated, they feel the loss for years, worry about one another, and would like to see one another more often (Whitaker *et al*, 1984) or find each other if lost. They may blame themselves for separation and believe they are being punished (Fisher *et al*, 1986).

Although in around four out of five cases surveyed by Wedge and Mantle workers aimed to keep the siblings together, for almost two-fifths of the children, no reason was given that related to the children themselves and then often only that a 'strong bond' existed between them. Where it was planned to split children up, this was typically recorded as being to meet the 'individual needs of the child' (p 39). As Selwyn's chapter suggests may still be happening, there was a strong suspicion that children were not being consulted. For only a small minority of children did their own views appear to influence the decision and this was more often recorded where the decision was to split the group. Even then, it is not clear that this was what all the siblings wanted or, indeed, what their views actually were on maintaining contact with one another. It is an indictment that this situation persists today.

Psychological research

As Wedge and Mantle (1991, p 73) point out, 'the relevance of sibling relationships to human development is . . . a largely unknown subject'. Certainly the key figure in what limited research has taken place in psychology, beginning in the 1980s and flowering in the early 1990s, Judy Dunn has been called 'the godmother of research in the area of siblings' (Treffers, 1992, p xii). The chief interests of this field of study (Dunn, 1992a) have been the nature of the sibling relationships themselves, their link with parent–child relationships, and their influence on individual adjustment and outcome.

A word of warning

It is important for social workers to remember that this whole area of research is derived from a discipline different from their own and that extreme caution is necessary in interpreting, and particularly in applying, findings arrived at through complex and unfamiliar methodology.

In all psychological research (and other studies that adopt the same, positivist paradigm), there are conventionally understated project design difficulties in deciding what to measure and how, derived from the more fundamental challenge of finding ways to render human behaviour and feelings into units of measurement. For example, in order to boil sibling relationships down to something researchable, Jenkins (1992) looked at how much time the siblings spent together and whether there was evidence of high levels of hostility or of warmth and closeness. Yet, clearly, such measures would not tell us whether the siblings in question mattered to one another or whether they might want a relationship later on. In such studies, children are unlikely to have been asked for their own views and perspectives; their adjustment is more likely to have been judged by carers, teachers or other adults or, at best, they may have been asked to respond to psychological tests based on questions thought relevant by adults. Deeming a sibling relationship less than positive on such measures cannot safely be read off into a practice decision as to whether or not siblings would benefit from being placed together – this is clearly a different and rather more complex issue in which professional judgement is bound to play a part.

When it comes to sampling and surveying, the bulk of published research will have been conducted on white, Western subjects, often in North America, and will not necessarily engage with issues of social justice or translate to other cultural contexts. Then, at the analysis stage, it is virtually impossible to infer causal relationships because so many other processes may be mediating the observed correlations and because, even where two factors do emerge as fairly clearly influencing one another, the direction of cause and effect cannot be known with certainty from the study. Finally, the eventual findings can tend to have a 'so what' feeling about them because only the general (and often the fairly obvious) is measurable in this way, not the infinite gradations of perceptions and narratives that are yielded by qualitative research.

It is important to bear all these limitations in mind when drawing on this school of research and also to remember that, struggling even to indicate general trends, *it does not have the capacity to predict anything about any individual child*. Hence, even if you start from what appear to be the clearest likelihoods, you will never know whether you are working with one of the rare exceptions to the suggested rule until events themselves unfold. This makes the application of such research in practice problematic, to say the least. With psychological influences currently in the ascendancy in social work, for example, through a whole armoury of "risk assessments", these words of caution may be particularly necessary.

Sibling relationships

Bearing in mind these caveats, what does the research report? Siblings may well have spent more time with one another in their early years than with their mother, and certainly more than with their father (Dunn, 1983). In many cultures, this includes a caretaking role (Dunn, 1983; see also Prevatt Goldstein, this volume). Even as very young children, siblings demonstrate affection towards one another, show concern and make practical attempts to help one another, although, because they can read each other's pain, distress and excitement, they know what will tease and annoy as well as what will comfort (Dunn, 1983). Their relationships appear to become more egalitarian in middle childhood (Dunn and McGuire, 1992) before they start turning away to peer groups in their teens. Not all brothers and sisters get on, either in childhood or later. Individual character and temperament, family events and the family constellation variables of birth position, age gap and gender can all potentially influence children's development through to adulthood (Dunn, 1983; 1992b) and presumably also their relationships with one another.

Siblings as a protective feature

What benefits do children derive from their siblings? They may learn social play, co-operation, ways to handle conflict, how to perceive the world through another's eyes and tune in to the way they feel, the impact of their own behaviour on others; they are helped to develop a sense of self. Younger ones watch and learn from older siblings (Dunn, 1983, 1992b; see also Selman and Mason, this volume). Children can support their brothers and sisters in times of insecurity (Dunn, 1983), stress and family disharmony, to a point that does seem able to help some avoid a pathological reaction and to grow up with fewer problems (Jenkins, 1992). They give and receive, and, when they are young, may confide in one another more commonly than in friends. Jones, in her chapter below, perfectly illustrates this in the behaviour of two sisters she observed in a Romanian orphanage. Children talk to one another about parental quarrels and use one another as a source of comfort, but the closeness of their relationship is the most important factor (Jenkins, 1992). One practical implication might be to make it well worth while working on improving sibling relationships (see Beckett *et al*, this volume), rather than assessing them at one point in time and taking decisions on that basis.

What comes through more consistently than any other finding is that even full siblings, despite their close relationships and living in the same family, are utterly different from one another in personality and adjustment (Dunn, 1983). Differential interactions with parents, between siblings, and between each child and a range of aspects in their family environment are all likely to be relevant in shaping the individual, including as each of these factors influences all of the others (Dunn, 1983). Children are also born with their own qualities and strengths, as any parent knows, and make their own impact on a world which reacts back to them. Their development is part of a two-way (and indeed multiply interactional), not a one-way traffic. As a consequence of all this, it is important to be aware of the needs, wishes and perceptions of each individual child and never to treat a sibling group as one homogeneous unit.

Who are siblings?

We are perhaps fortunate to have one shorthand word in the English language, "sibling", that covers so many varieties of relationship – provided we are prepared to make the effort to start unpacking its meaning in the light of present social constructions of family and kinship. Elgar, in the chapter which follows this one, does an expert job of that unpacking, while Kosonen suggests her own terms, categorising the manifold kinds of sibling and degrees of shared history and relationship into "core" and "kin". Prevatt Goldstein points out the diversity of meanings of terms of brotherhood and sisterhood among different ethnic and cultural groupings. It is crucially important to remember that our graspings towards making some sense out of all the half- and step-siblings in contemporary Western families may make no sense at all in other contexts. As Graham (1999, p 261) points out, for example, 'The notion of half-siblings . . . does not exist within an African-centred worldview' where 'the family structure . . . incorporates the lineage both of the mother and the father, and also includes members who are not biologically related and an extensive network of cousins'. She adds that working with children on ecomaps and life histories may be based on ethnocentric assumptions about family structures which do not translate into other contexts.

We would not get very far with writing a press release about siblings, grouped around the five key 'W' questions: Who, What, Where, When and Why? Not only do we have trouble defining what siblings' relationships are and keeping track of who they are in relation to one another, we often do not know where they are. As Kosonen explains, there are no statistics gathered on siblings, either in the nation at large or among the care (or adoptive) population, to use as a baseline, and record-keeping may lack essential information (Neil, this volume). At the root of this omission is the lack of child-centredness in public policy (Qvortrup, 1997). Children are recorded as part of an adult-run household or care setting, never in relation to one another.

Yet our relationships with our siblings are the longest lasting of our lives, longer than those with our partners (even if we stay with the same person), outliving those with parents (assuming a normal lifespan for all parties), and predating those with our own children. If we are lucky, surviving into old age and remaining in touch with our families, our sibling relationships traverse all the traumas not only of childhood but of adulthood too. It must surely be quite a dramatic decision to sever that link and – while I have heard one woman on *Home Truths* on Radio 4 bemoaning the fact that she could not divorce her siblings, with whom she felt she had nothing in common – such severance is most often imposed by adults (whether family members or professionals) on children, without the latter's volition or agency.

It is the norm in the wider community to have siblings (see Kosonen, this volume, and Kosonen, 1996) and this volume will show that it is equally, and tragically, the norm in the care system and in adoption to be separated from some or all of them, if not on entering care then on moving between placements (though a minority of moves do reunite children). The neglect of a child–child perspective extends into policy and practice in social work where it gives rise to other problems. Decisions about children's placements are made in terms of what adults can offer them, and do not incorporate the additional element of what benefits relationships with other children, notably siblings, might confer. Contact is most often thought about in parent–child terms, too, especially post-divorce, although there is perhaps just beginning to be a recognition of what siblings can give to one another. Sibling groups are typically regarded as a single unit in reports to the court (see the chapter by Selwyn) and, where individuals *are* singled out, it is because they are seen as a problem or a threat to the stability of a placement, for example, because of abuse (see chapters by Elgar and Head and by Farmer and Pollock) – not as a resource to the other child(ren).

Why do siblings matter?

Why do siblings search for one another, sometimes without ever having met in their lives before, as in John Lennon's case? Why do they feel that there is something special about being a sibling and what is the nature of that something special? The chapter in the last section of this volume by Pavlovic and myself reveals some of the answers. It is followed by chapters from practice and research by Hodgkins and Prynn which echo ours in the strength of the feelings of loss and the sometimes desperate need to search which separated siblings describe in adult life, particularly when kept apart by closed adoption.

Conclusion

One of the interviewees in my own joint study said she was sure the separation adoption had imposed on her and her siblings would not happen nowadays. Worryingly, the recent revival of political interest in adoption, under both Conservatives and New Labour, appears to show no awareness of the damage such partings can do in terms of severed relationships. This is not, of course, to write off family placements nor to underestimate the contribution of adopters in meeting the complex needs of children. Rather, it is to recognise that adoption is not a panacea nor a straightforward matter of finding good parents (as if that could ever be simple).

Children do not come, like Paddington Bear, with nothing but a nametag round their necks and a suitcase full of jam sandwiches. In fact, thinking about it, even Paddington Bear had strong memories of his past and an even stronger force of personality which made his new life totally his own. He also made immediate relationships with the two children in that new life who became his foster siblings. Children who are adopted or looked after in the care system do not leave their backgrounds behind in "Darkest Peru" like a fictional bear. They have flesh and blood relatives who care about them, who feel their loss, and who may want to reinstate contact in later years. They themselves have memories and may want to sustain contact or closer links through being placed together.

The sociopolitical forces that intervene in children's lives, and in which social work plays its part, would do well to be mindful of research findings that at least raise important questions about sibling and other family relationships, even if they do not have all the answers.

References

Berridge D and Cleaver H (1987) *Foster Home Breakdown*, Oxford: Blackwell.

Bilson A and Barker R (1992/3) 'Siblings of children in care or accommodation: a neglected area of practice', *Practice*, 6:4, pp 307–18.

Boer F and Dunn J (1992) *Children's Sibling Relationships: Developmental and clinical issues*, Hillsdale, NJ: Lawrence Erlbaum.

Boer F and Spiering S M (1991) 'Siblings in foster care: success and failure', *Child Psychiatry and Human Development*, 21:4, pp 291–300.

Borland M, Laybourn A, Hill M and Brown J (1998) *Middle Childhood: The perspectives of children and parents*, London: Jessica Kingsley.

Department of Health (1991) *Patterns and Outcomes in Child Placement: Messages from current research and their implications*, London: HMSO.

Dunn J (1983) 'Sibling relationships in early childhood', *Child Development*, 54, pp 787–811.

Dunn J (1992a) 'Introduction', in Boer F and Dunn J, *op. cit.*

Dunn J (1992b) 'Sisters and brothers: current issues in developmental research', in Boer F and Dunn J, *op. cit.*

Dunn J and McGuire S (1992) 'Sibling and peer relationships in childhood', *Journal of Child Psychology & Psychiatry*, 33:1, pp 67–105.

Farmer E and Parker R (1991) *Trials and Tribulations: Returning children from local authority care to their families*, London: HMSO.

Fenyo A, Knapp M and Baines B (1989) *Foster Care Breakdown: A study of a special teenager fostering scheme*, Canterbury: University of Kent at Canterbury, Personal Social Services Research Unit. Discussion Paper 616.

Fisher M, Marsh P and Philips D with Sainsbury E (1986) *In and Out of Care: The experiences of children, parents and social workers*, London: Batsford.

Fratter J, Rowe J, Sapsford D and Thoburn J (1991) *Permanent Family Placement: A decade of experience*, London: BAAF.

Graham M J (1999) 'The African-centred worldview: developing a paradigm for social work', *British Journal of Social Work*, 29:2, pp 251–267.

Haimes E and Timms N (1985) *Adoption, Identity and Social Policy*, Aldershot: Gower.

Harris P (1998) 'I am the sister John Lennon never knew', *Daily Mail*, 25 August, pp 18–19.

Hegar R L (1993) 'Assessing attachment, permanence, and kinship in choosing permanent homes', *Child Welfare*, LXXII:4, pp 367–78.

Jenkins J (1992) 'Sibling relationships in disharmonious homes: potential difficulties and protective effects', in Boer F and Dunn J, *op. cit.*

Kosonen M (1996) 'Maintaining sibling relationships: neglected dimension in child care practice', *British Journal of Social Work*, 26:6, pp 809-22.

Morrow V (1998) *Understanding Families: Children's perspectives*, London: National Children's Bureau.

Qvortrup J (1997) 'Childhood and societal macrostructures'. Paper presented at the second Programme meeting, 'Children 5–16: Growing into the 21st Century', 17 March, Keele University.

Rowe J, Cain H, Hundleby M and Keane A (1984) *Long-term Foster Care*, London: Batsford.

Rowe J, Hundleby M and Garnett L (1989) *Child Care Now*, London: BAAF.

Staff I and Fein E (1992) 'Together or separate: a study of siblings in foster care', *Child Welfare*, LXXI:3, pp 257–270.

Thoburn J and Rowe J (1988) 'A snapshot of permanent family placement', *Adoption & Fostering*, 12:3, pp 29–34.

Treffers P D A (1992) 'Foreword: sibling studies and sibling lore', in Boer F and Dunn J, *op. cit.*

United Nations (1989) *Convention on the Rights of the Child: Adopted by the General Assembly of the United Nations, 1989*, London: Stationery Office. (Implemented in the UK since 1991; this edition published 1996.)

Wedge P and Mantle G (1991) *Sibling Groups and Social Work: A study of children referred for permanent substitute family placement*, Aldershot: Avebury.

Whitaker D, Cook J, Dunne C and Rocliffe S (1984) *The Experience of Residential Care from the Perspectives of Children, Parents and Care-givers*, York: Department of Social Policy and Social Work, University of York.

2 An overview of siblings

Marian Elgar and *Ann Head*

Marian Elgar is Senior Lecturer, School of Social Sciences and Law, Oxford Brookes University. She is also a guardian ad litem.

Ann Head is a guardian ad litem and independent researcher.

According to George Orwell (1941: 1982 edition, Part 1, p 54) the family 'has its private language and its common memories and at the approach of an enemy it closes its ranks'. Families have so often been thought of as parents and children, but it is the siblings who outlive their parents and pass on the private language and common memories to a new generation, confirming and reframing them with each other.

Sibling relationships

Brothers and sisters to a greater or lesser extent share their identity and they are able to offer each other a sense of permanence. In terms of identity, siblings may share genetic inheritance; where they have grown up together they also share a common history and a common cultural inheritance and family values. Rebecca Hegar (1988) concludes in her literature review that brothers and sisters usually have meaning for each other that unrelated children lack. Owusu-Bempah *et al* (1997) describe how siblings are important even when they do not have contact with each other directly; siblings provide 'socio-genealogical connectedness'. They can provide a way of ensuring that children remain in touch with their background, enhance their sense of connectedness to their roots or belonging, and increase their sense of well-being. Children can have the opportunity of understanding their whole picture by being told about their siblings by others.

Siblings can also offer life-long support to each other and provide a sense of belonging and a long-term attachment. Clark and Anderson

(1967) report in their study that, while 38 per cent of people over 65 years of age had a living spouse, 61 per cent had living children and 93 per cent had living siblings still alive. It is not uncommon for siblings to live together after the death of their respective spouses or following the breakdown of relationships with partners. Indeed, Hegar (1988) found that sibling bonds are a major source of emotional support for many adults.

Definition of siblings

The concept of siblings encompasses a large variety of relationships, in terms of degrees of relatedness, contact, shared upbringing and legal status. For children of the same parents brought up with both parents in the same household, all these elements are held in common though, even then, age differences or life events may mean that not all experiences are shared or, certainly, they may be perceived and experienced differently. Many reconstituted families include full, half- and sometimes step-siblings in the same household and these children may have any combination of common genetic make-up and common history and culture, length of shared upbringing and legal parents. Equally, siblings may grow up apart and share only their genetic make-up but no common family experiences or values. In the case of adopted children, depending on their age at adoption, the child may share common experiences with other adopted children in the family or with children born to the family. These children also share full legal status and to some extent a common history, but not the genetic inheritance of the family in which they are brought up. Likewise, because of their shared history, foster children may become siblings with other unrelated foster children or children of the carers' family.

Thus siblings may be defined as children (and later as adults) with some degree of one, some or all of the following:
a) common genes;
b) common history, family values and culture; and
c) common legal status.

The possible combinations can be thought of as follows (and are shown in Table 1):

- *Full siblings* brought up with both parents $a+b+c$
  Full siblings brought up apart following separation in childhood $a + some\ b+c$
  Full siblings, one placed away from other(s) at birth $a+c$
- *Half-siblings* brought up as one family $some\ a + b$
  Half-siblings brought up apart having been separated during childhood $some\ a + some\ b$
  Child born to one parent but never having lived with half siblings $some\ a\ only$
- *Adopted children* – no common genes, but common history and legal status as full siblings $some\ b+c$
- *Step-siblings* – no common genes, some common history $some\ b\ only$
- *Foster children* non-related children – $some\ b\ only$

Table 1
Types of sibling relationships

	Common genes	Common history, family values, and culture	Common legal status
Full siblings brought up together	✓	✓	✓
Full siblings brought up apart/separated during childhood	✓	some	✓
Full siblings, one placed away from another at birth	✓	no	✓ (unless adopted)
Half-siblings, brought up together	some	✓	no
Half-siblings brought up apart/separated during childhood	some	some	no
Half-siblings – brought up by one parent – never lived with half-siblings	some	no	no
Adopted children	no	some	✓
Step-siblings	no	some	no
Foster children (non-related children)	no	some	no

Normal and abnormal sibling behaviour

Sibling rivalry is common in families and in all cultures. It can be of benefit to children because the rivalry can teach children to share, and the relationship between children and adults allows a safe process of adjustment and socialisation in the family which can then be extended into society at large. This healthy rivalry does not prevent an attachment from forming between the children that may be enduring; an attachment described by Ainsworth and Bell (1970, p 49) as:

> an affectional tie that a person forms between himself and another specific one – a tie that binds them together in space and endures over time.

For many siblings, these attachments are formed early in the child's life when children are very close, drawing apart in adolescence but, later in life, typically when the adult siblings have their own children, becoming close again.

Sibling rivalry can be harmful, however, if the siblings are too competitive, particularly if one child is perceived as favoured by the parent. Hegar (1988) concludes that exaggerated sibling rivalry is associated with parental behaviour and also with the specific characteristics of the children, especially where one child has culturally or socially acceptable characteristics such as, for example, higher intellectual achievement or more acceptable physical characteristics. She found, however, that there is no evidence that destructive levels of conflict are common between children.

Sibling caretaking, although criticised in some cultures where the older caretaking child may be perceived as taking too much responsibility for a younger sibling, is described as normal in many cultures and common in families. There is no real evidence to show that this is harmful for children.

Bank and Kahn (1982, p 507) emphasise the importance and enduring nature of sibling relationships in childhood and adult life:

> The power of sibling relationships is most clearly demonstrated when a fundamental change in the structure of the sibling group occurs. These structural changes have enormous consequences. Trauma such

as the marriage or death of a sibling, the onset of illness or even the divorce of a sibling from a spouse can jolt a brother or sister. Normal separations can have profound consequences in that the support and other important processes that buttressed the sibling relationship are no longer taking place or have changed.

Dunn and Plomin (1990) argue that no two siblings are alike and that siblings, despite being brought up within the same family group, have individual experiences of relationships which are unique. Each child's development results from experiences as well as from genetic make-up. These individual experiences become internalised to mould the personality. Relationships with caregivers, usually parents, are of particular importance but there are many other influences which play their part in the process. These include social influences such as school teachers, and more immediately, siblings. Dunn (1993) considers from her studies that sibling rivalries, jealousies and friendship are significant developmental experiences and, to some degree or other, common within families. Sulloway (1990) asserts that later born children identify less with their parents than their first born siblings. He argues, therefore, that they have more freedom and leeway to challenge the status quo within the home. There is evidence to support the argument that young children develop strong attachments to siblings, especially where they are involved in the child's care (Dunn, 1993). Equally, older children become attached to their younger siblings.

Hegar (1988, p 460) points out that 'a small proportion of siblings become sexually involved with each other with unclear consequences' . Her view is that separation may not always be necessary and that professionals need to make a proper assessment. Bank and Kahn (1982) conclude that sexual involvement may arise when siblings in a frightening environment cannot rely on their parents for comfort and protection. This may be particularly relevant for children in the child protection system where stress is often pronounced and parents are frequently unavailable or inaccessible.

Effect of separation on siblings

Kosonen (1994) reminds us that siblings provide the longest lasting relationships, often extending throughout a lifetime. Children growing up apart from brothers and sisters, lacking knowledge about their siblings, may be deprived of family support in adult life.

Hegar (1988, p 459) cites research by Isaacs (1941) of the placement of siblings evacuated from London to Cambridge during World War II. Significantly more children who were accompanied by siblings adapted well:

> *The presence of the child's own brother or sister in the foster homes is therefore clearly favourable to ease of adjustment to the new home, while so far as our figures show, the presence of other evacuated children . . . has no such effect.*

This suggests that it is not the presence of other children but the continuance of part of the child's own family life that is important.

Hegar also found that juvenile siblings are frequently able to help each other to learn and change and that the loss of a sibling is traumatic whereas the presence of a brother or sister may ease adjustment to other stresses or losses. This latter point is crucial when considering the placement of children outside the family.

Siblings in the care system

The Department of Health (1991) supports the placement of siblings together, for example, by removing the limit on the numbers of children that may be placed in a foster home in the interests of keeping siblings together (Volume 3, para. 4.6). Care plans for children in care or accommodated are set out in some detail; they have been widely adopted as the format for care plans presented by the local authority in court proceedings (Volume 3, para. 6.2.). Although the child's identified needs take precedence, thereby giving a wide brief, there is no mention of siblings in the outline care plan. Nor is there anything in the Children Act that sets out the child's right to have contact with siblings specifically, although s34(2) allows for contact between the child 'and any named person'.

The majority of children in care have one or more siblings. Rowe *et al* (1984) found that 84 per cent of children had full or half siblings; Bilson and Barker (1992) similarly found in their study of 1,068 children that 86.5 per cent of children in care or accommodated by the local authority had siblings or half-siblings. A number of studies, taken together, indicate that, although over 80 per cent of children in care have siblings, only between 25–33 per cent are living with one or more siblings.

Kosonen (1994) found in her study that, for the majority of children in a foster or adoption placement, the process of coming into care had led to separation of siblings. She found that, once separated, there was little chance of a reunification of siblings. Often, separation happened at the point of entry into the care system, when there had been little time to plan the admission properly, or otherwise siblings came into care at different times. In the latter case, attention was not necessarily given to placement together and contact between separated siblings was often not maintained.

Research on placement stability has considered the effects of siblings placed together or separated: As Thoburn (1988, p 66) states:

It is usually considered desirable in most cases to place siblings together, or to keep up contact between them if they are placed separately. Berridge and Cleaver's findings of a higher rate of foster placement breakdown for those placed away from other siblings in care reinforces this view, as does our study of children placed with permanent substitute families.

Although there is much we still need to learn about siblings, and the relationships between them, which vary widely both in type and in apparent significance at particular points in time, it is clear that separation from siblings is common in the family placement context and that both legislation and research argue against it. These themes will be further examined in later chapters.

References

Ainsworth M and Bell S (1970) 'Attachment, exploration and separation: illustrated by the behaviour of one-year-olds in a strange situation', *Child Development*, 41, pp 49–67.

Bank S P and Kahn M D (1982), *The Sibling Bond*, New York: Basic Books.

Bank S P and Kahn M D (1976) 'Sisterhood and brotherhood is powerful: sibling sub-systems in family therapy,' in *Annual Progress in Child Psychiatry and Child Development*, Chess and Thomas (eds), New York: Brunner/Mazel.

Bilson A and Barker R (1992/3) 'Siblings of children in care or accommodation: a neglected area of practice', *Practice*, 6:4, pp 307–28.

Children Act 1989 (1991) London, HMSO.

Clark M and Anderson B (1967) *Culture and Ageing*, Springfield, Illinois: Charles C Thomas.

Department of Health (1991) *Patterns and Outcomes in Child Placement*, London: HMSO, p 27.

Dunn J (1993) *Young Children's Close Relationships: Beyond attachment*, California: Sage.

Dunn J and Plomin R (1990) *Separate Lives: Why siblings are so different*, New York: Basic Books.

Hegar R (1988) 'Sibling relationships and separations: Implications for child placement', *Social Services Review*, September pp 446–67.

Isaacs S (ed) (1941) *The Cambridge Evacuation Survey: A wartime study in social welfare and education*, London: Methuen.

Kosonen M (1996) 'Maintaining sibling relationships: neglected dimension in child care practice', *British Journal of Social Work*, 26, pp 809–22.

Orwell George (1941) *The Lion and the Unicorn*, Penguin, 1982, Part 1 p 54.

Owusu-Bempah J and Hewitt D (1997) 'Socio-genealogical connectedness, attachment theory, and child care practice', *Child & Family Social Work*, 2, pp 199–207.

Rowe J, Cain H, Hundleby M and Keane A (1984) *Long-term Foster Care*, London: Batsford/BAAF.

Sulloway F (1990) 'Orthodoxy and innovation in science: the influence of birth order in a multivariate context'. Paper presented to the American Association for the Advance of Science, New Orleans, LA.

Thoburn J (1988) *Child Placement: Principles and practice*,' 2nd edition, Aldershot: Arena, 1994, p 66.

3 'Core' and 'kin' siblings
Foster children's changing families

Marjut Kosonen

Marjut Kosonen, originally from Finland, obtained her CQSW and MPhil in Social Work and Social Administration in 1977 at the University of York. She has worked as a child care and family placement social worker, manager and planner in the UK and, in between, lived in West Africa. She is a senior social work manager in Angus Council, Scotland, and a postgraduate research student at the Centre for the Child & Society, University of Glasgow.

Studies of looked after children summarised in two government publications (Department of Health and Social Security,1985; Department of Health,1991) suggest that their family backgrounds are complex and rapidly changing. Looked after children are likely to come from lone parent, poor, and larger than average families (Bebbington and Miles, 1989). Studies reviewed by Kosonen (1996a) show that 80 to 90 per cent of children who are looked after have one or more siblings and that their families are fragmented, with different types of siblings living in a variety of situations. However, little is known about looked after children's siblings (Department of Health, 1998). Social workers are required to record details of a child's siblings and their living arrangements as part of planning for a child's care. However, this information is not collated nationally to monitor the performance of local authorities, or to inform policy and practice. Nor is much known about how looked after children themselves define their family composition or whom they regard as their siblings.

There is a dearth of information about siblings in general. Family statistics are collected from the perspective of adults rather than children (Church and Summerfield, 1994; Pullinger and Summerfield, 1997). Consequently, no direct information is available on children's living arrangements at birth or changes in these following a birth outside marriage or marriage breakdown (Clarke, 1996). No national statistics exist regarding the numbers and types of siblings children have, or changes in the children's living arrangements in relation to their siblings.

We know from the statistics collected on "families" that the demographic changes occurring as a result of an increase in divorce, births outside marriage, cohabitation and remarriage in Britain have all led to increased disruption in children's family circumstances (Clarke, 1996). Family disruption can, in turn, lead to children experiencing more than one family during childhood. Simpson (1994), in his discussion of the complex restructuring of kinship arrangements which can occur following divorce and remarriage, refers to such restructured families as 'unclear families'. The real impact of changes in family structure on children's sibling relationships is not well understood. However, some writers suggest that these changes may have a negative impact on children, albeit as a result of the greater freedom and choice experienced by adults (Halsey, 1993; Clarke, 1996).

A decrease in the average number of dependent children in families obviously means that children are now likely to have fewer siblings. However, due to the increase in family disruption, children's kinship arrangements with their siblings are likely to be more complex. Despite demographic changes, most children (four-fifths of dependent children) are still brought up in a family with two parents and with other children. Almost four-fifths of dependent children lived with at least one other dependent child in 1995–96 (Pullinger and Summerfield, 1997). Some researchers suggest that the decrease in the number of siblings can be a mixed blessing, leading to reduced opportunities for companionship but an increased share of parental resources (Hernandez, 1993).

This chapter explores the multifaceted nature of foster children's sibling relationships in middle childhood, in the context of their disrupted early lives and complex family relationships. The children's relationships with their sisters and brothers will be considered *from the perspective of the child*, by comparing some of the findings of a sample of 21 children in foster care (referred to as the foster care sample) with a sample of 64 primary school children (referred to as the community sample). Some other aspects of this study have been reported previously

(Kosonen,1996b; Kosonen,1998; Kosonen, forthcoming). This chapter discusses the findings relating to: the children's descriptions of their family composition; their perceptions of what is a sibling; their experiences of separation and loss; the significance of siblings in relation to friends and others; their views on placement with or without siblings; and expectations of the continuity of sibling relationships in adulthood.

Sample and methodology

The study of sibling relationships of children in foster care presents particular conceptual and methodological challenges. These are rarely acknowledged in literature or statistics. Staff *et al* (1993) suggest that, because of the complexities inherent in the study of siblings in foster care, methodological issues such as how to define a sibling, and who to use as a subject of study – an individual child, a pair of siblings, or the sibling group – should be determined in accordance with the purpose of the study and made explicit. As the purpose of this study was to explore children's own perceptions of their siblings, the children themselves were asked to define which related children they regarded as their siblings. The study explored the perspectives of individual children about their siblings.

The *foster care sample* contained 21 children aged eight to 12 (mean age 10 years), who were in short-term foster care (3–12 months) in one local authority area in Scotland. There were seven girls and 14 boys in the sample. The sample was drawn from 11 families and included two groups of three siblings, six groups of two siblings, and three singleton children. Most of the children had full, half- and step-siblings elsewhere.

Information was obtained from the children by questionnaire, the administration of the Family Relations Test (Bene-Anthony, 1978), and an interview. A "Sibling Relationships Questionnaire" was developed with the aid of eight children and piloted in a local primary school. It included an illustrated explanation of the types of families found in contemporary Britain, as well as explanations of different types of sibling relations, e.g. full, half- and step-siblings. Information about the child's family background and the history of sibling relationships was obtained from the social worker by means of a second questionnaire. Where the children are referred to by name, their names have been changed to protect their anonymity.

The *community sample* contained children in a single primary school class in each of three schools. One child was withdrawn from the study by the parents. Two-thirds of the children lived in socio-economically disadvantaged urban housing estates in the same local authority area. The sample consisted of 69 children aged nine to 12 (mean age ten years and one month), of whom 64 had one or more siblings. The children who had siblings comprised 60 per cent of girls and 40 per cent of boys. Information from these children was obtained by the same questionnaire as the foster care sample.

Findings

Foster children's unclear families

Information about the foster children's family composition was obtained both from the children and their social workers. For the children in the community sample, information was obtained from the children only. The children were asked: 'Who belongs to your family, including people and pets, and lives at home with you?', and 'Are there any members of your immediate family such as mother, father, sister or brother not living at home?' Thus the family composition was considered from the perspective of the study child's relationships with adults and with other children in the family.

When the children's family composition and living arrangements were considered, differences emerged between the foster children's families and those of the children in the community. Over 80 per cent of the children in the community sample said their families included both mother and father (reflecting national statistics, Pullinger and Summerfield, 1997), whereas only one foster child did so. None of the foster children's biological parents lived together. The presence of the mother's new unmarried partner in the family home was proportionally more common in the foster children's families.

Retrospective data obtained from the children's social workers showed that the majority of foster children had experienced "serial" parenting by two or more of their mother's partners being involved in the child's life. Children identified with individual parents and their perceptions of their family composition reflected their divided loyalties. This was particularly the case in families where there had been conflict and violence between parents and where parental separations had been acrimonious (Kosonen, 1998).

Differences also emerged between the children's and their social workers' descriptions of the families. Some children included different members as part of their family from the social workers' descriptions; for instance, in one case where grandparents were recorded by the social worker as the main parent, the child did not include them as part of his family. Although he had been brought up by his grandparents, they had abused him and, consequently, he regarded his mother, with whom he wanted to live, as his main parent. Such differences of perception may be a result of a tendency for social workers to consider the looked after children's relationships with parents from the legal perspective of 'parental responsibility for the child' rather than from the perspective of the 'child's social and emotional relationships to adults'. Social workers were not always fully aware of the children's own perceptions of their family composition; sometimes they omitted family members or substituted others.

These findings accord with two recent studies of children's understanding of family. O'Brien *et al* (1996), based on two cohorts of children in the general population (average ages nine and 14), found that 'as with adults, children's concepts of family are complex, fluid and sometimes contradictory' (p 98). Morrow (1998), in her study of children's (aged eight to 14) constructions of the family, found that children defined the concept of family in terms of roles (what family members do for each other), relationships (love and affection), and structure (the people involved). The children were aware of a wide variation in family structures, and their definitions did not always centre around biological relatedness or the "nuclear" family. The key characteristics of family included love, care, mutual support and respect. These notions were also important to the foster children in this study.

Who are the foster children's siblings?

The Oxford English Reference Dictionary defines a sibling as 'each of two or more children having one or both parents in common' (Pearsall and Trumble, 1996). This appears to be a simple and straightforward definition. However, siblings can be further categorised into biological siblings (full and half), step-siblings, adopted siblings and foster siblings. Distinctions between siblings can also be made on the basis of whether siblings have ever lived together and, consequently, whether they have had an opportunity to develop a shared sense of identity and of belonging to each other. Considering the biological, emotional and social connections between siblings, and the child's and siblings' residential arrangements, there is potentially a range of different types of sibling arrangements. Treffers *et al* (1990) identified, as part of collating patient data in a child and adolescent psychiatric centre, 26 types of sibling a child can have. It is important to note that all the definitions in use have been constructed by adults.

As the aim of this study was to obtain an 'insider view' (Olson, 1977) of the children's sibling relationships, the children in the foster care sample were asked to include in the questionnaire all children they regarded as their siblings. They were also asked to create their family as part of the Family Relations Test. In the interview situation, the children elaborated on their relationships with their siblings. This allowed for the information on the children's siblings obtained by three different measures to be compared. In addition, social workers were asked to give information about all siblings (whether full, half-, step- or adopted) living with or apart from the child. The children's perceptions of their siblings were compared with the social workers' understanding of the children's sibling relationships.

'Core' and 'kin' siblings

The *foster children* named 57 siblings, with whom they lived currently or had lived in the past. Only a few children made a distinction between full and half-siblings, although they were more likely to use the term 'step-'. The information obtained from the social workers indicated, however, that half of the children's siblings were full siblings and another half were half-siblings. These 57 siblings, who had shared joint living arrangements in the past and who, to varying degrees, still shared their childhood with the study children, are called "core siblings" in the context of this study.

In addition, the children gave information about 35 other related children whom they also regarded as their siblings (27 half- and eight step-siblings – this information was obtained from the questionnaire, test and interview data, for instance where the child said their father had another family of four children whom their regarded as siblings, rather than the child using the term half-sibling). They had not lived with these siblings in the past, although with some there had been ongoing contact. Some of these siblings were located at the fringes of their families, for instance, living with a grandparent; others were living further away, and some were in another country. The children expressed a sense of kinship to these "external" siblings and, for this reason, they are called "kin siblings" in the context of this study. All together, the foster children mentioned a total of 92 siblings, an average of 4.4 siblings per child. The average number of core siblings was 2.7 per child.

A complex picture emerged when the details of siblings obtained through the questionnaire, the Family Relations Test and the interview were compared. The children included all their core siblings in all the research measures used. Some children, however, included and excluded individual kin siblings in different measures used, for instance, by including in the test situation a kin sibling they had not mentioned in the questionnaire. Although a kin sibling received a low test score indicating low emotional involvement, nevertheless, they were regarded by the child as their sister or brother. Similarly, some children talked in the interview about the importance of their kin siblings, with whom they had only infrequent contact. Some of the "kin siblings" floated in and out of the children's families and, as the children talked about their siblings, they were making sense of these fragmented and complex sibling connections.

The question, *Who are the children's siblings?*, was further compli-cated by some children within the same family (only three study children had no siblings in the sample) defining their family composition differ-ently from one another. They included different kin siblings in their descriptions of their families, and indicated different degrees of emotional closeness to them.

Differences also emerged when the information given by the social workers was compared with that from the children themselves. The children's social workers were unaware of the existence of 21 kin siblings (nearly one-third of all siblings) mentioned by the children. In respect of one family group of children, neither the children nor the social worker were aware of additional kin siblings living elsewhere. The children's foster carer volunteered information on half-siblings living in the locality (belonging to the biological father) whom she had cared for in the past. This further illustrates the complex and multifaceted nature of foster children's sibling relationships.

By contrast, the *children in the community* sample who had siblings had fewer of them. They gave information about 152 siblings, averaging 2.4 siblings per child. Forty-one (27 per cent) of the children's siblings were living away from the child's family home. These included 11 full, six half- and 24 step-siblings. Although not all children differentiated between sibling types, particularly between full and half-siblings, it was possible to deduce this information from the children's answers to other questions. Reasons for the siblings living apart from the child included the following: siblings were grown up; they lived with another parent; siblings were fostered or lived with a relative; or the child had never lived with the step-siblings. It is acknowledged that information was obtained from the children by a questionnaire only. A fuller picture was obtained of the foster children's siblings by the use of multiple methods and sources of data.

Children's fragmented lives – separation and loss

Children entering local authority care have experienced a great deal of disruption in their lives. Changes in the children's families often continue while the child is being looked after (Fisher *et al*, 1986; Millham *et al*, 1986; Packman *et al*, 1986; Stone, 1995). Such changes have an impact on the development and maintenance of sibling relationships. Research on the "non-shared" influences (environmental influences not shared by siblings) on the qualitative aspects of sibling relationships for children in intact families is well documented (Dunn and Plomin, 1991; Hetherington *et al*, 1994). For this reason, it was considered useful to enquire into the changes the study children had experienced in the past and continued to experience while in foster care.

Social workers were asked detailed questions about the child's family background and the history of the child's family relationships. The children's chronological histories (a list of changes affecting the child maintained in chronological order in the child's case file) were also perused.

Information on the following changes affecting the child's relationships with siblings was analysed: separations from parents; parental separations from one another; separations from siblings in foster care; previous separations from siblings; and changes in the child's family composition and living situation. All foster children had experienced a great deal of change in all the areas studied; however, this chapter focuses primarily on the disruption of sibling relationships.

Separations from siblings

Separation from siblings was remarkably common; only five of the 21 children were living in foster care with all of their core siblings, and even then, not with all of their kin siblings. By the end of the study period, further separations from core siblings had occurred and only two siblings were still together. The remainder of children lived apart from one or more of their core siblings.

When the foster children's previous living arrangements in relation to their siblings were considered retrospectively, it was found that only two children were now and had in the past lived continuously with all of their core siblings. However, even they had an older half-brother who had grown up with their grandmother. Although they had not been separated from their core siblings, they were thus living separately from a kin sibling.

The length of separations from the individual core siblings ranged from five weeks to three years (separations of less than two weeks were excluded). When the length of separations was considered in relation to the child's age, it was found that younger children were separated from their siblings for proportionally longer periods than were their older siblings. For younger children, a separation of three years may represent over one-third of their life-time. Also, the age and developmental stage of the child and their siblings is important when considering the potential effects of such separations, taking into account young children's relatively rapid development. The study found that, although separation from siblings was fairly common for the children in the community, continuity of sibling relationships was considerably *more* difficult for the foster children to maintain.

Family disruption

The majority of children had experienced extended separations from their parents and parental separations. For over a third of the children, separation from mother had occurred before the age of two, and half the children had experienced parental separation before the age of five. Some children had experienced more than one parental separation, having lost their father and subsequently a stepfather. Some parents continued the process of splitting up and getting back together over a number of years. The parents' relationships were marked by conflict and domestic violence.

Few children had remained in the same community they lived in at birth. The number of known changes of children's living situation, including previous episodes of being looked after, ranged from four to 36 (average 13.3). Few of the recorded changes were pre-planned; most occurred as a result of a crisis in their parents' lives. The changes had adverse effects on the children beyond their practical living arrangements. Changes of family home led to the loss of familiar people and places, changes of school, and often changes of male figures in the household. Some children lost all or most of their pets, toys and personal belongings in unplanned family disruptions. Less than half of the foster children had in fact had pets prior to coming into foster care, and these were of a limited range. By contrast, two-thirds of the children in the community had pets and these were more varied.

Continued family disruption

Changes in the foster children's birth families continued while the children were in foster care, despite the short period of time the children had been away from home (an average of six months). Two-thirds of the children experienced changes in family composition and in parents' and siblings' living situations. Such changes resulted in children experiencing further losses: of family home; of personal possessions, toys, photographs and childhood mementos; and, for some, of contact with siblings, grandparents and other relatives. At the same time, new people entered some children's families through cohabitation and marriage. These findings reflect previous research on returning children home (Farmer and Parker, 1991; Bullock *et al*, 1993). Bullock *et al* (1993) caution about potential difficulties encountered by children returning home to a changed family situation and suggest that changes in children living at home can be even more significant than changes relating to adults, taking into account the relatively rapid developmental changes occurring in childhood. The study children's experiences of family change were primarily characterised by loss of contact with siblings, rather than the arrival of new siblings. The children who acquired new baby half-siblings welcomed their contact with them.

Siblings in the context of a network of relationships

Children's networks of important people

The subjective importance of foster children's sibling relationships was considered by asking the children to think about their family, friends, pets and other people they knew (like teachers and neighbours) and to write down those who were most important to them. The children's answers were analysed in terms of the proportion of children who saw people and pets as important to them, rather than according to their relative importance. Although the picture emerging from the questionnaire findings provides only a snapshot in time, it was felt worthwhile to compare their answers with those of the community sample. The following aspects of the children's network of relationships were considered in this way: the size of children's networks of relationships; the importance of siblings in relation to other people; children's friendships; and friendships shared with the child's siblings.

Only a marginal difference was found in the size of the foster children's networks of important people (average five) compared with those of the children in the community sample (average 5.8). However, one-fifth of the foster children's relationships were with the members of the foster family. These were inevitably of a temporary nature. When relationships with the foster family were excluded, the foster children enjoyed, on average, four important relationships with members of their birth family and others.

The mother and siblings were most often mentioned as important people, followed by foster mother and father. Three-quarters of the foster children (75 per cent) compared to 83 per cent of the children in the community sample mentioned at least one of their siblings as important to them. However, it is suggested that foster children's lack of relationships with the wider family (particularly with grandparents who were notably absent from the children's lives) made siblings proportionally more important to them.

Children's networks of friends

The children in foster care had smaller friendship networks than the children in the community. Taking into account the gender balance in the two samples (two-thirds of the foster children were boys compared to less than half of the children in the community), this may be due partly to the relatively smaller friendship networks of the boys rather than girls. Also, foster children enjoyed fewer friendships with children of their own age or older, compared to the children in the community.

The children were asked how many of their friends were also friends of their siblings. The findings regarding the community sample had suggested that the maintenance of shared friendships with siblings was difficult for children who did not live with their siblings. The relatively small proportion of joint friendships with siblings enjoyed by the foster children again reflects their fragmented living situations.

Disruption in foster children's lives inevitably makes it difficult for them to develop and maintain supportive relationships with friends, wider family and significant others. Because of the smaller networks of supportive others, and the almost total absence of grandparents, siblings hold an even greater importance to foster children than they do to other children. The findings suggest that *because of* the children's fragmented lives, siblings continue to be important to children in foster care, whether they are living with them or not. Siblings are one of the few constants in foster children's rapidly changing families and lives.

39

Continuity of sibling relationships

Previous research suggests that continuity of relationships with siblings is difficult to maintain for children in foster care due to separation from and lack of contact with siblings (Bilson and Barker, 1994; 1998). Children are likely to be separated *on entry to and on leaving care* and, where separations have occurred, there are rarely plans to reunite siblings in care (Kosonen, 1996a). The outcome of qualitative studies of children in care (Weinstein, 1960; Thorpe, 1980; Rowe *et al*, 1984; Whitaker *et al*, 1984; McAuley, 1996) suggest that, in general, children value being placed with their siblings and that, when separated, they miss one another.

We also know from retrospective studies of the experiences of adults, who as children were brought up in care or grew up adopted (Ferguson, 1966; Meier, 1966; Triseliotis, 1980; Triseliotis and Russell, 1984), that continuity of sibling relationships is important for children separated from their parents. A more recent study by Mullender and Kearn (1997) of birth relatives' views on contact with adopted adults, found that birth siblings of all ages were seeking to make contact through the Adoption Contact Register for England and Wales with their adopted sisters and brothers. Birth siblings of adopted people were searching for their sisters and brothers, some of whom had never had a physical presence for them, yet '. . . they considered the adopted person as a part of their family and part of themselves, and they were deeply grieved at the loss of that person in their lives' (p 143). Birth siblings felt that they had been deprived of an essential ingredient in their lives.

Although we have retrospective data such as the above about adults' views on separation from their siblings, little is known about children's expectations of the continuity of their relationships with their siblings. One of the aims of this study was to explore children's expectations of the continuity of relationships with their sisters and brothers. This was done by asking the children about their preferences regarding a place-ment with or without siblings and contact with separated siblings; and about their expectations of the continuity of their relationship with their siblings in adulthood. Some of these areas were explored in the question-naire and elaborated in the interviews, others were covered by one measure only.

Placement in foster care – with or without siblings?

Despite, or perhaps because of, their complex sibling arrangements and fragmented lives, children who were in a joint placement with their siblings valued the presence of their sisters and brothers and some worried about separation from them. The few children who had remained together throughout their childhood, or who had experienced only short separations from their siblings in the past, valued the continuity of these relationships. This reflects the findings of previous qualitative studies referred to earlier in this chapter.

Children's preferences on being placed with or without their siblings generally reflected qualitative aspects of their relationships with their siblings already reported by the author (Kosonen, 1998), and mirrored the positive, negative and mixed patterns of these relationships. Some children's views were ambivalent. They acknowledged their difficulties in living with their siblings, such as fighting and domination by the siblings, particularly where their relationships with siblings were intense. Many wanted to be close to their siblings, ideally living in a different foster home 'across the road', 'next door' or 'two doors away'. For some, their views reflected their split family situation and they expressed clear preferences about being placed with a particular sibling or siblings and not with others. Where children had hostile or detached relationships with their siblings, these were reflected to a degree in their views on placement. For the three children who did not have any of their siblings in foster care, the question of a placement with siblings did not arise.

Significantly, however, children's views did not in all cases reflect their current placement situation. Some children were separated from their most preferred sibling(s), and others were placed with a sibling or siblings from whom they wanted to live apart. This is illustrated by the views of three siblings: eight-year-old twins, Judy and David, and their older brother Arron. When no suitable placement was found to take the three siblings, an assumption (albeit a common one) was made that the twins should be placed together, and Arron in a separate foster home.

This arrangement did not accord with any of the children's wishes as expressed to the researcher. Both Judy and David found it too intense an experience to live together. There was a lot of conflict between them (although this could have been worked on), and David complained that

Judy 'mothered' him. Judy would have preferred to live with her older brother, and David with neither sibling. He wanted to live near, but not in the same foster home. Arron wanted to live with both twins in a previous foster home, where he felt the three siblings had been happy.

In this situation, it appears that the placement decisions were made by using "conventional wisdom" rather than based on an assessment of the sibling relationships and the consideration of the children's views. Where one of the siblings lacks a niche among the siblings, as was the case for Arron, separation from siblings can further isolate the child from them.

Contact with siblings

Maintaining contact between the foster children and their siblings living apart involved a number of individual arrangements and considerable effort and resources by social workers and foster carers. The contact arrangements mirrored the unclear nature of the children's families. Some siblings maintained contact with different parents and step-parents, siblings and members of the extended family. For others, contact between separated siblings had already been infrequent before the child's arrival in foster care. Simpson (1994) suggests that one implication of the multiplicity of sibling relationships which occur in "unclear" families is the immense amount of energy and other resources required to enable children to maintain relationships with their various siblings.

From the children's perspective this can make an exhausting schedule of movement . . . and . . . low income families may have considerable problems in maintaining kin relations in anything other than the discrete nuclear family variant (p 846).

Social workers were generally aware of the need to maintain contact with the child's core siblings, and some went to considerable effort to ensure that regular contact took place. However, maintenance of contact with kin siblings was generally not taken into account by the social workers.

Expectations of sibling relationships in adulthood

The children's expectations of their relationships with their siblings in the future was explored by asking them to consider: when they grew up how near to their sibling they would like to live; how often they thought they would see them; whether they would do a lot together; whether they would have great fun together; and whether they would miss their sibling if they never saw them again. These questions were asked about each individual sibling rather than about their siblings in general. These areas were further explored with the children during the interviews.

The questionnaire findings show that the children perceived their siblings to hold a considerable importance in their lives in the longer term. The children expected to live relatively close to their siblings, to maintain contact with them, and to enjoy each other's company when they grew up. Proportionally more foster children (79 per cent) wished to live near their siblings than was the case for the children in the community sample (50 per cent). Only one foster child expressed a wish to live far away from his siblings. Over two-thirds of the children expected to see their siblings 'often', one third 'not often' and none of the children expressed a wish to see their siblings 'never' in the future.

Foster children also held higher expectations of their joint activities with their siblings when they grew up than was the case for the children in the community. Over two-thirds (70 per cent) of the foster children, compared to fewer than half (44 per cent) of the children in the community, expected to 'do a lot together' ('for instance, go shopping, baby-sit for each other, go to football, help each other in other ways') with their siblings. A higher proportion of foster children (73 per cent) also expected to enjoy their contact with their siblings ('we will have great fun together') than was the case for the children in the community (45 per cent). The importance of siblings to the study children was further evident in their response to the question about whether the child would miss their siblings if she or he never saw them again. The great majority both of the children in the community (82 per cent) and of the children in foster care (87 per cent) expected to miss their siblings.

The interview data revealed a more detailed picture. Children with generally positive sibling relationships perceived their siblings as likely to be an important part of their lives in adulthood. Andrew said about the future: 'We'll see each other quite a bit, every day or something . . .' Some children's expectations were characterised by ambivalence, the child wanting to live near siblings, but not too close. Nina said: 'I'd like to be next door to them or maybe a few miles up . . .' For many, their expectations also reflected their divided loyalties to their parents and their identification with individual siblings. For the children with negative or detached relationships with their siblings, their expectations were more complex. Arron, despite his generally negative perceptions of his siblings, wanted all five siblings (two were grown up) to 'live just about half a mile from each other . . .' By contrast, Fraser wanted nothing to do with his when he grew up. Two children were unable to visualise their future, and three others were preoccupied by their future relationships with their parents.

Findings suggest that, despite disrupted past sibling relationships, foster children's expectations of their siblings in the longer term were similar, and in some respects surpassed the expectations of the children in the community. The children's expectations of their siblings are likely to reflect their past family experiences and norms. The findings of a recent study of families and kinship (McGlone *et al*, 1998) suggest that the family continues to be perceived in contemporary Britain as an important source of support in adulthood. Contact with adult siblings continues to be important, particularly for people with dependent children. Although social class differences were not found to be large, the researchers suggest: 'Contact with relatives is a more prominent part of working class life than of middle class life' (p 29). Information was not obtained about the background of the children in the community sample; however, we know that two-thirds of these children lived in working class communities. Thus, the differential expectations of the two groups of children cannot be attributed to the differences in social background.

Conclusions

The findings of this study suggest that there is a need for increased attention to be paid to children's sibling relationships by researchers, policy makers, child care managers and practitioners. The focus of attention should include the following:

- *Definitions* – We do not have a common understanding of which related children are regarded as siblings for statistical, research or practice purposes.
- *Children's views on whom they regard as their siblings* – The current typology of siblings was not commonly used by the children them-selves. We need to obtain a better understanding of whom children regard as their siblings, and find ways of expressing these in child-centred ways.
- *Demographic data* – There is a need for statistics both on looked after children and on children in the general population to be collected, using a child as a unit of observation. Children's sibling relationships are currently hidden within family and household statistics.
- *Impact of family change and disruption* – More needs to be known about the effect of family disruption on the children's sibling relation-ships. Disruptions to family relationships potentially increase the range of influences impacting on the qualitative aspects of children's sibling relationships and on their development of a sense of identity and kinship.
- *Social workers' understanding of children's families* – Information collated by social workers should include the child's perspective on their sibling relationships. Kin siblings living at the fringes or outside the child's immediate family should be included, although it is accepted that the main parent may not wish any contact to take place with such siblings.
- *Sibling contact as a means of continuity* – Because of children's experiences of separation and loss, contact with siblings can be one element of continuity for children in foster care. Siblings are poten-tially a resource to each other in terms of developing identity, main-taining knowledge of self and family, and providing support in shared adversity.
- *The diverse and complex nature of sibling relationships* – The needs and best interests of a child will from time to time conflict with those of one or more of their siblings. Because of this intrinsic conflict of interest in some sibling relationships, it is vitally important that those making decisions about children in foster care have a good

understanding of the individual child's relationships.

- *Potential for change over time* – Although established early, relationships with siblings may change over time, depending on a diversity of influences bearing on the child, their siblings, and external circumstances. It is important to acknowledge the potential for change, and to find imaginative and supportive ways of working with children and their siblings. Children should not be separated merely because 'they don't get on'. It is useful to remember that many parents in intact families have to manage sibling conflict, particularly between siblings who are 'high access' (closely spaced, same gender), without resorting to separating sisters and brothers (Kosonen,1994).

- *Continuity of relationships in the long term* – Any decisions regarding looked after children taken in the context of assessment, care planning and review procedures should consider the potential impact of these decisions on the child's relationships with their siblings in the short, medium and long term. Even short-term decisions can have implications for sibling relationships that persist over a lifetime. Children should be involved, according to their level of understanding, in all decisions which affect their relationships with their siblings.

This study was undertaken under the auspices of the Centre for the Child and Society, University of Glasgow.

References

Bebbington A and Miles J (1989) 'The background of children who enter local authority care', *British Journal of Social Work*, 19:5, pp 349–68.

Bene E and Anthony J (1978) *Family Relations Test: Children's Version*, revised edition, Windsor: NFER-Nelson, (originally published in 1957).

Bilson A and Barker R (1994) 'Siblings of children in care or accommodation: a neglected area of practice', *Practice*, 6:4, pp 307–18.

Bilson A and Barker R (1998) 'Looked after children and family contact: reassessing the social work task', *Research, Policy and Planning*, 16:1, pp 20–7.

Bullock R, Little M and Millham S (1993) *Going Home: The return of children separated from their families*, Aldershot: Dartmouth.

Church J and Summerfield C (eds) (1994) *Social Focus on Children*, London: HMSO.

Clarke L (1996) 'Demographic change and the family situation of children', in Brannen J and O'Brien M (eds), *Children in Families: Research and policy*, London: Falmer.

Department of Health and Social Security (1985) *Social Work Decisions in Child Care: Recent research findings and their implications*, London: HMSO.

Department of Health (1991) *Patterns and Outcomes in Child Placement: Messages from current research and their implications*, London: HMSO.

Department of Health (1998) *Children Looked After by Local Authorities: Year ending 31 March 1997 England*, London: The Government Statistical Service.

Dunn J and Plomin R (1991) 'Why are siblings so different? The significance of differences in sibling experiences within the family', *Family Process*, 30, pp 271–83.

Farmer E and Parker R (1991) *Trials and Tribulations: Returning children from local authority care to their families*, London: HMSO.

Ferguson T (1966) *Children in Care – and after*, Oxford: Oxford University Press.

Fisher M, Marsh P, Phillips D and Sainsbury E (1986) *In and Out of Care: The experiences of children, parents and social workers*, London: BAAF/Batsford.

Halsey A H (1993) 'Changes in the family', *Children & Society*, 7:2, pp 125–36.

Hernandez D J (1993) *America's Children: Resources from family, government, and the economy*, New York: Russell Sage Foundation.

Hetherington E M, Reiss D and Plomin R (1994) *Separate Social Worlds of Siblings: The impact of non-shared environment on development*, Hillsdale, NJ: Lawrence Erlbaum.

Kosonen M (1994) 'Sibling relationships for children in the care system,' *Adoption & Fostering*, 18:3, pp 30–5.

Kosonen M (1996a) 'Maintaining sibling relationships: neglected dimension in child care practice', *British Journal of Social Work*, 26, pp 809-22.

Kosonen M (1996b) 'Siblings as providers of support and care during middle childhood: children's perceptions', *Children & Society*, 10, pp 267–79.

Kosonen M (1998) 'Foster children's sibling relationships – compensation and/ or reflection of adversity', in BAAF, *Exchanging Visions: Papers on best practice in Europe for children separated from their birth parents*, London: BAAF.

Kosonen M (forthcoming) 'The role of siblings in relation to children in residential care', in Chakrabarti M and Hill M (eds), *Residential child care: International perspectives on links with family and peers*, London: Jessica Kingsley.

McAuley C (1996) *Children in Long-term Foster Care*, Aldershot: Avebury.

McGlone F, Park A and Smith K (1998) *Families and Kinship*, London: Family Policy Studies Centre.

Meier E G (1966) 'Adults who were foster children', *Children*, 13:1, pp 16–22.

Millham S, Bullock R, Hosie K and Haak M (1986) *Lost in Care: The problem of maintaining links between children in care and their families*, Aldershot: Gower.

Morrow V (1998) *Understanding Families: Children's perspectives*, London: National Children's Bureau.

Mullender A and Kearn S (1997) *"I'm Here Waiting": Birth relatives' views on Part II of the Adoption Contact Register for England and Wales*, London: BAAF.

O'Brien M, Alldred P and Jones D (1996) 'Children's constructions of family and kinship', in Brannen J and O'Brien M (eds) *Children in Families: Research and policy*, London: Falmer.

Olson D H (1977) 'Insiders' and outsiders' views of relationships: research studies', in Levinger G and Raush H L (eds) *Close Relationships: Perspectives on the meaning of intimacy*, Amherst: University of Massachusetts Press.

Packman J, Randall J and Jacques N (1986) *Who Needs Care? Social work decisions about children*, Oxford: Blackwell.

Pearsall J and Trumble B (eds) (1996) *The Oxford English Reference Dictionary*, Oxford: Oxford University Press, 1996.

Pullinger J and Summerfield C (eds) (1997) *Social Focus on Families*, London: The Stationery Office.

Rowe J, Cain H, Hundleby M and Keane A (1984) *Long-term Foster Care*, London: Batsford.

Simpson B (1994) 'Bringing the "unclear" family into focus: divorce and re-marriage in contemporary Britain', *Man (N.S.)* 29, pp 831–51.

Staff I, Fein E and Johnson D B (1993) 'Methodological issues in studying sibling placement', *Social Work Research and Abstracts*, 29:2, pp 35–7.

Stone J (1995) *Making Positive Moves: Developing short-term fostering services*, London: BAAF.

Thorpe R (1980) 'The experience of children and parents living apart: implications and guidelines for practice', in Triseliotis J (ed), *New Developments in Foster Care and Adoption*, London: Routledge and Kegan Paul.

Treffers P D A, Goedhart A W, Waltz J V and Kouldijs E (1990) 'The systematic collection of patient data in a centre for child and adolescent psychiatry', *British Journal of Psychiatry*, 157, pp 744–8.

Triseliotis J (1980) 'Growing up in foster care and after', in Triseliotis J (ed) *New Developments in Foster Care and Adoption*, London: Routledge & Kegan Paul.

Triseliotis J and Russell J (1984) *Hard to Place: The outcome of adoption and residential care*, London: Heinemann.

Weinstein E A (1960) *The Self-image of the Foster Child*, New York: Russell Sage Foundation.

Whitaker D S, Cook J M, Dunn C and Rockliffe S (1984) *The Experience of Residential Care from the Perspective of Children and Parents and Caregivers*. Report to the ESRC, York: University of York.

4 The sibling relationships of adopted children and patterns of contact after adoption

Elsbeth Neil

After gaining two years post qualifying experience in a child care social work team, Elsbeth Neil is now studying full time for her PhD and tutoring on various courses in the School of Social Work at the University of East Anglia in Norwich. Her doctoral research is about contact arrangements for young children with their birth relatives after adoption. Her thesis is due to be completed at the end of 1999.

Introduction

When people grow up with their siblings, most people choose to maintain the relationship as a source of affection and support throughout their adult life (Cicirelli, 1982). Even when children are very young, sibling relationships have been found to be psychologically and developmentally important (Dunn, 1988).

Adoption very often separates children from existing or future siblings in their birth family. Adopted people may experience the loss of siblings with whom they have a significant emotional relationship. They may also experience the more covert loss of never knowing their brothers and sisters. It is generally accepted that adopted people need to have knowledge of their biological background and the reasons why they have been adopted (e.g. Triseliotis, 1973) in order to establish a strong sense of their own identity. It is also argued that every adopted person must at some stage deal with the loss of their birth family (Brodzinsky, 1990). The concepts of identity and loss are key components of what is termed the "psychology of adoption" (e.g. Triseliotis *et al*, 1997 pp 34–42). Issues of identity and loss are, however, generally discussed with reference to birth parents rather than siblings. The effects of the maintenance or loss of sibling relationships after adoption have received some attention, but research is scarce and sometimes contradictory.

Research on siblings has tended to look at the issue of whether to place siblings together or separately. Some studies have looked at the effect of such decisions on placement outcomes, and what evidence is available suggests that the placement of siblings together has a positive or neutral effect on placement outcomes (e.g. Barth and Berry, 1988; Borland *et al*, 1991; Fratter *et al*, 1991; Wedge and Mantle, 1991; Boer *et al*, 1994). It is further argued that the placement of siblings together can act as a protective factor because they can provide a source of emotional continuity (Howe, 1998). The reflections of young people raised in care demonstrate the value such individuals place on sibling relationships and the strong negative reaction to separation from siblings (Triseliotis and Russell, 1984; Masson *et al*, 1996).

The other angle from which researchers have examined the issue is through the feelings of siblings who have grown up separated by adoption. Feast and Howe (1997) found that 25 per cent of a sample of 366 adopted people who sought information through The Children's Society had gone on to make contact with a birth sibling. Some researchers have found that such reunions with siblings are in almost all cases experienced positively (Humphrey and Humphrey, 1988; Sachdev, 1992). Pacheco and Eme (1993), in their study of 72 adoptees who had successfully completed a search, found that over a third of the sample said they got more from meeting siblings than from a reunion with a birth parent. Mullender and Kearn (1997), in their study of birth relatives' use of the Adoption Contact Register, found that ten per cent of birth relatives using the Register were siblings of an adopted person.

The research described in this chapter cannot at this stage offer any insight into the outcomes of adoption in relation to sibling issues. What it does aim to do is to illustrate the sibling relationships of adopted children, to look at patterns of contact between siblings after adoption, and to explore how arrangements for contact differ according to where and with whom siblings live.

Outline of the research study

The information about the children who are the subject of this chapter has been collected in the 'Contact after Adoption' study. This study, being carried out by the author under the supervision of Professor June Thoburn, is stage one of a longitudinal study of children aged less than four at the time of placement for adoption. The sample has been gathered through the co-operation of ten participating agencies, two of which are in the voluntary sector. The children in the sample were all adopted or placed for adoption by these agencies in a twelve-month period from July 1996 to June 1997. Additional cases of children having face-to-face contact with adult birth relatives have been sought outside of this study period and from other agencies, but such additional cases are excluded from *this* analysis. Neither children adopted by birth relatives nor children adopted from abroad are included in the research. Detailed information on each child has been collected by means of a postal questionnaire to social workers. In total, 209 children are included in the study, which is still in progress. This chapter is based on 124 questionnaires that have been returned to date, a response rate of 77 per cent of the cases where the adoption order has been made.

A profile of children in the sample

From the questionnaires returned so far, a picture is emerging of the kinds of young children who are being adopted, the circumstances of their birth families and of their adoptive families. In terms of the reason why each child needed to be adopted, the cases fall into three main categories. Firstly, there are the "straightforward baby adoptions". Despite the young age of all the children in the research, the proportion of such adoptions is small (16 per cent). The second category, containing 20 per cent of the sample, consists of cases where parent/s had requested adoption for their child, but in very complicated circumstances. For example, the request may have been made when the child was older and had been cared for at home for a period, or because the birth parent/s had mental health problems. Other cases in this category are where the adopted child was the youngest child in the family and other children remained at home with parents. The third and largest category of children are those whose parents had not requested adoption; this group makes up 64 per cent of the sample. Such children were placed for a variety of reasons, such as maltreatment, parents' mental illness, learning disability, or drug and alcohol problems. In many cases, a combination of these factors was present.

More than half (60 per cent) of the 124 children have been subjects of care orders. A smaller proportion of children (43 per cent) has been described by their social workers as having experienced one or more forms of maltreatment prior to their placement for adoption, this indicating that some children come into care and are adopted because of the risk of future significant harm. Forty-three per cent of the children had been looked after by three or more main carers before being placed for adoption. The troubled backgrounds of the children are further illustrated by looking at their functioning at the time of placement in the adoptive home. Well over half (60 per cent) of children had at least one developmental problem at the time of placement. Problems known to be associated with poorer outcomes in adoption, namely behavioural problems and emotional problems, were noted in 16 per cent and 21 per cent of the sample respectively. Sixteen per cent of the children have one or more physical, learning or sensory disability.

The ethnic origin of 81 per cent of the children is described as white. The second biggest category of children is those classed as "mixed parentage". In this category are all children whose birth parents are of different ethnicity to each other, not just children with one white parent and one black parent (but not including children with two white parents of different nationality/ethnic origin). Table 1 shows the proportions of children in the three main categories of white, black and mixed parentage.

Turning to the birth parents of the children, a high level of personal, social and financial disadvantage can be seen. Sixty-six per cent of birth fathers and 68 per cent of birth mothers were described as having one or more personal difficulties. The list of difficulties on the questionnaire included mental health problems, learning difficulties, drug and alcohol problems and criminal convictions. In response to an open question about the nature of the birth parents' relationship, in 30 per cent of cases where birth parents had an ongoing relationship (n = 92), social workers

Table 1

The ethnic origin of children in the study

Child's ethnicity	n	%
White (both birth parents are white)	100	81
Mixed parentage (birth parents are of different ethnic origin to each other)	16	13
Black (both birth parents are black and of the same ethnic origin)	8	6
Total	**124**	**100**

mentioned that violence, usually against the woman, was a factor.

Relative to birth parents, the adopters of the children in the study have better housing, income and employment. The vast majority of children in the study (96 per cent) have been adopted by married couples. The main motivation to adopt for the majority (88 per cent) of adopters was because they were unable to have a child or a further child by birth. Eight per cent of children in the sample had been adopted by their foster carers. In five cases (4 per cent), the adopters were adopting the child because they had, at an earlier stage, adopted the child's older sibling.

Sibling relationships of the children in the study

How many children have birth siblings?
Counting full and half-siblings, 68 per cent (n = 85) of the 124 children have birth siblings. This is lower than the 80–90 per cent suggested by Kosonen (1996) in her review of the literature. This is probably explained by the young age and recency of placement of the children included in the present study. It is quite probable that the 32 per cent of children in the study who are currently the *only* child in their birth family, will subsequently have siblings born into their birth family.

Looking now at whether children have full siblings or half-siblings, we can see that 39 per cent of the children with siblings have full siblings. In the sample of children with siblings, over three-quarters (76 per cent) have half-siblings with the same mother (maternal siblings) and 34 per cent of the children have half-siblings with the same father (paternal siblings). All these figures refer to siblings that the child is *known* to have. It is very likely that many more children have paternal siblings, but there is a paucity of information about fathers and consequently about such siblings. These categories do overlap, with some children having both half- and full siblings. Table 2 attempts to further clarify the pattern of siblings.

Table 2
The pattern of full siblings and maternal and paternal siblings of sibling sample

Types of siblings	n	%
Full siblings only	10	12
Maternal siblings only	31	36
Paternal siblings only	4	5
Full siblings and paternal siblings	6	7
Full siblings and maternal siblings	15	18
Full siblings, maternal and paternal siblings	2	2
Maternal siblings and paternal siblings	17	20
Total	**85**	**100**

The mean number of siblings that children in the study have (of those who have siblings) is approximately three, with 95 per cent of the children having between one and five siblings (mean = 3.15, sd = 1.92, range = 1–10). Table 3 shows how many siblings the children have.

Table 3
Numbers of siblings of children in the sibling sample

Number of siblings per child	n	%
1	19	22.3
2	19	22.3
3	15	18
4	13	15
5 or more (maximum 10)	19	22.3
Total	**85**	**100**

Two-thirds (67 per cent) of the children with siblings are the youngest in their family. Eight per cent of children only have younger siblings and 22 per cent have both younger and older siblings. One set of twins have no siblings apart from each other.

In summary, the sibling relationships of the children are a further illustration of the complex family backgrounds of these adopted children. Whilst a large proportion (44 per cent) of children are born of parents who have lived together, such relationships are commonly not the first nor the only partnerships the birth parents have been involved in. The result of this is that many children (48 per cent) have siblings in more than one "branch" of their birth family. Over time, the complexity of relationships within birth families is likely to increase as further children are born.

How many children are placed with siblings?
Twenty-seven of the children with siblings are placed with one or more of their brothers and sisters (the largest group of siblings in the same placement is three). This constitutes 32 per cent of children with siblings and 22 per cent of the whole sample. Twenty-one (78 per cent) of these children were placed at the same time as their siblings (this includes four sets of twins); the rest were placed at different times. These results suggest that placement with siblings is more likely to be considered when children are needing adoption at the same time. Arrangements to place together siblings who need adoption at different times are made less often. Table 4 looks at the children placed with a sibling.

Table 4
The placement of children with a sibling

Children placed with a sibling (n=27)	Number of children	Both sibs in study sample?
Placed same time as twin	8	4 pairs
Placed same time as younger or older sib	13	2 pairs
Joined by younger sib later	2	no
Followed older sib placed earlier	4	no

Thoburn (1991), in her study of 1,165 adoption and permanent fostering placements, found that 40 per cent of *all children* in the sample were placed with a sibling. Whilst it is not known how many of the children in the sample actually had siblings, it nevertheless seems likely that the rate of placement with siblings in Thoburn's study is higher than in the current research. Kosonen's sample of 337 children in all types of placements found that 40 per cent of those *with siblings* were placed with a sibling. It is difficult to compare in a meaningful way the proportion of children placed with siblings in the present study with the findings of such other research studies because of differences in the populations of children. It is interesting to speculate, though, as to why the children in the current study have a relatively lower rate of placement with siblings. For example, is it because they are *adopted* as opposed to *fostered?* Is it that the young age of the children means that they can be placed more quickly alone than with older siblings?

As the questionnaires were focused on the index child, not the siblings, it is not possible in every case to say *why* children are not placed with siblings but three main themes do emerge, as follows:

- *Siblings are not in care or adopted.* It is apparent that in more than half (n=31, %=53) of the 58 cases where the child is not placed with one or more siblings, none of the index child's siblings are in care or adopted.
- *Siblings do not enter care at the same time.* In many cases, the children have come into care sequentially, rather than at one time. Often, in such situations, the siblings will never have lived together. A not uncommon example of this type of situation is when the first one or two children in a family are taken into care and adopted because of concerns for their welfare. Subsequent children born into the family are then removed at birth and adopted because of the likelihood of significant harm. In 62 per cent of cases in the sibling sample, there were concerns for the child's welfare because of the previous treatment of older siblings. It appears to be unusual (only six cases in this sample) that arrangements are made for younger siblings to join older ones in an adoptive home, although the reasons for this are not clear.
- *Siblings have never lived together.* It is not possible in all cases to tell when siblings have and have not lived together as the questionnaire

only collects information about current rather than past placements of siblings. However, it is clear that 22 children had definitely lived with siblings (26 per cent), nine probably had (11 per cent) and 54 (63 per cent) definitely had not. There are 12 children in the sample who are now separated from one or more siblings with whom they have lived in the past.

Where are the siblings living?

The complexity of children's relationships with siblings is further illustrated by looking at where the siblings are living. Only four children with siblings have no other siblings apart from those they are placed with. This means that, of all the children with siblings, 95 per cent have one or more siblings with whom they do not live. Even of the children who do live with a sibling, 85 per cent have more siblings living elsewhere. A further layer of complexity is that these other siblings are frequently not in only one other location. Overall, more than half of the 85 children with siblings (51 per cent) have siblings elsewhere in two or more different places.

Table 5
The number of locations of the siblings of children in the study

Number of different places where the child has siblings	n	%
0 – all siblings are placed with child	4	5
1	37	43
2	21	25
3	13	15
4, 5 or 6	7	8
Number of locations unknown	3	4
Total	**85**	**100**

More than half (51 per cent) of the children with siblings have one or more siblings who are also placed away from the birth family, either in foster care, residential care or a different adoptive home. An even higher proportion of the sample (76 per cent) have a sibling who lives with a birth parent or other relative. The next table looks in more detail at where the siblings are now living. Many children have siblings in more than one of the categories below.

Table 6
Type of living situations of the siblings

Where siblings are living	Number having a sibling in this situation	% (of 85)
In foster care	19	22
In a different adoptive home	28	33
At home with birth mother	23	27
At home with birth father	7	8
At home with both birth parents	5	6
At home with another birth relative of index child	15	18
Living independently or in residential care	13	15
At home with a relative (not of index child)	26	31

The most usual arrangement for children in the category "at home with a relative (not of index child)", is that paternal siblings are at home with *their* mother.

Contact with siblings

Overall level of contact with siblings

Of the 81 children who have birth siblings outside of their adoptive family, 42 per cent have contact with all of their siblings, or the potential for contact via contact with the parent/s or carer/s of such siblings. Twenty-three per cent of the children have contact with some of their siblings, but have no contact with others. Thirty-five per cent have no contact with any siblings and no contact with the parents or carers of such siblings. Adding the last two groups together, then, it can be seen that well over half (58 per cent) of the children in the study will have one or more siblings who live elsewhere with no means of contact arranged.

Sibling contact and the location of siblings

On taking a closer look, it can be seen that arrangements for contact with siblings vary according to where the siblings are growing up. To begin with, it can be seen that more arrangements for contact, especially face-to-face contact, are made for siblings who are also adopted or looked after than for siblings who live with relatives. Table 7 illustrates this.

Table 7

Variations in contact according to whether siblings live with birth relatives or are looked after or adopted

Type of contact with sibling	Siblings are "looked after" or adopted		Siblings living with their family	
	n	%	n	%
Face-to-face	20	46	6	11
Indirect	8	19	20	32
No contact	15	35	32	52
Missing data	0	0	3	5
Total	**43**	**100**	**61**	**100**

In this table "indirect contact" refers to the exchange of written information or greetings between the siblings, and to cases where the child has indirect contact with the carer of a sibling and it is known that siblings are involved in this. The information in Table 7 shows that the children in the study are more likely to have indirect contact with a sibling living with relatives than a sibling looked after or adopted. This higher level of contact is largely via links with the parents or carers of such siblings, and in most cases is set up to keep the child and adult in touch rather than specifically the siblings. Indirect contact with siblings in other placements, however, is more often a direct child–to–child link, arranged specifically to meet the needs of children rather than their carers. The children in the study are much less likely to actually *see* a sibling who lives with relatives than a sibling who is also out of their birth family. Overall levels of contact are also different, with over half the children having no contact with siblings *with relatives* as opposed to a third having no contact with siblings *in other placements*.

Within these two broad groups, however, there are variations between different situations. Table 8 attempts to tease out further differences in contact arrangements according to where siblings live. In this table "indirect contact" has a broader meaning. Wherever the index child is indirectly in touch with the parent or carer of a sibling this is coded as "indirect contact" with the sibling. It is acknowledged that in some cases siblings may be excluded from this link, but there is at least a potential route for them to make contact in the future. This kind of contact, or potential for it, accounts for almost all cases of "indirect contact" with siblings who are at home with the birth mother.

Table 8

Variations in contact according to eight types of living situations of siblings

Living situation of sibling/s	Face-to-face contact		Indirect contact		No contact		Totals	
	n	%	n	%	n	%	n	%
In foster care	9	47	3	16	7	37	19	100
In a different adoptive home	12	43	6	21	10	36	28	100
At home with birth mother	1	4	17	74	5	22	23	100
At home with birth father	0	0	1	14	6	86	7	100
At home with both birth parents	1	20	3	60	1	20	5	100
At home with birth relative of index child	3	20	3	20	9	60	15	100
Independent or in residential care	2	15	3	23	8	62	13	100
At home with a relative (not of index child)	3	11.5	3	11.5	20	77	26	100

N.B. the figures in this table cannot be summated vertically as many children have siblings in more than one category.

Although it is acknowledged that in some categories in this table there are very small numbers, nevertheless, some themes can be identified from both Table 7 and Table 8 that merit an airing.

- *Lack of contact with paternal siblings.* There are 29 children in the study who have paternal siblings. Such siblings commonly live with the ex-partner of the father. However, there are also some paternal siblings in foster care, adopted, living independently and living with the birth father. Regardless of such living arrangements, there are *no* cases where the child in the study sees a paternal sibling and only one case where indirect contact is maintained. There are five children with paternal siblings who have indirect contact with the birth father, but in none of these cases do the paternal siblings live with the father and in all cases the fathers' contact with the siblings is either non-existent or unknown. These paternal siblings, therefore, are almost invariably "lost" to the adopted children in the research. It is acknowledged that such siblings might well not have been in contact even if the index child were not adopted, but this relative lack of attention given to paternal siblings seems part of a wider pattern of the lack of involvement of fathers in adoption matters generally. In the current sample of 124 children, only 17 per cent of fathers had parental responsibility for their child. In 16 per cent of cases the identity of the father was not known by the adoption agency. In many more cases where the identity was known, very little other information was available. After adoption, three times as many mothers as fathers have any kind of contact with the child. The extent to which fathers are not involved through their own choice, through the birth mother's choice, or as a matter of social work practice is not clear. However, a similar lack of involvement of non-resident fathers with their children after divorce or separation has been found in a number of studies (Rodgers and Pryor, 1998).
- *Siblings living in the maternal versus paternal family.* Related to the point above, it seems that, when siblings live with relatives, there is a definite tendency towards more contact if the siblings live in the maternal birth family than in the paternal family. This seems to be largely because adult relatives in the maternal family, especially birth mothers, have more direct and indirect contact with the children after adoption than relatives in the paternal family. This illustrates the general inter-relationship between adult relative contact, sibling con-

tact and the location of siblings. When siblings live in the birth family, contact generally occurs as a "by-product" of contact with parents, grandparents, aunts and uncles. Where the relatives caring for the sibling are not related to the index child, sibling contact is much less likely to happen. When siblings are adopted or looked after, i.e. when siblings are separated from the birth family, sibling contact is "separated" from contact with adults and is therefore uncomplicated by considerations of the suitability or otherwise of contact with the child's carers.

- *Siblings with birth parents versus other relatives.* A third theme is that when siblings live with relatives, the index child is more likely to see that sibling if he or she lives with a relative *other* than a birth parent. This may indicate that sibling visits are not arranged when siblings live with birth parents because face-to-face contact with the birth parent/s is not seen as desirable and sibling contact is not seen as feasible without birth parent contact. Whether this is actually the case might be open to question. This way of thinking may also partly explain why looked after and adopted siblings have more contact than those at home.

Conclusions

This research project cannot, at this stage, increase our knowledge of any relationship between sibling issues and outcomes in adoption. However, this first stage of the research can already provide a sketch of current practice in this area. Also, the study has identified a representative sample of young adopted children and there is the potential to follow up these cases at a later date.

The key points indicated by the research so far are as follows:

- Children needing adoption today often have very complicated histories and many different needs that must be considered.
- Children needing adoption today also often have very complex sibling relationships. Many children have numerous siblings of different types and living in different locations.
- In this young age group many children do not know or remember their siblings.

- In this young age group more siblings come into care sequentially than at the same time.
- More arrangements are made for contact with siblings in other placements than those living at home.
- In many cases no arrangements are made for contact with siblings after adoption. Paternal siblings are particularly likely to be "lost".

It is hard to say, from the current body of research knowledge, to what extent it will matter to these adopted children that they have siblings whom they have no means of knowing (though see chapter by Pavlovic and Mullender, this volume). What this research suggests is that the loss of relationships with siblings for adopted children in this age group is more likely be a "covert loss" as many children have not lived with any or all of their siblings. This phrase was used by Nickman (1985) to describe the nature of the loss of birth parents for people adopted as infants. It is argued that the loss, although not apparent at the time of placement, awakens as the child's understanding of the meaning of adoption grows. The available evidence suggests that, for some adopted people and their non-adopted or separately adopted siblings, it will be a concern in the future that they have grown up apart and with no contact, so this notion of "covert loss" may also apply to sibling relationships. What cannot be known for certain is to what proportion and to which individuals this will apply. This in itself could be an argument for building into placements some means for siblings to have contact either now or in the future and for greater attention to be paid to the document-ation of family information.

What this research has shown is that agencies are making such efforts in some cases, even in situations where there are several siblings living in different families. However, well over half of children have siblings with whom there are no built-in arrangements for contact either now or in the future. In many cases, social workers completing questionnaires for this research had very little information about siblings, especially those siblings not adopted or looked after. Presumably, then, if the adopted person were to seek information through their files in adulthood they might not always find what they were looking for. In some cases the lack of information about, and of contact with, siblings is a problem being stored up for the future.

In many instances contact with siblings is out of the direct control of agencies arranging adoptions, as the siblings who are not looked after are not their responsibility. Furthermore, after the order is made, agencies cease to be responsible for the adopted child. Obtaining and recording more information about siblings or arranging for contact with siblings will, in these situations, necessitate the involvement and co-operation of other people, especially birth relatives and adopters. The difficulty involved in making these efforts may be significant and the benefits not immediately apparent, but actions taken at this stage of placement may be of significant importance to some adopted people and their relatives in the future.

Another learning point from this research is the finding that, in many cases, children from the same family will need placement for adoption at different points in time. While social workers cannot see into the future to determine if and when future children will be born and will need to be adopted, in some cases there will be indicators that this is likely. It may be possible, more than is happening at present, to find families who would be willing to consider adopting subsequent siblings should this be appropriate (see chapter by Jones, this volume, for an example of this happening).

When decisions are made about the needs of children requiring placement for adoption, social workers have many factors to consider. The immediate developmental needs of children will probably, and understandably, be highest on the agenda. However, we do know from research into the outcomes of adoption that issues of loss, rejection and identity will surface at some time in the future for many adopted people. Brothers or sisters may be important sources of support for adopted people in addressing such matters. What is already clear from this research is that obstacles to current and future contact between siblings are currently arising by default. Learning how and when such problems come about is a first step in making arrangements that may overcome them.

References

Barth R P and Berry M (1988) *Adoption and Disruption: Rates, risks and responses*, New York: Aldine de Gruyter.

Boer F, Versluis-den Bieman H J M and Verhulst F C (1994) 'International adoption of children with siblings: behavioural outcomes', *American Journal of Orthopsychiatry*, 64, pp 252–62.

Borland M, O'Hara G and Triseliotis J (1991) 'Placement outcomes for children with special needs', *Adoption & Fostering*, 15:2, pp 18–28.

Brodzinsky D M (1990) 'A stress and coping model of adoption adjustment', in Brodzinsky D M and Schechter M D (eds) *The Psychology of Adoption*, New York: Oxford University Press.

Cicirelli V G (1982) 'Sibling influence throughout the life span', in Lamb M E and Sutton-Smith B (eds) *Sibling Relationships: Their nature and significance across the lifespan*, Hillsdale, NJ: Lawrence Erlbaum.

Dunn J (1988) 'Sibling influences on childhood development', *Journal of Child Psychology & Psychiatry*, 29:2, pp 119–27.

Feast J and Howe D (1997) 'Adopted adults who search for background information and contact with birth relatives', *Adoption & Fostering*, 21:2, pp 8–15.

Howe D (1998) *Patterns of Adoption*, Oxford: Blackwell.

Humphrey H and Humphrey M (1988) *Families with a Difference: Varieties of surrogate parenthood*, London: Routledge.

Kosonen M (1996) 'Maintaining sibling relationships: a neglected dimension in child care practice', *British Journal of Social Work*, 26, pp 809–22.

Masson J, Harrison C and Pavlovic A (1996) *Working with Children and 'Lost' Parents: Putting partnership into practice*, York: Joseph Rowntree Foundation.

Mullender A and Kearn S (1997) *"I'm Here Waiting": Birth Relatives' views on Part II of the Adoption Contact Register for England and Wales*, London: BAAF.

Nickman S L (1985) 'Losses in adoption: the need for dialogue', *Psychoanalytic Study of the Child*, 40, pp 365–98.

Pacheco F and Eme R (1993) 'An outcome study of the reunion between adoptees and biological parents', *Child Welfare*, 72:1, pp 53–64.

Rodgers B and Pryor J (1998) *Divorce and Separation: The outcomes for children*, York: Joseph Rowntree Foundation.

Sachdev P (1992) 'Adoption reunion and after: a study of the search process and experience of adoptees', *Child Welfare*, 71:1, pp 53–68.

Thoburn J (1991) 'Survey findings and conclusions', in Fratter J, Rowe J, Sapsford D and Thoburn J (1991) *Permanent Family Placement: A decade of experience*, London: BAAF.

Triseliotis J (1973) *In Search of Origins*, London: Routledge and Kegan Paul.

Triseliotis J and Russell J (1984) *Hard to Place: The outcome of adoption and residential care*, London: Heinemann.

Triseliotis J, Shireman J and Hundleby M (1997) *Adoption: Theory, policy and practice*, London: Cassell.

Wedge P and Mantle G (1991) *Sibling Groups and Social Work*, Aldershot: Avebury.

5 Sibling separation and contact in permanent placement

Cherilyn Dance and *Alan Rushton*

Cherilyn Dance is a researcher at the Institute of Psychiatry. She has a degree in developmental psychology and her background is in nursing and health visiting. Since joining the research team in 1989 she has been involved in a variety of studies relating to adoption and fostering. More recently, along with Alan Rushton, she has begun to conduct research into parenting and child development among general population samples.

Alan Rushton is also at the Institute of Psychiatry. He has worked for many years in mental health social work. He currently directs the MSc Programme in Mental Health Social Work based at the Maudsley Hospital/Institute of Psychiatry in London. His research interests cover a wide variety of topics related to social work. His particular research interest is late permanent placement. With colleagues, he has recently published 'Joining New Families: A study of adoption and fostering in middle childhood' (Quinton et al, 1998).

The material for this chapter is drawn from a study which examined the first year of placement of looked after children who joined new, unrelated families during their middle childhood with the intention of permanence. The study had a broad scope, but we focus here on two features of placement that are related to the sibling status of the children: firstly, the ways in which children come to be placed with siblings or alone and secondly, planning for contact between separated children. These factors are important, since there is growing evidence that some singly placed children are at increased risk of experiencing more difficult placements and potentially a higher proportion of disruptions (see, for example, Barth and Berry, 1988; Holloway, 1997; Quinton *et al*, 1998). Additionally, although evidence from prospective research is not yet available, studies of self-selected adult adoptees are suggesting that placing children separately from siblings, at least in the past, has all too easily resulted in the children being virtually isolated from each other (Mullender and Kearn, 1997).

The main guidance on policy towards sibling group placement is to be found in the Children Act 1989 which states that siblings should be accommodated together whenever 'reasonably practicable and consistent with [the child's] welfare' (section 23 (7)(b)). Where only one child of a family needs to be accommodated on a long-term or permanent basis, there is clearly no option about placement alone; however, studies are consistent in reporting that a large proportion of looked after children do have siblings who are placed elsewhere in the care system (Bilson and Barker, 1992/3; Kosonen, 1996). The factors most frequently mentioned by social workers as important in decisions to maintain sibling groups are the mutual bond between the children, the degree of difficulty presented by the children and the influence of birth parents (Boer and Spiering, 1991). Reasons for separation, as reported by social workers, frequently focus on the individual needs of children, although children's views and limited placement availability may play a part (Wedge and Mantle, 1991). In Kosonen's (1996) study, the most frequently given reason for separation was that the siblings had entered care at different times. From her analysis Kosonen concluded that points of entering and leaving care, whether for return home, independence or for adoption, were especially likely to be associated with separation of siblings.

Of course, the research outlined above has examined all looked after children, whatever the placement plan. The children in the study reported here were entering placements that were planned with permanence as the goal. As such, the choices and plans made for them at placement may be expected to endure for the majority. In this context, the extent to which social workers were achieving the principle of maintaining sibling groups was a particularly important question.

The aims and methods of the research study

The study was prospective in design, taking referrals from 16 local authorities at the time a match was agreed between waiting children and their new family. All of the children were placed subsequent to the implementation of the Children Act 1989. Over a period of 21 months we collected a sample of 32 singly placed children and 40 sibling groups. Each placement included at least one child who was between five and 11 years old. Interviews were conducted with the new family, the children's social worker and the family placement social worker at three months and at one year after placement.

The majority of the information in this chapter comes from the initial interview with the children's social workers in which we explored the structure of the children's birth families and documented the characteristics, whereabouts and contact plans for any siblings from whom they were separated. Depending on the placement type, we also explored with the social workers decisions about separation, maintenance or reunion of sibling groups. In the course of talking to the new families we investigated their understanding of the plans for sibling contact and the extent to which these plans were realised in the course of the first year. We also sought their views on how the placed children reacted to seeing or hearing from their siblings.

Terminology

Before we move on to describe the findings we need to clarify the terms used in this paper. Firstly, we have employed the terms 'separated siblings' and 'other siblings' to indicate those from whom the sample children had been separated. Secondly, when discussing decision-making, we have chosen to concentrate on siblings who were under 17 years old at the time of data collection (described as 'dependent'), in order to capture only those placements where the placed child could reasonably be expected to know the sibling and where there might be a possibility of joint placement. The siblings who were 17 and over are referred to as 'independent'.

Placement decisions for children with siblings who were looked after

Aside from removing children from their parents, taking decisions about separating or maintaining siblings together in placement must be one of the most taxing demands on child care social workers. They must try to balance the competing needs of the children themselves, their parents, the views of other professionals and the likelihood of finding a placement where large groups of possibly difficult children could be accommodated. We were interested to explore the patterns of separation and reunion, the reasons that lay behind past decision-making, and the factors that influenced the practitioners in their plans for the permanent placement.

When it came to placing children for permanence, we found that the majority of the study placements represented a continuation of previous arrangements. Just two of the 32 singly placed children had been in their previous placement together with a sibling, with a decision then taken to separate them on planning their permanent placements because of either behavioural or relationship difficulties. Of the 40 sibling groups, 26 moved to their new placement with no question of changing the placement configuration, while for eight groups there had been considerable discussion about separating the children, although they eventually moved together, and in six cases the children were reunited.

Reunion possibilities for separated children

Of the 72 study placements (40 sibling groups and 32 individual children), the great majority (58) had at least one sibling living elsewhere. However, as illustrated in Figure 1, in only a minority of cases, 11 singly placed children and 13 sibling groups, were there other siblings who were looked after in the care system.

All but one of the singly placed sample children who had other looked after siblings, had been with one or more of their siblings at some point while "in care". On average, these children had been on their own in foster care for a little over two years (mean 25.27 months; sd = 15.59; range 0–53 months). Only two of these children had been separated for the permanent placement. Considerable thought had usually been applied to the initial separation of these children and, in seven of the nine cases of long-standing separation, some consideration had been given to the possibility of reunion.

The 13 sibling groups who also had other siblings elsewhere in the care system, in contrast to the singly placed children, tended to have been together for most of their care careers, but in only one case had they ever been placed with other siblings as well. While over half of the

Figure 1

The whereabouts of "siblings elsewhere" for 72 study placements

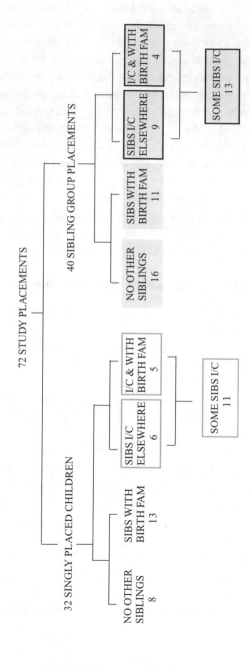

separations in respect of sibling groups were ascribed to the needs of the children involved, the others had occurred as a result of circumstantial factors, such as different times of entry to care or availability of placements (see Table 1). Re-examination of the possibility of reunion for these splintered sibling groups occurred in six out of 13 cases. At first glance it appears that much less attention was given to the circumstances of some sibling groups than others. However, a closer look at the characteristics of the children and the reasons for separation reveals a somewhat different picture.

Table 1
Reason for sibling separation in the past

	Sibling groups	Singletons	Total
A child's needs	7	5	16
Relationship between siblings	–	4	–
Reception dates different	5	1	6
Placement availability	1	–	1
A child's wishes	–	1	1
Totals	**13**	**11**	**24**

Starting with the children's needs for separate placement, these were usually described as problems with either the behaviour of one child or the relationship between children. Where one of the children had severe behavioural problems or there was a high level of conflict between children, this was sometimes thought to reduce the chances of finding a family and/or increase the risk of disruption. However, these views were clearly not applied consistently since there were, among the sample, sibling groups who demonstrated a good deal of conflict and bad feeling towards each other and some children who were jointly placed who showed considerable behavioural difficulties. We have not been able to identify any specific factors that discriminate between those who were separated and those who remained together despite difficult behaviour or relationships. It is possible that factors like the tolerance of carers or practitioner commitment to maintaining sibling ties come into play.

Factors associated with separate placement

When examining the characteristics of the sibling groups that had been separated, we found that the number of other looked after siblings ranged from one to six, varying similarly for both singleton and sibling group placements. Clearly, the possibility of finding one family able to accommodate some of the larger groups would have been unlikely. However, the extent to which reunion possibilities were discussed was not associated with the number of other siblings for either singletons or placed sibling groups.

Neither the extent to which the placed children knew siblings placed separately, nor indeed the quality of relationship between them, appeared to be associated with consideration of reunion. Perhaps surprisingly, deliberation about this was more likely when past separation had been due to children's needs rather than different reception dates or placement availability. In exploring the possible reasons for this, we found that age gaps between placed groups and separated children tended to be larger when separation was due to these more practical factors. Although the age differences were not significant, they may have discouraged reunion in some cases.

Thoughts of reunion were more likely when separated children were full siblings to those placed ($\chi^2 = 6.1$; df = 1; p<0.05). This was true for both sibling groups and singly placed children. In just over half of the cases, separated children were half-siblings to those placed. However, among the sample children, we found that one-quarter of sibling groups included at least some half-siblings, suggesting that this relationship does not necessarily exclude the possibility of joint placement. Among sibling groups in particular, there was a tendency for half-siblings looked after elsewhere to differ substantially in age from sample children. Although numbers are too small to apply statistical tests, it seems that a combination of age differences and the biological relationship between children may explain why less thought was given to reuniting some of the splintered sibling groups in this sample. They may have seemed in many ways more like siblings from separate families.

Since the singly placed children in the sample were almost always separated on the basis of perceived individual needs, we were somewhat surprised to find that, in half of the six cases of splintering that were due to practicalities of admission, the placed sibling groups had only one other sibling in care. However, on closer inspection, there were substantial age differences and substantial gaps between admission dates in these cases. Thus some of these separated children may have been well settled in their own placement at the time the sample children entered care.

Bearing in mind that most of the sibling groups in our sample did not have other siblings who were looked after in the care system, it seems that social workers were for the most part operating within the guidance which encourages maintenance of sibling groups. Where it occurred, separation usually resulted from the social workers' assessment of the needs of individual children. The exceptions were those cases in which the separated siblings were markedly different in age and only had one birth parent in common with the placed children.

Plans for contact with separated siblings

While accepting that separation may sometimes be unavoidable, there remains the question of contact between siblings. Wherever placement together is not possible, there is general agreement that some form of contact should be maintained between related children, in order that they know of each other's lives and have the opportunity to develop their relationship as they grow up.

We were keen to establish the extent to which arrangements had been made for separated siblings to stay in touch with each other and whether this varied according to where the siblings were living. Children in 58 of the 72 sample placements had brothers and sisters elsewhere. This includes ten cases where the only other siblings were independent at the time of placement. Separated siblings were all with the birth family in nearly half the cases, elsewhere in the care system in just under one-third and had some siblings in each in 20 per cent of cases. It was disappointing to find that, overall, definite plans for face-to-face contact with at least one other sibling had been made in only 29 cases. There were two cases in which the placed children were to have some postal contact with their sibling/s but no meetings.

The whereabouts of the other siblings were found to be significant, especially for singly placed children. Where there were separated siblings who were looked after elsewhere, definite plans for contact had been made with at least one brother or sister for all of the singly placed children and for eight of the 13 sibling groups. However, where all of the other siblings remained with the birth family, contact arrangements had been made for fewer than half of the sibling groups and only one quarter of singleton placements.

Because we are dealing with quite a small number of children, many of whom have complex sibling networks, we have included in these figures any occurrence of a plan for contact. In some cases this was a plan to meet only one sibling, where there may have been many. This raises the question of whether what was planned was sufficient to meet the children's needs. In five cases, the level of contact was thought to be insufficient, in the view of the social worker, and there were concerns that lack of contact might lead to difficulties for the placed children. Of the cases where no definite arrangements had been made for sibling contact, social workers felt that, in all cases, this could be a cause of difficulty for the placed children.

While singly placed children were no more likely than others to have contact arrangements with their siblings, there was a tendency for social workers to feel that lack of sibling contact would be potentially more problematic for singletons ($\chi^2 = 6.0$; df=2; p<.05). Lack of contact with siblings at home was clearly associated with lack of contact with the birth parent. Sometimes this was due to birth parents refusing to see the placed child, making it difficult for social workers to effect contact between the siblings.

It was of interest to explore whether the contact plan was associated with the reason for separation. For example, it might have been that those separated for reasons of poor relationship or difficult behaviour were thought better off without ongoing contact. However, this was not the case; where there were other siblings who were looked after, plans for meetings were in place for all of the children who had been separated from other siblings because of individual needs assessments, but this was only true for two of the six sibling groups who were splintered for reasons of different admission dates or placement availability. These four groups of children who were to lose contact were those for whom there had been no consideration given to reunion.

In the past it has been common for levels of contact with birth family members to decrease and sometimes to cease completely when children are placed for adoption. We explored the data to see to what extent the sample children would experience a reduction in contact. We found that although sample children who had been in contact with brothers or sisters prior to the move were likely to remain in contact with some siblings, there was a reduction in the number of other children many of them were likely to see. Table 2 illustrates the proportion of other siblings who were described by social workers as known to the placed children, the proportion that had been in contact in the past, and where plans were in place for future meetings. Regardless of whether other siblings were living with birth parents or other substitute carers, there was a decrease in the numbers of other siblings who would remain in touch with the children. Thus, although most of the placed children who had siblings who were looked after elsewhere were in touch with some, there were still 40 per cent of these separated children for whom further contact with the placed children was unlikely. The different level of contact

Table 2

The proportion of siblings maintaining face-to-face contact with the placed children according to place of residence

	Whereabouts of siblings elsewhere								
	Birth family n=59		Extended family n=11		Independent n=21		In care n=55		Significance of group differences
	n	%	n	%	n	%	n	%	
Known to the placed children	40	68	9	55	11	52	49	89	χ^2 =8.6, df=3, p<·05
Contact in past	20	34	4	36	12	57	43	78	χ^2=24.0, df=3, p<·001
Contact in future	10	17	4	36	9	43	33	60	χ^2= 20.6, df=3, p<·001

NB As the categories are not mutually exclusive, columns do not total.

planning according to where the other siblings were living was also thrown into stark relief by this comparison.

By examining the data available concerning the other siblings, of whom there were 154 in total, we were able to establish that a plan for contact post placement was more likely when the children knew each other reasonably well and were relatively close in age.

Contact with siblings during the first year of permanent placement

Of course, planning for contact does not necessarily mean that it will happen. We only followed the placements for the first year, but one would expect that contact with siblings would happen in that time frame. According to the new parents' or carers' reports at the end of the year, sibling contact had taken place as planned in the majority of cases. Plans made for singly placed children were more likely to be fulfilled although not significantly so. In only one singleton placement had there been a contact plan that had not materialised, whereas planned contact had not happened in four sibling group placements (see Figures 1a and 1b).

On the whole, sibling contact was viewed very positively by parents and carers in both groups (see Figures 2a and 2b), although parents of jointly placed children reported that contact with siblings had a mixed or negative effect on a slightly higher proportion of their children. In both groups, the proportion of families reporting mixed or negative effects of sibling contact reduced over the year as all parties adjusted to the experience. Negative parental assessments of sibling contact which endured throughout the year occurred when their children were exposed to "mixed messages" or undesirable lifestyles or where the children were frightened of their siblings. The major obstacle to sibling contact arose during negotiations with the carers of the "other" siblings. There were examples of resistance from both custodial birth parents and adopters or foster carers. Overall, the new parents of the study children were very open to facilitating contact between the placed children and their siblings, although practicalities could be considerable in cases where many children, different placements and sometimes large distances were involved.

Figure 1a and b
The extent of sibling contact during the year for singly and jointly placed children

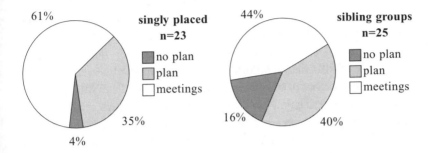

Figure 2a and b
The effect of sibling contact during the year for singly and jointly placed children

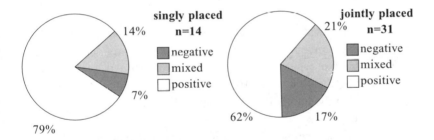

Note: Numbers of placements and children are reduced because one year data were not available for some cases. For sibling groups the extent of contact is based on the number of placements; the effect of contact is presented according to the number of children who were placed in sibling groups.

Discussion

The major point to take from this paper is that the majority of children placed in this study (two-thirds) did not have siblings from whom they were separated by the care system. Indeed, because relatively few of the children were separated, our ability to tease out the associated factors was limited; nevertheless the findings presented above do raise some important issues.

Where it occurred, separation of children was usually instigated or perpetuated as a result of social work planning – the practitioner's perceptions of the children's individual needs with regard to either behaviour problems or difficulties within the sibling relationship being the major reasons for this. Behavioural difficulties have repeatedly been shown to threaten the stability of placements and, indeed, data from other areas of this study suggest that enduring problems between siblings can negatively affect new parents' and carers' reports of satisfaction with the placement. We would not wish to underestimate the difficulties and dilemmas involved in planning for children requiring placement, but it seems, from the findings outlined above, that the need to achieve permanency may in some cases be in competition with the aim of maintaining siblings together. Bringing together these aims would only be feasible if there were sufficient professional time and skill available. However, a greater emphasis on improving the behaviour of children or the relationships between them might reduce the need for separation. This might, of course, entail a wider use of other professional resources. While there are obviously limitations on the numbers of children that can be placed with any one family, it may be possible to establish placements with an agreement between the authority and carers that further children from the same family could be placed at a later date, if necessary or appropriate.

The data concerning sibling contact revealed that nearly half the placements were made without any definite plan for contact and that, where there was a plan, this rarely included all possible siblings. For singleton placements in particular, social workers felt that losing touch with siblings was likely to pose additional difficulties for the children. Lack of any sibling contact at all was usually because the other brothers and sisters remained with the birth family. This points to a need for social workers to work both with birth parents and their children towards the development of contact arrangements that are sufficient to meet the needs of the placed children. We have no data about how the children who remained with their own parents may have reacted to either losing or maintaining contact with the sample children; indeed, this is an area which has, thus far, been relatively unexplored (though see chapter by Hodgkins, this volume).

On the whole the new families we spoke to reported a good deal of sympathy with the aim of maintaining relationships with the children's brothers and sisters. They were prepared to accommodate considerable upheaval in family life to support the contact. A minority of families drew attention to problems such as their children's fear of their siblings or worries about the behaviours to which children were exposed during meetings or the character of the interaction between the children. These cases underline the fact that it is not sufficient simply to establish contact arrangements. Ensuring they are positive for all concerned would entail active social work involvement with all those participating at the setting-up stage and also the continued availability of social work assistance should circumstances change.

We have concentrated here on face-to-face meetings between children and their siblings, largely because there were so few examples of other means of contact. The children in our study were mostly of an age to be able to appreciate some form of written communication and certainly old enough to talk to siblings on the telephone. Yet, while cards were exchanged and 'phone calls made when there was also face-to-face contact, these methods were rarely employed on their own as a means of keeping children in touch. These more indirect methods might be well worth considering when direct contact is not deemed advisable.

Conclusion

Much thought and exploration of options had been applied in this study to planning for children, particularly those who were placed alone. It is evident that separation of siblings for permanent placement was not routinely due to poor practice or lack of resources. Indeed it usually resulted from an attempt to balance the twin principles of achieving placements that were likely to endure on a long-term basis and the desirability of keeping related children together. However, some siblings were separated on the grounds of difficult behaviour or poor relationships between them, while others with similar problems were placed together.

It is clear that different decisions are being made despite what appear to be very similar characteristics in the children and their relationships.

References

Barth R and Berry M (1988) *Adoption and Disruption: Rates, risks and responses*, New York: Aldine de Gruyter.

Bilson A and Barker R (1992/3) 'Siblings of children in care or accommodation: a neglected area of practice', *Practice*, 6:4, pp 307–318.

Boer F and Spiering S (1991) 'Siblings in foster care: success and failure', *Child Psychiatry and Human Development*, 21:4, pp 291–300.

Holloway J (1997) 'Outcome in placements for adoption or long term fostering', *Archives of Disease in Childhood*, 76, pp 227–230.

Kosonen M (1994) 'Sibling relationships for children in the care system', *Adoption & Fostering* 18:3, pp 30–35.

Kosonen M (1996) 'Maintaining sibling relationships: a neglected dimension in child care practice', *British Journal of Social Work*, 26, pp 809–822.

Mullender A and Kearn S (1997) *'I'm here waiting': Birth relatives' views on Part II of the Adoption Contact Register for England and Wales*, London: BAAF.

Quinton D, Rushton A, Dance C and Mayes D (1998) *Joining New Families: Establishing permanent placements in middle childhood*, Chichester: John Wiley & Sons.

Wedge P and Mantle G (1991) *Sibling Groups in Social Work: A study of children referred for permanent substitute family placement*, Aldershot: Avebury.

6 The role of sibling group structure on adoption outcomes

Celia Beckett, Christine Groothues and
Thomas G O'Connor

Celia Beckett is a research worker in the Department of Child and Adolescent Psychiatry, Institute of Psychiatry, University of London. Her background is in family placement work and research and she is an adoptive parent of a sibling group.

Christine Groothues has been a research worker in the Department of Child and Adolescent Psychiatry, Institute of Psychiatry, for a number of years. Her background is in family research and social work.

Thomas G O'Connor is Lecturer in Developmental Psychology in the Departments of Psychology and Child and Adolescent Psychiatry at the Institute of Psychiatry.

Introduction

The influence of sibling group structure (the combination of related and non-related siblings) on outcomes in adoption is an important focus for further research. Policy makers look to the limited available research on sibling constellations for guidance on which placements are more likely to succeed.

Interpretation of research findings on adoption placements is limited for a number of reasons, such as a single variable rather than a multivariate approach, looking at the influence of one factor rather than a combination of factors (see discussion in Groothues *et al*, 1999) and the shortage of longitudinal studies of outcome. A further limitation is created by policy and practice, which permit only specific types of placement. In particular in the adoption of babies, which has declined substantially over the past 30 years, placement agencies are extremely selective and the majority of agencies will only consider childless couples who are infertile (Dance, 1998). It is atypical for two children to be placed at the same time for adoption unless they are biological siblings. Placements in families who already have birth children are usually only made when the age gap between the birth child and the adopted child is a minimum of three years. Families with birth children are generally only considered as adopters of children with special needs or older children, perhaps adding to the stresses in the family through the formation of new sibling relationships.

One widely reported finding from research in fostering and adoption is that the presence in the family of birth children of the adoptive or foster parents, particularly if those children are close in age to the adopted or foster child, increases the risk of poor outcomes (Trasler, 1960; Parker, 1966; George, 1970; Berridge, 1987; Barth and Brooks, 1997; Quinton *et al*, in press), but this finding was not replicated in other studies (Zwimpfer, 1983; Boyne *et al*, 1984; Festinger, 1986).

This study seeks to add to the research literature on the role of different sibling constellations in adoption by examining a sample of families who adopted children from Romania in the early 1990s.

The families included in the Romanian study (Rutter *et al*, 1998) are atypical adoptive families in several respects. For example, although some families were initially motivated to adopt because of their own childlessness, many adopted because of a humanitarian response to the plight of children in Romanian institutions. In addition, families frequently identified a child or children before completing a home study assessment with their local authority and gaining approval from the Department of Health (DoH). These factors not only resulted in important differences between these adopters from overseas compared with domestic adopters, but also meant that many of the adopting parents in the current study went through an application process that diverged from existing DoH guidelines (1997). For instance, contrary to DoH recommendations, 15 per cent of the sample adopted more than one unrelated child within a short time period (a further six per cent adopted related children). Forty per cent of the families had their own birth children living in the household and, of these, half were within 36 months of the age of the adopted child. In addition, half the mothers and more than half of the fathers would have been considered too old to adopt a young child, if guidelines generally used by UK adoption agencies had been followed. The families in this study also adopted children with a high risk of developmental and social difficulties as almost all the children had experienced very poor previous care.

The circumstances surrounding these adoptions from Romania have provided a unique opportunity to examine empirically the value of current policies and guidelines on the role of age spacing and sibling group composition in the adjustment to adoption and to relate this to child characteristics.

The sample

The study sample of 165 children was drawn from the 324 Romanian children identified from Home Office and DoH records adopted into families living in England between February 1990 and September 1992. The adopters travelled to Romania and arranged the placements of the children; some looked after the children for a period in Romania, either in institutions or elsewhere. We have used the date they returned with the child to the UK to categorise the children by age bands, and this is referred to as age at entry.

Stratified sampling was applied to attain a target number of 13 boys and 13 girls aged between 0–3 months and 3–6 months at entry to the UK, and thereafter ten boys and ten girls in six month age bands to 24 months. Relatively few families adopted children at an older age, so all the children who entered the UK between 24 and 42 months were selected for the study. This gave a total of 117 children below 24 months at entry and 48 children between 24 and 42 months. Eighty-one per cent of the families who were approached agreed to take part in the study and, when a family refused, the child was replaced by the next child of a similar age and sex, thereby sustaining the overall sample size of 165. The 165 children in the sample were adopted into 148 families (17 having adopted two children in the study).

Those children younger than 24 months at entry have been assessed at four and six years of age; those joining adoptive families at 24 months or older were only assessed at six years of age. The assessment consisted of a detailed interview with the child's primary caregiver (in most cases the mother) and a comprehensive developmental assessment of the child (see Rutter *et al*, 1998). Most of the children were adopted from Romanian institutions; only a minority (n = 24) were adopted directly from their birth families. Over 80 per cent of the children who had been in an institution were placed there at birth or shortly afterwards. The conditions within the institutions were extremely severe; they were understaffed and under-resourced and the children suffered from global physical and psychological deprivation. Reich (1990) describes conditions in the institutions and the socio-economic factors resulting in children being placed in institutional care. As a consequence of the early privation, at the time of entry to the UK most of the children were extremely developmentally delayed and malnourished. In brief, half were below the third percentile for weight at placement and the majority were seriously developmentally delayed. Nevertheless, at four years of age the majority had made a very significant physical and cognitive recovery (Rutter *et al*, 1998).

The background of the children and the adopters

We do not have systematic data on the children's background, but adoptive parents reported that the children from Romanian institutions all experienced extreme poverty. In 85 per cent of the cases, poverty seemed to be the reason for the child being relinquished by the birth parents to an institution. Adoptive parents reported that 16 of the children had an important relationship with a sibling in Romania, but only five of those 16 children were placed with that sibling.

The mean age difference between the adopting parents and the adopted child was 35.5 years for the mothers (range 24–53 years) and 38 years (range 23–57 years) for the fathers. Although there are no specific age criteria for adopters from overseas, in domestic infant adoptions a maximum age difference between adoptive parent and child of 35 years is used as a general guideline. Half of the mothers and two-thirds of the fathers exceeded this age gap.

The adoptive parents were of higher social status compared with the general population. Only one in ten families was headed by a parent whose employment status was semi-skilled or unskilled. This is to be expected given that families adopting from abroad are required not to have 'recourse to public funds' (DoH, 1997) and that they must bear the additional costs associated with these adoptions such as legal fees and travel.

Two-thirds of the adopters had enquired about adoption or applied to adopt in the UK. Of these, only 14 per cent had been approved to adopt children in the UK and four had already adopted; the remainder either did not pursue domestic adoption in the UK or withdrew for a variety of reasons (e.g. lack of available placements, their age, already having birth children in the family).

Measures

The measures used to evaluate the adoptions were taken from the interview and questionnaires completed by the mother. Ratings were made of the parental satisfaction with the adoption. Positive and negative evaluation were each rated separately, based on parental responses about the most rewarding aspects of having the child in the family and, on the other hand, about things that had not worked out as hoped. In addition, there was a question about any aspects they had found particularly surprising or disconcerting. Ratings were made on a scale from 0 to 3, indicating "not at all", "minor", "moderate" or "marked".

The impact on the family, the effects of the child's arrival on each of their new siblings, and how well the child got on currently with the sibling were rated using separate 0 to 3 scales. A target child, closest in age to the study child, was selected for the analysis of the sibling relationship, but separate analyses were also run for other children in the family who were more widely spaced, and an overall score for the level of intensity of the sibling relationships was calculated, indicating whether it was negative to a moderate or marked degree and whether this involved more than one sibling.

An index of the children's current behavioural problems was assessed using the Revised Pre-school Behaviour Questionnaire, revised for use with parents (with the pro-social items from Weir and Duveen, 1981; Elander and Rutter, 1996). This questionnaire provides a total problem score as well as sub-scales for emotional, oppositional and hyperactivity problems.

Findings at age four

Parental evaluation

When the children were aged four years (having lived with their adoptive families for between two and four years) there was a high level of reported satisfaction among all the adopting parents. Eighty-nine per cent reported 'marked satisfaction' with the adoption, and a further ten per cent 'moderate satisfaction'.

There was wider variation in parental report of negative evaluation at the four-year-old assessment. Although 88 per cent reported minimal or no negative evaluation, 12 per cent expressed marked or moderate negative evaluation with the adoption. Negative evaluation was associated with age spacing and constellation of sibling groups. The families with their own birth child closely spaced to the adopted child expressed more negative evaluation than families who had other adopted children closely spaced to the study child, or widely spaced birth children, with 32 per cent reporting marked or moderate negative evaluation (see Beckett *et al*, 1998).[1] In addition, the level of negative evaluation expressed by families was correlated with the degree of the children's behavioural problems, notably hyperactivity and conduct.[2]

The families who had adopted two younger children from Romania in the sample expressed very little negative evaluation of the adoption; none of these families reported either moderate or marked dissatisfaction with the adoption. Similarly, of the families who had widely spaced birth children, only one expressed moderate dissatisfaction with the adoption.

Interestingly, despite the wide variation in the age at which children joined their families, this was not a significant predictor of negative evaluation.

---

[1] F (2.78) = 7.29, p<.01 (Beckett *et al*, 1998)
[2] correlations: hyperactivity r =.28, p<.01, conduct r =.34 p<.01

Sibling conflict at four

When the children were assessed at four years old, the level of conflict between siblings was associated with the age gap between the children, with closely spaced children engaging in more conflict.[3] At age four, the children who were closely spaced had the highest level of sibling conflict, with 34 per cent of the parents reporting that the adopted child and their birth or adopted child close in age had a moderate/marked level of sibling conflict. Widely spaced siblings had a lower level of conflict, with only six per cent of parents reporting a moderate/marked level of sibling conflict. The degree of sibling conflict was also related to the negative evaluation of the adoption.

Overall, 27 per cent of the sample seen at four years described relationships between the study child and their sibling closest in age as moderately or markedly conflicted. The age at which the child joined the family was, once again, a factor in determining the level of sibling conflict.

Findings at six-year follow-up

Parental evaluation

When the children who were first seen at four years old were followed up at six years, they had been living with their parents for between four and six years. Parents continued to report a high level of satisfaction with the adoption. There had been an overall decline in the percentage of parents reporting a marked or moderate negative evaluation, from 12 per cent to six per cent. This decline was most marked in the group of families who had adopted a child close in age to their own birth children, for whom negative evaluation fell from 32 per cent to nine per cent.[4] There had not been a corresponding decline in the level of behavioural problems at age six, so the decline in the negative evaluation at six was not accounted for by a change in the children's behaviour.

There were still differences between the levels of negative evaluation of the different sibling constellations but, when the behavioural difficulties of the child were considered, these differences were

---

[3] $F_{(1,81)} = 8.53$, p<.01 (Beckett et al, 1998)
[4] $t(21) = 2.34$, p<.05

no longer significant at the six-year interview.

The families who had adopted two closely spaced adopted children continued to express very little negative evaluation, with none reporting moderate or marked negative evaluation of the adoption and fewer behavioural difficulties being experienced.

Families with widely spaced birth children also continued to report very little negative evaluation, none reporting moderate or marked negative evaluation with the adoption at the six-year interview.

Sibling conflict at six

Some of the most interesting points to arise from the study were, firstly, that, at age six, there were no longer any significant differences between closely and widely spaced siblings in the level of sibling conflict. While the overall level of sibling conflict had not decreased between the ages of four and six, there had been some changes within different sibling groups which brought them closer together on this measure. Thus, at age six, the number of parents of widely spaced siblings reporting moderate or marked conflict had increased from six per cent to 18 per cent, but that of the closely spaced children had fallen from 34 per cent to 26 per cent.

Second, and importantly, one moderating factor on the degree of sibling conflict was identified at age six. The families were asked whether they were able to set aside special times for their adopted child, and if so how often. Sibling conflict was highest in families who did not set aside a special time for the individual child. Thirty-six per cent of those families who set aside no special time to spend with their adopted child reported moderate or marked sibling conflict, compared with two per cent of those families who said they set time aside on more than three days a week.[5] This finding was not moderated by family size. The finding regarding time set aside will be further discussed below.

Findings for the older children

Parental evaluation

The children who were over two years old when they joined their families

---

[5] $F_{(3,83)} = 3.13$, $p < .05$

had, at the time of the interview at six years, been living with their new families for between two-and-a-half and four years. The parents expressed a high level of satisfaction with the adoptions, with 85 per cent expressing marked satisfaction and a further 13 per cent moderate satisfaction.

As with the adopters of the earlier adopted children, there was greater variation in the level of negative evaluation, with 20 per cent of the families with later placed adoptees expressing moderate or marked dissatisfaction with the adoption. They expressed significantly more dissatisfaction with the adoption than the adopters of the youngest children who were less than six months when they joined their families.[6] There were no differences in the level of negative evaluation between the oldest group and those aged between six and 24 months when they joined their families. Nor were there any differences in dissatisfaction according to the type of sibling structure, but the numbers in each group were relatively small.

Sibling conflict

Twenty-eight per cent of the adopters of older children (i.e. those aged over 24 months at placement) reported marked or moderate sibling conflict.

As had been found with the younger children, and again importantly, the time the family was able to set aside specifically for the child was a significant factor in reducing sibling conflict. Seventy-one per cent of the families who did not set aside specific time for the adopted child reported moderate or marked sibling conflict, compared with only 17 per cent of those who set aside time more than three times a week.[7]

Findings for whole sample

Within-family comparison of sibling conflict

The levels of sibling conflict were analysed for the relationship with one sibling in each family, the closest in age to the study child. Where there

---

[6] $F(2,160) = 3.86$, $p<.05$
[7] $F(3,30) = 4.93$, $p<.01$

were two or more siblings in the family, a comparison was made between the levels of sibling conflict of a closely and widely spaced sibling. It was found that the level of conflict between the widely spaced siblings was less marked than that of the closely spaced siblings within the same family.[8] In a very small number of families (n = 3), the degree of conflict for both closely and widely spaced siblings was moderate or marked, and this appeared to be contributing to the level of dissatisfaction with the adoption, with the mothers reporting moderate or marked dissatisfaction with the adoption.

Summary and discussion

This study reveals a complex and changing relationship between sibling constellation, the age at placement, the child's behavioural difficulties, and the evaluation of the adoption. There were differences in reported levels of dissatisfaction according to the sibling group composition at the age of four. In particular, families who had closely spaced birth children reported higher levels of negative evaluation at age four, though this had markedly declined by age six.

Adopters of the older children, who have only been seen at six, reported higher levels of dissatisfaction than the younger group at follow-up, with significantly more dissatisfaction than the adopters of the youngest children, who joined their families under six months of age (see footnote 6). The levels of conflict between the older children and their siblings were not different from that of the younger children and their siblings. A further follow-up is planned when the children are 11 years old. At that stage, it should be possible to judge whether the higher level of reported dissatisfaction among the older group is related to the age at placement or to the length of time the children have been in placement. It will also be possible to ascertain whether levels of dissatisfaction decline generally as the placement progresses, or whether this finding only applies to the younger children. At the 11-year-old follow-up, it will also be possible to judge whether the early difficulties in adjustment for families with birth children have any impact on the future

---

[8] $t = -2.85$, $p < .01$ (Beckett et al, 1998)

success of the placements. It is not possible to conclude at this stage whether the stresses of adopting a child close in age to a birth child improve over time or whether they change at different developmental stages.

On the basis of the study findings, it is possible to make some tentative comments regarding the progress of different family placements. First, families with two adopted young children (either related or unrelated) were very satisfied when the children were four years old and continued to report very little negative evaluation when the children were six years old. This suggests that there may be no greater risks to the adjustment of unrelated children than of related children, placed simultaneously, provided the children are both very young.

Second, the families whose birth children were close in age to the adopted child expressed a comparatively high level of dissatisfaction at four but, by age six, this had declined and was no longer different from other families. The majority of these families appear to have experienced an improvement in sibling relationships over the two years though, for small minority of the families where there were continuing difficulties between one or more siblings, the negative evaluation was still high.

Third, families with widely spaced birth children described a low level of sibling conflict at four but this had increased by age six. This did not appear to have any impact on the reports of parental dissatisfaction, however, which were very low.

Finally, for the older groups of children, who have only been seen once at age six, there does not appear to be any connection between the type of sibling group composition and outcome measures, as they all expressed higher levels of dissatisfaction. It may not be possible to ascertain whether sibling constellation has any impact on outcome for this group until a further follow-up is completed at 11. It is not clear whether the adoption of two older children is more difficult because of the greater difficulties of adopting an older child, or because of the potential for additional stress in taking on two placements. Any analysis is also limited because of the smaller number of children adopted over the age of two years.

Families who adopt more than one child, or who integrate an adopted child into an existing or growing family, are taking on additional demands and pressures and need to ensure that they have the time and commitment to devote to that child's individual needs. If they do not, this is likely to have an impact on the relationships between siblings. The older the child and the more complex the problems, the more demands will be made on a family, and therefore the ability to make this individual commitment is increasingly important.

References

Barth R and Brooks D (1997) 'A longitudinal study of family structure and size and adoption outcomes', *Adoption Quarterly*, 1, pp 29–57.

Beckett C, Groothues C, O'Connor T G and the English and Romanian Study Team (1998) 'The experience of adopting from Romania: the role of siblings in adjustment', *Adoption & Fostering*, 22:2, pp 25–34.

Berridge D and Cleaver H (1985) *Foster Home Breakdown*, Oxford: Blackwell.

Boyne J, Denby L, Kettenring J R and Wheeler W (1984) *The Shadow of Success: A statistical analysis of outcomes of adoptions of hard-to-place children*, Westfield, New Jersey: Spaulding for Children.

Dance C (1998) *Focus on Adoption: A Snapshot of adoption patterns in England–1995*, London, BAAF.

Department of Health (1997) *A Guide to Inter-country Adoption: Guidance on Practice and Procedures*, London: Department of Health.

Elander J and Rutter M (1996) 'Use and development of the Rutter parent's and teacher's scale', *Journal of Methods in Psychiatric Research*, 6, pp 63–78.

Festinger T (1986) *Necessary Risk: A study of adoptions and disrupted adoptive placements*, Washington: Child Welfare League of America.

George V (1970) *Foster Care: Theory and practice*, London: Routledge & Kegan Paul.

Groothues C, Beckett C and O'Connor T G (1999) 'Outcomes of adoptions from Romania: predictors of parental satisfaction', *Adoption & Fostering*, 22:4, pp 30–40.

Home Office, Entry Clearance Procedures leaflet *RON117*.

Parker R (1966) *Decision in Child Care: A study of prediction in fostering*, London: Allen & Unwin.

Quinton D, Rushton A, Dance C and Mayes D (1998) *Joining New Families: Establishing permanent placements in middle childhood*, London: John Wiley & Sons.

Reich D (1990) 'Children of the Nightmare', *Adoption & Fostering*, 14:3, pp 9–14.

Rutter M and the English and Romanian Study Team (1998) 'Developmental catch-up and deficit following adoption after severe global early deprivation', *Journal of Child Psychology & Psychiatry*, 39:4, pp 465–76.

Trasler G (1960) *In Place of Parents*, London: Routledge & Kegan Paul.

Weir K and Duveen G (1981) 'Further development and validation of the Prosocial Behaviour Questionnaire for use by Teachers', *Journal of Child Psychology & Psychiatry*, 22:4, pp 357–74.

Zwimpfer D (1983) 'Indicators of adoption breakdown', *Social Casework*, 64, pp 169–77.

7 Children being looked after and their sibling relationships
The experiences of children in the working in partnership with 'lost' parents research project

Christine Harrison

Christine Harrison is Lecturer in Applied Social Studies at the University of Warwick. She previously worked as a social worker in child care and child protection and as a guardian ad litem. Her research interests include children in the looked after population and their parents, as well as feminist perspectives in child protection. During 1993–96, she conducted a major research study, jointly with Professor Judith Masson and Dr Anita Pavlovic, on restoring working partnerships with parents of children in the public care where contact had been lost.

Introduction: siblings and being looked after

This chapter explores the significance of sibling relationships for a group of children separated from their parents – those being looked after on a long-term basis by local authorities. Families of children in the public care experience considerable disadvantage and discrimination (Bebbington and Miles, 1989; Ahmad, 1990; Langan, 1992; Booth and Booth, 1994; Parton, 1996) and, in addition, looked after children may have experienced abuse or neglect before and after their reception into care (Millham *et al*, 1986). They are also likely to have endured considerable losses before, during and after care. This includes not just the loss of people significant to them, serious though the implications of this are, but other familiar and important aspects of their lives, like friendships and familiar community and culture. Singly or in combination, these losses may undermine a sense of personal, familial and ethnic history and have a negative effect on identity (Harrison, 1999).

Research has continued to raise fundamental concerns about social work intervention with children and families, and specifically about the quality of care given to children being looked after by local authorities (Department of Health, 1991; Utting, 1991; Stevenson, 1992; Ward, 1995). For children and young people in the public care on a long-term basis, care has frequently been characterised by instability, disruption and sometimes abuse. This has had persisting effects on their identity and self-esteem as adults (Stein and Carey, 1986; Biehal *et al*, 1992; Fowler *et al*, 1996). Evidence further suggests that the needs of disabled children and black children, in particular, have not been met (Morris, 1995; Barn *et al*, 1997).

This accumulating knowledge has precipitated a re-evaluation of the care of children away from their families, and has shifted views about attachment, permanence and the significance and form of contact with parents, siblings and other people important to the child. One factor which is now considered to assist with many of the above problems is that of maintaining links with parents, brothers and sisters, and other family members. Not only is family contact often the key to discharge from care (Milham *et al*, 1986; Bullock *et al*, 1993), but contact and knowledge of family of origin can be crucial to a child or young person's well-being while in long-term care. This has challenged the belief that security and a positive sense of identity for those being looked after lies in the severing of all links and in placement for adoption (Ryburn, 1993). It is now accepted that there are different routes to permanence (Triseliotis, 1985; Thoburn *et al*, 1986, 1990 and 1994) and that children can maintain attachments to a number of significant people in their lives (Schaffer, 1990; Fratter, 1996). Maintaining contact with parents appears to contribute to placement stability (Fanshel and Shinn, 1978; Mullender, 1991; Ryburn, 1994) and to reduce the rate of foster home breakdown (Berridge and Cleaver, 1987; Fratter *et al*, 1991).

Despite these understandings of how important knowledge of family history is for a child or young person's identity, reflected in the provisions of the Children Act 1989 in England and Wales, social workers still encounter difficulties in retaining or restoring relationships with people significant to a child (Masson *et al*, 1999). The attrition rate in relationships, including those with siblings, for children and young people in long-term care remains unacceptably high.

This chapter examines how social work theory and knowledge have approached siblingship and how this has influenced social work practice with children and families. It draws on the findings of a three-year research project on working in partnership with 'lost' parents. As the title suggests, a primary objective of the research was to examine how parents had lost relationships with children in the care system. However, a prominent theme emerging from the research process related to siblings. It was possible to review official accounts of how and why siblings became estranged from one another and to contrast this with the accounts of young people themselves. For the young people, dealing with the most difficult of histories and living in adverse circumstances, siblings occupied a place frequently unrecognised by the agencies that looked after them, or were looking after them.

A fundamental argument advanced is that marginalising children and young people's perspectives on sibling relationships has profound implications for some of those in long-term care. An assumption that sibling relationships are of negligible value can obscure the meaning they hold for the child or young person. This can result in the failure to acknowledge the impact of loss on a child or young person or may deny a child access to an important source of emotional protection and well-being. It poses questions, too, about the ways in which we work with children and young people and make decisions about their lives. The chapter also assumes that the study of any aspect of childhood will be partial if it does not seek to incorporate the life experiences of children themselves (Mayall, 1996; Morrow, 1998).

Siblings in the 'lost' parents research

Although not unequivocal, there is evidence that placement with siblings contributes to placement stability (Berridge and Cleaver, 1987; Wedge and Mantle, 1991). Despite this awareness, and despite the legal and philosophical changes generated by the Children Act 1989, Bilson and Barker's (1992/3) census of 1,068 children found that sibling groups in care are frequently separated and that a large proportion subsequently lose contact with each other. Only 37 per cent of those placed separately were in regular contact and three per cent had no contact at all. The study reported below had similarly worrying findings.

The 'lost' parents research (Masson *et al*, 1997, 1999) considered the lives of 62 children and young people who were being looked after by ten local authorities. This included 31 girls and young women and 31 boys and young men; five were black and 20 black and of mixed parentage. Their age when they entered the care system was between a few days and almost 16 years and, at the beginning of the research process, they were between three and 17 years old. They were both older and had spent longer being looked after than the generality of children in the care system; 25 of the children and young people in the study had spent at least three-quarters of their lives being looked after. The complexity of family relationships in general and sibling relationships in particular reflects the larger study by Bilson and Barker (1992/3).

From interviews with social workers and analysis of case records of the 62 children and young people, the following picture emerged of the pattern of sibling relationships at the time of their most recent entry into the care system.

Table 1

Number of siblings that the study children had at their most recent entry to care

	n	*%*
Only children	8	13
One sibling	24	39
Two siblings	17	27
Three or more siblings	13	21
Total	**62**	**100**

Table 2

Number of siblings with whom the study children most recently entered care

	n	%
Only child and therefore entered alone	8	13
Had siblings but entered alone	25	40
With some sibs	15	24
With all sibs	14	23
Total	**62**	**100**

During their most recent period in care, parents of 33 of the children had other children born to them who were half or full siblings of the looked after children; just six children remained only children. However, by the end of the study, over half of the children and young people who had siblings had no contact with some or all of them.

For some, this loss had occurred before or at the point of reception into the care system, when they were placed separately. With the unplanned nature of many receptions of children into public care and the associated disruption, there were sometimes initial difficulties in placing siblings together. For others, once looked after they were seen to have different needs from their siblings and plans were made which resulted in their separation. This frequently happened when an older child was presenting more difficult behaviour to carers. Once children were separated, they encountered the kind of non-specific barriers to contact described in *Access Disputes in Child Care*: 'hostility, distance and inaccessibility' (Millham *et al*, 1989, p 3). Fourteen children and young people had (usually younger) siblings who had been adopted. Where efforts were made to maintain important relationships, parental relationships tended to be privileged, although even this proved problematic and 45 children in the study had lost contact with both parents.

There were organisational and resource implications in maintaining contact. Where parental involvement or sibling contact was thought to threaten placement stability, this invariably over-rode other considerations and contact was consequently attenuated. For adopted children, contact with siblings had usually ceased prior to the adoption. Adopters had sometimes defaulted on agreements made about sibling contact and children were powerless to affect this.

For few of the children, as in the Wedge and Mantle (1991) study, did case records contain detailed assessments of the quality or significance of sibling relationships or of siblings' related or individual needs. Nor was it always clear how these had been taken into account in decisions either to separate or to place together. Once children had been separated, the same ambiguity was found in relation to maintaining links, which seemed to wither through default or inaction.

The social workers involved in the 'lost' parents research participated because they wanted to re-establish a working relationship with a parent, but many of them were also concerned about what had happened to other important people, including siblings. For the majority of children and young people who had lost contact with a sibling, the current social worker was dealing with the inheritance of past practices and did not always know whether the young person wanted contact with their sibling(s) or *vice versa*.

The views of children and young people in the 'lost' parents research

A small number of qualitative interviews were undertaken with children and young people to gain their detailed accounts and perspectives. No claims are made that they are representative of children and young people being looked after. There is an assumption, however, that their views about their lives may be relevant to the care of other children. Nine young people were interviewed who were between the ages of 11 and 20 years at the time of the interview. They all had siblings, although only one pair of siblings was interviewed together. Each of the others, whether in or beyond care, was living without their siblings. The family compositions of these young people tended to be complex and difficult to describe. Some of the young people had several siblings, not just full siblings but half-siblings and step-siblings. Indeed, one young woman struggling to explain to the interviewer her family composition commented that she had 'too many brothers and sisters'.

All of them had spent the majority of their lives in the care system, most experiencing disruption while in care and painful and damaging experiences before and after admission. Even where entry to care had provided initial relief, for example from sexual abuse, this was often subsequently replaced by more negative and ambivalent feelings. Foster care, for eight of these children, had been associated with feeling different and being badly treated.

Her [foster carer's] daughter was just perfect and I was . . . just like . . . the rotten child (young white woman aged 18).

When you were naughty you had to put your hand up, your leg up . . . And if you put your hand down they used to hit you. But they didn't do that to their children, though (young black woman aged 13).

Respondents described the ways in which being looked after is not only stigmatising in itself, but compounds other forms of oppression and a sense of worthlessness. Each of the black children interviewed described experiences of racism that permeated every aspect of their daily lives.

School was a nightmare as well 'cause . . . like everyone was white and I was the only black girl in the school . . . and it was in a dead posh area. So I used to get hassled by the other kids . . . they called me racist names . . . and when I started to fight back it was like in the teacher's eyes I was the trouble maker because I was in care (young black woman aged 19).

Siblings

The significance of sibling relationships was evident from the discussions with the young people who were interviewed, as they all mentioned brothers or sisters, their concerns for, and worries about them. Some of the young people were explicit that a sibling relationship was more important to them than contact, direct or indirect, with a parent. For these young people, there was no necessary correlation between the amount of their life that they had lived together with a sibling (in the birth family or while in care) and the importance they attached to them, nor were they less interested in a half-sibling than a full sibling. Their comments about siblings were woven into the accounts of their lives before, during and after care and were an essential part of those lives, even if they had last had contact some time ago.

Coming into care

Of the young people interviewed, one was an only child, one had already been separated from siblings before their entry to the care system, four had come into care and left siblings behind, and the remaining three had come into care as part of a sibling group and had been separated from some or all of the others at, or shortly after, the point of placement.

When I came into care there was me and my two brothers and my little sister... She was only about six months old the last time I saw her (young white woman aged 17).

For the young people interviewed, many factors had conspired to generate successive and repeated losses as differential plans had been made for children in sibling groups, influenced by ideological as well as pragmatic considerations. One young woman had pictures of her brothers and sisters and one of her whole sibling group around her living room. The children had come into care together in particularly traumatic circumstances in which, as the eldest, she had tried to take care of her brother and sisters. The group was split up quite soon after their reception into care, the reasons for which she was unsure, and she had lost contact with some of them. The photographs, taken some years before, kept her family perpetually frozen at the time when she had last had contact with them. She showed the interviewer these pictures, talking about missing her sisters and brothers and her hopes for a reunion. Her case records indicated that a critical factor for her, as for other children in the study, had been a view that the younger, sometimes the youngest, child/ren in the group could be placed for adoption.

That one [picture of whole group] was a few years ago... My brother Michael, he's living in [nearby district], he's adopted there. Not five minutes away over the fields and we don't know where... I think I bumped into him once. Well, it looked like him. I don't know whether it was or not... It might be hard, finding each other like... I've got two sisters in [county some distance away]... well, they were in children's homes down there . . . I don't know why they took them all the way down there (young white woman aged 18).

Another young woman had similar and perplexing recollections of the fragmentation of her family.

I wish they'd have let me see my family . . . my brothers and sisters. 'Cause a few of them are adopted and I can't really see them like . . . and that's Sarah, when she was fostered with me and my brother . . . and then they decided to put Samantha in the foster home with Louise and Mark . . . and then they had her adopted out, for no reason at all, to tell you the truth (young white woman aged 17).

Leaving siblings behind

For young people who had experienced abuse before their entry into the care system and who had left siblings behind, there were real concerns about those that had remained in the family. These young people continued to feel, not just a sense of loss, but of guilt and responsibility. They felt that they had left a sibling behind to have experiences similar to their own.

I've definitely lost my mum and I've definitely lost Lee. By rights he's my half-brother . . . Contact will never be there, basically . . . And I do worry about him a hell of a lot . . . because he's nearly the age that I was [when the abuse started] . . . I haven't any pictures of him or anything (young white woman aged 19).

After I came into care I didn't see my brothers. So I asked to see my brothers and I saw them. And I wished they had gone into care as well, the way they were treated. I've worried about them a lot, you know. I would have liked to see them under better conditions, but unfortunately it wasn't in my power to do anything (young white man aged 15).

For those still in contact

A constant refrain from all the children and young people interviewed was that the care system does not allow the living of a normal life. They gave many examples of the intrusions, constraints, restrictions, stigmatisation and discrimination that they felt were associated with being in care. As already indicated, for some young people this meant losing contact with siblings when different plans were made or because their contact had not been actively promoted. Where siblings had been placed at some distance, it was more or less impossible for children themselves to maintain contact. Where contact had taken place, young people also had feelings about the restrictions placed on their relationships. Some of the young people were unhappy about the level of contact they had with a sibling, or the arrangements they had to comply with in order to have contact. Organisational strictures failed to take into consideration the importance or the "normality" of the relationship for the young person.

I've been told by a social worker that I have to give four weeks notice for contact. That's a bloody month's notice. That's to see my own sister (young white woman aged 18).

Where children and young people had been able to stay in contact or had remained looked after together, they were positive about the value to them of this. A sister (age 13) and brother (age 11) had come into care together; throughout the interview they checked out with each other how they were describing what had happened to them, making sure that different as well as similar experiences were captured. Each of them was clear about the importance to them of being placed together.

My sister – I tell my sister everything (young black man aged 11).

I would say never split up the children who come into care. I think they get on more in life if they have each other. . . as long as they have each other. . . And I told him [her brother] as soon as anyone does anything to him, always come and tell me (young black woman aged 13).

Adopted siblings

Where a young person had taken a substantial caring role, then separation left very painful feelings, especially when a younger sibling had been adopted. There were strong parallels with the experiences of birth mothers.

I think basically it's important because they're my sisters . . . with

Susan, when we was living with our parents I looked after her most of the time . . . so there's more of a bond there . . . I have always looked after her because when she was born I was six . . . even though they are my sisters, I feel more of a mother to them . . . because I have been a mother to them (young white woman aged 18).

This young woman's sister, Susan, had been adopted and, while wanting her to benefit from this, the research respondent in question also missed her dreadfully. Throughout the interview she reiterated several times that she had been like a mother to Susan, who had been like a daughter to her.

Knowledge, loss and identity

Although the lives of these young people were diverse, significant themes of change, disruption and loss emerged. While they were actively attempting to reach an understanding of their life and construct a positive sense of identity in the face of rejection and abuse, they often referred to "gaps" that they could not fill. Losing contact with a sibling represented not just the loss of the relationship but also being deprived of a source of information, a potential sense of belonging and, for some young people, the opportunity to continue in a caring role. The stigmatising and "dehumanising" effects of the care system were set out in detail, together with the powerlessness and confusion engendered. In young adulthood, all these young people referred to difficulties in trusting other people and to a continuing sense of exclusion which might have been offset, if not ameliorated, by the maintenance of some form of sibling relationships.

Conclusions

This chapter has explored the significance of being a sibling and of having a sibling for children who live out their lives in the public care system. It does seem that for children and young people being looked after the meaning of having siblings is irrevocably shaped by the difficult experiences many of them have had. It is this which can be easily overlooked or dismissed as symptomatic of the level of disruption and the adverse circumstances endured by children and young people who are looked after on a long-term basis away from their families. The importance of sibling relationships (Boer and Dunn, 1992) may be amplified by changes and losses frequently beyond their control; this may be more so where relationships with parents have been lost, attenuated or characterised by abuse or rejection.

Young people's accounts are a powerful testimony to their struggle to develop and maintain a positive sense of identity in the face of considerable disadvantage. If their lives are considered holistically, the significance of their relationships with and thoughts about siblings have frequently been marginalised. The factors pushing these relationships to the periphery of professional recognition are multiple and complex. They reflect ideological, organisational and resource priorities that either leave little room for the views and perspectives of children and young people or displace them in favour of official constructions. This may reflect a general lack of significance placed on children's relationships with people other than mothers and fathers (though these, too, have frequently been attenuated (Masson et al, 1997) and particularly with other children. It is also a feature of agencies driven by the imperatives of a child protection system that attempts to improve the lives of children in the care system are frequently undermined by competition for resources. Planning has proved difficult to achieve; placement stability has been regarded as an overweening goal which, once achieved, can become a rationale for inaction.

There are many consequences for children and young people being looked after of this lack of attention. The impact of losing a sibling through separation, including adoption, may remain unrecognised and unattended to. For some of the children interviewed, their grief was evident and similar to feelings experienced by relinquishing birth mothers (Howe et al, 1992). Some did not know why different plans had been made for them and their siblings. Others, although they felt that adoption was in the best interests of their brother or sister, still yearned for them and had not been afforded the kind of information or support that a birth parent might have been given, even where their feelings were clearly comparable. Whatever the reasons for separation, they surely cannot justify not responding to the depth of emotions generated, nor leaving young people to search for resemblance in the faces of strangers.

Children who had been abused by a parent or step-parent carried considerable worry about the child left behind. If it had happened to them, it could happen to a sibling still at home. Along with this worry, they held feelings of responsibility and guilt which continued to preoccupy them. They felt that if they had stayed at home they might have offered some protection and that, in being protected themselves, they had exposed a brother or sister to danger. Again, little response appeared to have been made to these worries or fears.

A final concern is that the importance of siblings to a child or young person's sense of identity, which comes from shared parentage, shared history and sometimes shared difficulties, is undervalued. While it has been acknowledged for some time that placing siblings together can have a protective effect, this may yet be underestimated. Additionally, the importance of maintaining contact and the contribution this can make to a positive sense of identity may similarly be being neglected. Where deep ambivalence is felt by a child or young person about a parent, then a sibling offers a sense of belonging which is potentially less compromised or less confusing.

The accounts of these young people also demonstrate that theoretical perspectives about children's experiences and relationships must be grounded in the realities of their lives. The difficulties they contend with are not always ameliorated, and are sometimes exacerbated by coming into care. For social workers, the tasks involved in promoting a positive sense of identity in children and young people being looked after may appear daunting in the face of different organisational priorities and resource limitations. The Looking After Children documentation (Ward, 1998), the advent of Children's Services Plans and the Quality Protects initiative have all helped raise the profile of children in the care system. To help make such aspirations a reality, it is hoped that impetus can be given to good intentions by the individual and collective accounts from children and young people reported here.

References

Ahmad B (1990) *Black Perspectives in Social Work*, Birmingham: Venture Press.

Barn R, Sinclair R and Ferdinand D (1997) *Acting on Principle: An examination of race and ethnicity in social services provision for children and families*, London: BAAF.

Bebbington A and Miles J (1989) 'The background of children who enter local authority care', *British Journal of Social Work*, 19:5, pp 349–368.

Berridge D and Cleaver H (1987) *Foster Home Breakdown*, Oxford: Blackwell.

Biehal N, Claydon J, Stein M and Wade J (1992) *Prepared for Living? A survey of young people leaving the care of three local authorities*, London: National Children's Bureau.

Biehal N, Claydon J, Stein and Wade J (1995) *Moving On: Young people and leaving care schemes*, London: HMSO.

Bilson A and Barker R (1992/3) 'Siblings of children in care and accommodation: a neglected area of practice, *Practice*, 6:4, pp 307–18.

Boer F and Dunn J F (eds) (1992) *Children's Sibling Relationships: Developmental and critical issues*, Hillside, NJ: Lawrence Erlbaum.

Booth T and Booth W (1994) *Parenting Under Pressure: Mothers and fathers with learning disabilities*, Buckingham: Open University Press.

Broad B (1997) *Young People Leaving Care: Life after the Children Act 1989*, London: Jessica Kingsley.

Bullock R, Little M and Millham S (1993) *Going Home*, Aldershot: Dartmouth.

Department of Health (1991) *Patterns and Outcomes in Child Placement: Messages from current research and their implications*, London: HMSO.

Fanshel D and Shinn E B (1978) *Children in Foster Care: A longitudinal study*, New York: Columbia University Press.

Fowler S, Harwood S and Reegan F (1996) *Too Much Too Young: The failure of social policy in meeting the needs of care leavers*, Ilford: Barnardo's.

Fratter J, Rowe J, Sapsford D and Thoburn J (1991) *Permanent Family Placement*, London: BAAF.

Fratter J (1996) *Adoption with Contact*, London: BAAF.

Harrison C (1999) 'Young people, being in care and identity', in Masson J, Harrison C and Pavlovic A, *Lost and Found: Making and remaking working partnerships with parents of children in the care system*, Aldershot: Arena.

Harrison C and Masson J (1994) 'Working in partnership with lost parents: issues of theory and practice' *Adoption & Fostering*, 18:1, pp 40–44.

Howe D (1996) *Attachment and Loss in Child and Family Social Work*, Aldershot: Avebury.

Howe D, Sawbridge P and Hinings D (1992), *Half a Million Women: Women who lose their children by adoption*, Harmondsworth: Penguin.

Langan M and Day L (1992) *Women, Oppression and Social Work*, London: Routledge.

Masson J, Harrison C and Pavlovic A (1997) *Working with Children and Lost Parents: Putting partnership into practice*, York: York Publishing Services.

Masson J, Harrison C and Pavlovic A (1999) *op. cit.*

Mayall B (1996) *Children, Health and the Social Order*, Buckingham: Open University Press.

Millham S, Bullock R, Hosie K and Haak M (1986) *Lost in Care: The problem of maintaining links between children in care and their families*, Aldershot: Avebury.

Millham S, Bullock R, Hosie K and Little M (1989), *Access Disputes in Child Care*, Aldershot: Gower.

Mullender A (ed) (1991) *Open Adoption: The philosophy and the practice*, London: BAAF.

Morris J (1995) *Gone Missing? A research and policy review of disabled children living away from their families*, London: Who Cares? Trust.

Morrow V (1998) *Understanding Families: Children's perspectives*, London: National Children's Bureau/Joseph Rowntree Foundation.

Parton N (1996) *Social Theory, Social Change and Social Work*, London: Routledge.

Ryburn M (1993) *Adoption in the 1990s: Identity and openness*, Birmingham: The Press.

Ryburn M (1995) *Contested Adoptions: Research, law, policy and practice*, Aldershot: Arena.

Ryburn M (ed) (1994) *Open Adoption: Research theory and practice*, Aldershot: Avebury.

Schaffer R (1990) *Making Decisions about Children: Psychological questions and answers*, Oxford: Blackwell.

Stein M and Carey J (1986) *Leaving Care*, Oxford: Blackwell.

Stevenson O (1992) 'Social work intervention to protect children: aspects of research and practice', *Child Abuse Review*, Vol. 1, pp 19–32.

Thoburn J, Murdoch A and O'Brien A (1986) *Permanence in Child Care*, Oxford: Basil Blackwell.

Thoburn J (1994) *Child Placement: Principles and practice*, Aldershot: Arena.

Thoburn J (1990) *Success and Failure in Permanent Family Placement*, Aldershot: Avebury.

Triseliotis J (1985) 'Adoption with contact', *Adoption & Fostering*, 9:4, pp 19–24.

Utting Report (1991) *Children in the Public Care: A review of residential child care*, London: HMSO.

Ward H (1995) *Looking After Children: Research into practice*, London: HMSO.

Wedge P and Mantle G (1991) *Sibling Groups and Social Work: A study of children referred for permanent placement*, Aldershot: Gower.

8 Local authority planning and decision-making for looked after siblings

Shelagh Beckett

*Shelagh Beckett works independently as a trainer and consultant special-
ising in family placement and acts as an expert witness on foster
care and adoption. She has developed a particular interest in sibling
placements. In 1993 she undertook a small-scale piece of research into
local authority practice and decision-making with sibling groups, while
studying for a Masters Degree in Social Services Management at the
University of Birmingham.*

This chapter considers sibling relationships in the context of local
authority planning and provision for sibling groups in public care. While
all children share some common needs, there is increased professional
recognition that children benefit from services targeted in ways which
better meet their individual needs in terms of their identity, their stage
of development, ethnicity, culture and background. Relationships between brothers and sisters are arguably of importance not only to the
children involved but also to their parents and carers.

Planning service provision for siblings

There is remarkably little material available about siblings who enter
the looked after system. This is perhaps surprising, given that 80 per
cent of the general population have one or more siblings. Various
estimates have been made about the numbers of children in public care
who are part of a sibling group. Berridge and Cleaver (1987), in their
study of foster home breakdowns, estimated that three-fifths of children
aged under 11 when they entered care were accompanied by one or
more siblings. For siblings in short-term foster care, more than half were
separated from at least some of their brothers and sisters.

The Department of Health Report, *Patterns and Outcomes in Child Placement* (1991), stated that between one-third and one-half of all admissions to care involved sibling groups and that the majority of these were concentrated in the pre-adolescent age range. Clearly, estimates vary. It is also important to recognise that there is a difference between the numbers entering care and those who remain in care over the longer term.

With regard to separation in the context of adoption planning there are no reliable data available at a national level. Wedge and Mantle (1991) conducted a study of siblings referred for permanent family placement which provided valuable information about planning for siblings and outcomes. The BAAF Adoption Statistics Project (Dance, 1997) found that 43 per cent of the adopted children had been placed with a sibling, while noting that it has been established (Wedge and Mantle, 1991) that 82 per cent of families of looked after children have at least one other sibling. This led Dance to conclude that, while in many cases real efforts are being made to secure placements for sibling groups, 'the proportion of children placed with a sibling seems somewhat low'.

Whether or not children are placed together has potentially far-reaching implications. Little is known about the impact of such decisions on the likelihood of achieving restoration home. The separate placement of siblings will not only affect the children themselves, but may also reduce the frequency of parental contact which is recognised as important both to children's well-being and to rehabilitation. Farmer and Parker (1991) also noted that the presence of "new" siblings in the changed household to which children were returning decreased the likelihood of success. Other research studies have found differing rates of foster and adoption placement disruption for children placed with or without siblings (Barth and Berry, 1986; Berridge and Cleaver 1987; Wedge and Mantle, 1991). Berridge and Cleaver's study of foster care found a higher rate of disruption for children who were completely separated from siblings, compared with those who were accompanied by some or all of their siblings. This finding applied in respect of short-term, intermediate and long-term fostering, in all of which children fared better when placed with siblings.

Research on the psychology of sibling relationships has found supporting evidence that siblings can provide comfort and reduce distress in a range of circumstances. Examples include admission to residential nursery (Heinicke and Westheimer, 1965); being left by a parent in a "strange", unfamiliar situation (Stewart, 1983); and coping with the aftermath of divorce (Wallerstein, 1985). Murray Parkes *et al* (1991) reviewed attachment across the life cycle and noted that there had been little systematic research into siblings as attachment figures. Dunn and McGuire (1992) have also highlighted gaps in our current understanding and have reviewed evidence on the impact of differential maternal treatment which increases the level of conflict between siblings. However, our knowledge base in respect of siblings in public care is even more limited. The impact of parental neglect and abuse on sibling relationships requires further study. Some patterns of behaviour, such as high levels of aggression, conflict or sexual activity between siblings, may make it extremely difficult for carers to cope. Separating children may be, or seem to be, the only option.

However, if it is acknowledged that local authority services should aim to place siblings together, then a range of support services need to be in place. Similarly, when there are concerns about the viability of maintaining siblings within a single placement, a clear assessment of needs is necessary. Arguably, such an assessment should always occur in order to inform the placement plan. To date, only one assessment framework has been published (Department of Health, 1991) and its use is far from routine.

Looked after children are among the most disadvantaged in our society (Bebbington and Miles, 1989) and increased professional attention has focused on the importance of reducing any secondary damage that might be caused by the experience of being "in care".

The Department of Health (1991) has recognised that sibling relationships merit closer attention, acknowledging that there were 'few references to siblings in local authority policy documents or practice guides' (1991, p 27). The extent to which local authorities have since responded positively to the Children Act requirement (s. 23(7)(b)) to place children with their siblings 'so far as is reasonably and consistent with [their] welfare', or to the wider needs of sibling groups is difficult to determine.

However, my own survey of 16 local authorities indicated that the majority still had little or no provision which specifically targeted the needs of siblings.

The research – methodology

There were essentially two types of material I wanted to examine. Firstly, I wanted to ascertain whether social services departments had in place information systems, guidelines and policies which recognised the sibling dimension. Secondly, I wanted to obtain more detailed data about the particular dilemmas for social workers working with sibling groups. The chosen methodology for the research needed to address both objectives. Initially, I conducted a questionnaire survey of local authorities and then selected a sub-sample for the second stage of the research which incorporated the use of semi-structured interviews with staff.

Questionnaire sample

The questionnaire was sent to 32 local authorities and a response was received from 16 (50 per cent) of these. The sample comprised all local authorities within the Midlands region and a random sample constituting the same number of authorities drawn from across England and Wales. The questionnaire was accompanied by a covering letter directed at a named manager with responsibility for fostering and adoption in each agency. The willingness or not of the authority to co-operate in the second stage of the research was elicited in the original questionnaire. It is also important to note that authorities were specifically asked to respond even if the information which they were able to provide was likely to be patchy or in some cases non-existent, for example, if records on siblings were not maintained.

The questionnaires were designed to obtain basic data relating to siblings, the use of fostering and other resources, and the existence of any policy framework or mechanisms for decision-making in respect of siblings.

Interview sample

In order to interview a range of staff and to try to allow for variation in local authority practice, interviews were conducted in three local authorities. The sample was selected on the basis of:

- willingness to participate in the second stage of the research;
- including at least one authority that made some use of residential provision in respect of siblings and at least one that did not;
- including at least one authority that stated it had no written policies or guidelines relating to siblings and one authority which stated it did have these in place;
- representing some diversity in terms of area, size and population served.

Each of the three participating authorities was asked to select a minimum of three area-based social workers to be interviewed, based on the following criteria:

- each social worker had been employed by the authority for at least two years;
- each social worker was currently working with at least one sibling group that was in accommodation/looked after;
- the social workers were drawn from more than one team in each of the authorities.

I anticipated that some social workers would have more than one sibling group on their caseload. In these cases, the interview questions addressed issues in respect of up to three separate sibling groups. To tackle any more than this was felt to be unrealistic, given the depth of information being sought.

A semi-structured interview format was used with all the social workers. The initial stage of the interview allowed for collecting basic data on the sibling groups with whom the worker was involved. Information was recorded in respect of children's age, gender, ethnic origin, any disability, the length of time accommodated/looked after, the plan for the future and whether or not children were currently placed together.

A series of open-ended questions was then used to elicit greater detail. For example:

Can you tell me about your involvement – what have been the issues about them as a sibling group? Are there any differences compared with your work with single children in care?

What about contact arrangements? (including the worker's experience of maintaining contact between separated siblings)

What has helped/hindered you? (prompts given: policy? finance? resources?)

How have decisions been made? What has been the process? Who was involved, who has had most influence? (carers? parents? staff?)

Is there anything you would do differently – or plan differently – if you were starting from the point of entry into care with a sibling group?

Would you have liked further guidance, clearer policies, more resources. If so, what sort?

Is there any knowledge or research which you have found helpful? What about any training you may have had?

Are there any values or assumptions that have influenced your practice with siblings? (prompts: "Do you think that 'as a general rule' siblings should be placed together? Has your own experience – of being part of a sibling group/single child – influenced you at all?").

At the end of the interview, social workers were asked whether they had any other comments to make or wished to raise any additional issues.

Findings

Information systems
Only five out of 16 responding authorities said that they monitored information relating to siblings. Those that did were asked for more detail as to how they did so. It emerged that what was recorded was often scant and/or applied only to some placements for example: 'only short-term placements' or 'information about the cross references of children looked after (including siblings) is maintained but not analysed'.

Respondents were asked to provide information about the numbers of siblings in their care and to give a breakdown in terms of ethnic origin and placement patterns (i.e. together, placed with at least one sibling, or as a complete group). Only one-quarter of local authorities were able to provide any details and, of these, half could give full information while the remaining half could only provide some.

Written policies and guidelines

Authorities were asked to provide a copy of any existing policy of guidelines in respect of siblings. Ten of the 16 authorities had none. Of the six who said they had 'something in writing', only four sent a copy. The nature of policy statements varied; one agency had two lines in its procedures which addressed the need to place siblings together 'unless this is part of a well thought out plan based on the children's needs'. However, no guidance was given as to how this plan should be developed or decisions reached.

Two departments addressed the issues in a more comprehensive manner, for example, having several pages of guidance for social workers working in the context of sibling groups needing permanent placement. This aspect seemed more likely to be considered than the needs of siblings in short-term care. One department had an assessment format to help social workers address issues such as their own views, the siblings' roles in relation to one another, the strength of attachment, and resource implications.

Use of residential provision

Just over half the sample said that they did make some use of residential provision but most acknowledged that this was very limited. Also, the actual use of provision tended to be restricted in practice by age factors; that is, residential provision was only actually available for children over ten years (in three authorities) or over 13 (in two authorities). Only three authorities said that they were *currently* making use of residential provision to keep siblings together.

Availability and use of foster care resources

Local authorities were asked to provide information about their total number of foster carers and a breakdown in terms of carers able to take one, two, three or more children. Just under half (seven out of nine) of the authorities monitored their foster care resources in such a way as to enable them to provide this information.

Authorities were also asked whether they made planned use of foster carers to take siblings. For example, did they make use of retainers to reserve carers for sibling groups? The majority (12 out of 16) did not reserve or use carers in this type of planned way. Of the four who did, they noted that it was not typical practice, commenting that this was 'rarely' or 'very occasionally' considered.

Contact between separated siblings

Local authorities were asked how they tried to promote contact between separated siblings. Three respondents did not complete this section which may indicate that they lacked knowledge about the means by which contact would be maintained. Very few were able to give much information. Most acknowledged that there was little or no specific provision or requirement to look at the issue positively. Typical comments included:

Addressed in reviews.

Foster carers can be paid an enhancement to promote links.

As there are no written guidelines this is approached on an ad hoc basis.

No common policy here – dependent upon the will of the social worker and the reviewing officer, consequently practice is piecemeal.

Decision-making

Whether or not siblings are placed together is likely to have far-reaching consequences for the children concerned and for their families. I was therefore interested to know how such decisions were reached and, in particular, whether there was a clear and recognised framework. Local authorities were asked if there was a defined process for deciding whether or not siblings should be placed together. If there was, they were asked to outline what it was. While three-quarters of the sample said that they had some process, their more detailed response called this into question. The majority of 'defined processes' related solely to adoption planning and involved the Adoption Panel considering social work reports and recommending whether or not siblings would be placed together.

The children being worked with

Interviews were conducted with eight social workers and three managers in three local authorities. The social workers were currently working with a total of 14 sibling groups, which included 52 children. There were 27 boys and 25 girls with an average age of nine years. All but five of the children were white. There were five mixed parentage children; four had Asian and white parents, and one child had African-Caribbean and white parents.

None of the children was described as having a physical or mental disability; however, approximately one-fifth of the group had learning difficulties and were subject to a Statement of special educational needs.

Forty-six children were on care orders and six were accommodated. However, social workers stated that many of the children now subject to care orders had initially been accommodated. The average length of time that children had been accommodated/looked after was two years and seven months. Some children had been looked after for as little as two months, while others had been in public care for over four years. Approximately half of the group had been in care for more than three years. For 21 of the children rehabilitation home was planned. A further three children were placed long term with grandparents. For the remaining 28 children, the plan was long-term placement with foster carers or adoption.

Twenty-two of the children were placed in intact sibling groups, while 18 were placed with at least one sibling and 12 alone. The 22 children placed all together included two groups of five. Of the 12 children placed alone, on the other hand, some had only one sibling. Clearly, then, the size of the group was not the only factor influencing whether or not children were placed together.

Table 1
Size of sibling groups

Number of children	Number of groups
2	4
3	3
4	2
5	3
6	2

Interviews with social workers

As mentioned above, eight social workers were interviewed. These interviews confirmed that the main factor in placing children apart had often been lack of resources at the point of entry into care. However, in shaping future plans it was clear that social workers had a powerful role to play.

Case examples

A family of five children had been maintained together when they had first entered care. This had been made possible through the use of a small residential unit, there being no foster home available to take all five at that point. As time went on, the social worker had felt under extreme pressure from senior staff who wanted to close the unit. When the authority closed the residential unit, the children had been split between several foster homes. The social worker remained committed to reuniting them within a permanent placement and was actively seeking this, together with colleagues in homefinding.

In another case, a social worker spoke of how a sibling group of five had been split between separate foster homes and the children had been distressed by this. She had since managed to reunite the children within a single placement which had subsequently become available.

Current contact

Most of the social workers spoke of the problems they experienced in maintaining regular and "real" contact between separated siblings. They felt that an hour or two once a week or a fortnight – or less – was far from adequate.

However, the practical obstacles alone which needed to be overcome in promoting contact were often significant and required considerable commitment on the part of social workers, foster carers and the department overall. For example, visits involved: identifying a suitable venue; arranging transport, escorts and safety for children (baby seats or restraints); adequate supervision; and so forth. Social workers employed in departments with family aides or social work assistants spoke positively about the role such staff played, as they were often used to support sibling contact. The role of foster carers in promoting sibling contact was also recognised; social workers spoke of some carers being particularly "good" at helping out. However, carers were typically doing this on an informal basis, rather than the additional tasks they were undertaking being recognised and paid for.

Future placements
Plans for permanence outside the family often included separating siblings. There were 28 children for whom the plan was permanence. Placement plans were at different stages. A sibling group of five children had recently been placed with foster carers recruited through national advertising. This placement was intended to be permanent. For the remaining 23, the plans were less advanced, were complex and involved various placement arrangements. For seven of the children, the plan was that they would be placed individually while, for their siblings, the plan was still rehabilitation home. A further 11 children were assessed as needing permanent placement separately from their siblings. There was only one group of five children for whom permanent placement was still being sought for the group as a whole.

It would seem that entering public care may have significant implications for sibling relationships. Within this small-scale study, siblings were at great risk of being separated whether the plan was rehabilitation home to family or permanent placement elsewhere.

Contact and separated siblings: permanent placements

Social workers expressed reservations about whether it would be possible to maintain contact and, if it were, at what sort of level. They often seemed to see the attitude of the adopters or new family, when identified, as being the determining factor, together with geographical proximity and the perceived degree of difficulty in placing the children. Typical comments included:

Haven't got a clue . . . it's really up to the adopters.

It will depend on how near they are.

It's going to be hard enough to sell these kids.

What helped social workers in planning

The following were some of the factors that proved helpful in keeping siblings together or in contact:

- financial support to keep siblings together, e.g. enhanced payments to foster carers, or a commitment to pay an inter-agency fee for a suitable adoptive placement;
- supervisory and ancillary support, e.g. recognition of the extra tasks involved in working with siblings in separate placements;
- a clear framework for planning, e.g. a common review structure, or knowing where to go to get early decisions made;
- responsibility for planning and decision-making being "shared" – the needs of siblings then became recognised as an issue for the agency, rather than just for the individual social worker, e.g. planning across team structures so that family placement staff and district social workers worked together from an early stage.

The benefit of hindsight

When asked if there was anything they would now do differently, social workers said that they would have wanted more departmental support in planning for siblings, and that they would have liked to have been able to use the experience of others in the department. Staff had often felt they were having 'to do things from scratch' or they spoke of 're-inventing the wheel'; they wanted to be able to avoid similar experiences for other staff in the future. A recurring theme was that of recognising the sibling relationship from the outset, while still taking account of children's individual needs.

Knowledge base

In general, social workers felt they had very little knowledge about sibling relationships and relevant research (for example, that on placement outcomes) and would have welcomed more training. Typical comments included:

> There has been lots of training on child protection but none on issues like this.

This awareness sat uncomfortably with the enormity of the decisions which they were having to make, often with little support.

Value base

Although the sample was small, it was noticeable that social workers of sibling groups which were intact, or where the plan was to re-unite them, tended to express stronger views about the value of the sibling relationship. In the absence of policy or a corporate response to planning for siblings, the values and commitment of individuals appeared to wield considerable influence.

Other issues

The social workers who were interviewed were given an opportunity to raise any additional issues. Most used this as an opportunity to reiterate points about which they felt strongly, such as the heavy responsibility they felt in working with large sibling groups. A small number of other issues were raised:

- the need for frameworks which could be used in assessment work with sibling groups;
- the need for a more systematic approach to recruiting foster carers and adoptive families for sibling groups;
- the need for foster carers to receive more specialist training, e.g. on caring for siblings from sexually abusive families;
- the importance of clarity with regard to 'who was responsible for what tasks';

- the need for caseload weighting systems to take account of the extra demands presented when working with sibling groups (especially when siblings were placed separately);
- the need for research into whether or not separating siblings affected their likelihood of achieving rehabilitation.

Interviews with managers

The three managers who were interviewed all acknowledged that there were shortcomings in the way their department currently addressed the needs of sibling groups. Two of the three referred to major inadequacies in departmental information systems which essentially treated children as singletons. Other problems highlighted were the lack of clear policy and the limited use or unavailability of residential provision.

With regard to the decision to keep children together or separate them, two of the three managers felt that this should be determined by the Adoption/Permanency Panel which either had taken on, or was in the process of taking on, this role. In one case, the Panel had a clear view as to how the assessment should be undertaken and what issues ought to be considered. Some social work resistance had been encountered to the Panel's role in scrutinising placement plans. Both these managers felt that their department was at a relatively early stage in recognising the needs of sibling groups. The third manager saw the decision as being more appropriately taken at social worker/line-manager level, regarding this as more consistent with the devolved decision-making and devolved budgets to which the department was committed.

Conclusion

This small-scale piece of research found limited evidence that departments were either recognising or responding positively to the particular needs of siblings in public care. This is worrying on several counts. Whether or not children are placed together has potentially far-reaching implications and long-term consequences. Children may be deprived of significant relationships which can lead to an enduring sense of loss in adult life.

In order to achieve the best outcomes for children, there is an urgent need to develop assessment skills and frameworks and to evaluate their contribution to practice. It seems fundamentally wrong to deprive a child of the opportunity to grow up with his or her siblings in the absence of a clear assessment to the contrary. We will also need to develop our understanding of how best to support carers looking after sibling groups. This would include distinguishing those behavioural difficulties which are likely to be short term, from those which are of a more chronic long-term nature. For those children who are separated, issues concerning their continuing relationship must still be addressed. This requires much greater emphasis to be placed on contact and imaginative ways of working with children in groups.

The task of planning for children in public care is an onerous and complex one which is fraught with difficulty. In order to plan effectively, it is crucial that departments recognise the particular needs of siblings and take steps to address these.

References

Barth R P and Berry M (1988) *Adoption and Disruption: Rates, risks and responses*, Hawthorne, NY: Aldine de Gruyter.

Bebbington A and Miles J (1989) 'The background of children who enter local authority care', *British Journal of Social Work*, 19:5, pp 349–368.

Berridge D and Cleaver H (1987) *Foster Home Breakdown*, Oxford: Basil Blackwell.

Dance C (1997) *Focus on Adoption: A snapshot of adoption patterns in England – 1995*, London: BAAF.

Department of Health (1991) *Patterns and Outcomes in Child Placement: Messages from current research and their implications*, London: HMSO.

Dunn J and McGuire S (1992) 'Sibling and peer relationships in childhood', *Journal of Child Psychology & Psychiatry*, 33:1, pp 67–105.

Farmer E and Parker R (1991) *Trials and Tribulations: Returning children from local authority care to their families*, London: HMSO.

Heinicke C M and Westheimer I (1965) *Brief Separations*, New York: International Universities Press.

Murray Parkes C, Stevenson-Hinde J and Marris P (1991) *Attachment Across the Life Cycle*, London: Routledge.

Stewart R B (1983) 'Sibling attachment relationships: child input interactions in the strange situation', *Developmental Psychology*, 19, pp 192–199.

Wallerstein J S (1985) 'Children of divorce: preliminary report of a two year follow-up of older children and adolescents', *Journal of American Academy of Child Psychiatry*, 24, pp 545–553.

Wedge P and Mantle G (1991) *Sibling Groups and Social Work – A study of children referred for permanent substitute family placement*, Aldershot: Avebury.

9 Planning for sibling continuity within permanency
Needs led or needs unmet

Marion Ellison

Marion Ellison is Lecturer in Social Policy and Sociology at the University of Sunderland. Specialising in looked after children and their families, her research interests centre upon comparative social policy. She continues to work closely with Danish Government agencies at national and local level.

Introduction

Although the requirement that siblings be accommodated together whenever 'reasonably practical and consistent with [the child's] welfare' is written into section 23(7)(b) of the Children Act 1989, neither the Act nor its accompanying regulation and guidance documentation makes direct reference to sibling continuity planning in terms of placement together or of contact as a proactive and deliberate means of maintaining such links.

In practice, proactive commitment to the importance of sibling relationships can be demonstrated in a range of forms of care planning for sibling groups. Having revealed a lack of any tangible policy or practice theories, the research reported here progressed to a more detailed focus upon decision-making processes as they impacted upon practice and as they were perceived by looked after sibling groups, their families, social workers and carers, so as to ascertain what professionals were actually doing.

Few social work studies have focused on sibling relationships within placements or related practice concerns (Gustafsson, 1993). However, studies on the periphery of the discipline, mainly from psychology, do provide a reference point on issues involved in separation (Harrison, 1979; Bagnell, 1980; Quinn, 1990). The importance of sibling relationships, particularly at the crucial point when the child is initially taken into care, is reinforced, for example, by evidence from Lewis and Karen (1990). Their work demonstrates that siblings can be a mutual resource in everyday life, as well as in emotional crises, so that it is especially important that siblings are emotionally available to each other.

Earlier social work research indicates that being with a sibling may have a positive impact on placement stability (see summary in Mullender's introductory chapter, this volume). However, variations in practice make it apparent that sibling continuity planning warrants closer attention. Clearly, the role of sibling relationships as part of individual case management and family intervention strategies needs to be addressed in a more coherent way, particularly within permanency planning.

Methodology

The principal aim of the author's research (Ellison, 1998) was to explore, analyse and explain the impact of contrasting political, legal and economic frameworks on social work practice in relation to looked after siblings. The focus was a comparative analysis and exploration of needs and rights-based social policy frameworks, child care law, resource distribution and the impact upon the timing, mode, and purpose of intervention in relation to looked after siblings.

An extensive data collection exercise was undertaken in regional conurbations in Britain and Denmark. This covered sibling placement, contact, and sibling continuity planning. The sample consisted of a cohort of 115 children from four agencies in an urban conurbation in Denmark and a cohort of 180 children from four agencies in a comparable area in Britain. A questionnaire survey and examination of case files were followed by a series of interviews with parents, children, social workers, foster carers and other care professionals. Only the British data are reported in this chapter.

Research findings

It's always a very difficult question when you've got siblings because, obviously, your heart tells you that children should remain in contact at least with their brothers and sisters, if nothing else. But, sadly, there are cases, and this is one of them, where that just is not possible. In an ideal world, one would have looked to all three children being placed together and that didn't work because grandparents were only able to take Paul and not the other two, and I don't think prospective adopters would have taken Paul because of his difficult behaviour. And, at the end of the day, contact would have had to be stopped anyway – I can't see any way that would have carried on (a British social worker).

The study revealed that decision-making in Britain was typically service led rather than needs led. The lack of specialised placements for siblings with special needs and for larger sibling groups was clearly identified by social workers as an impediment to effective sibling continuity planning. As the case study extract above shows, the implications of this are particularly important when the purpose of placement is adoption. For the sibling group alluded to, feelings of loss resulting from separation were described by the grandmother of the 11-year-old boy in this case as being severe: 'I know he misses them [his sisters]. He is always talking about them, and sometimes I can hear him crying at night.' During this case study investigation, it was found that the degree of information given to this looked after boy, his grandmother and his two sisters who had been freed for adoption was negligible. The information consisted of the argument that it was in the "best interests" of the girls to be placed separately. Clearly, decision-making in this case was service led.

Such examples are important in focusing on the rights of looked after siblings in relation to contact with their adopted siblings. The extent to which partnership with social workers, parents and looked after siblings is achieved in arranging and ensuring an adequate frequency of contact very often depends upon the wishes of the adoptive parents. Professional assessment in relation to the possibility of continuity is therefore heavily related to the lack of specialised placements for these children. Any semblance of partnership becomes diluted by the service-led nature of decision-making, and inadequate placement provision undermines a proactive approach to sibling continuity planning in practice.

This view of social work is supported by evidence that social workers may:

... sometimes be under pressure to fit people's problems into the particular services their departments can provide. They often feel constrained to conceptualise an individual's unique set of problems as a need for the available services. The individual's or family's problems are thus conceptualised in terms which dovetail neatly with the framework of existing organisational boundaries which are consistent with service availability. Service-oriented assessments are administratively convenient but pay scant attention to the individual's own conception of their problems (Biehal *et al*, 1996, p 114).

Adoption, and particularly the resulting separation of looked after siblings, raises key issues in relation to sibling continuity planning. In this study, the purpose of placement was identified as adoption in 25 per cent of cases. Within the cohort as a whole, of the 44 children who were to be adopted, 29 were separated from some or all of their looked after siblings. A major issue of concern was identified in the degree to which partnership between parents, social workers and siblings could be maintained in cases where looked after children were separated from one or more adopted siblings. This was found to be critical to contact. Tensions arose particularly in cases where siblings were separated as a result of a lack of suitable adoptive placements. In this context, the current plan, the purpose of placement, and the type of placement designated within the care plans of sibling groups all impacted in different ways upon sibling placement, sibling contact and continuity planning.

Placement provision, permanency planning and sibling continuity

The Children Act stresses the general importance of continuity in family relationships and includes siblings within this. Yet the present research demonstrates that the possibility of continuity can vary enormously between different types of placement. As Stone (1995) argues, greater use of short-term and respite placements could be beneficial to siblings. Figure 1 reveals that a third of the children in the British cohort of the present study were in short-term placements. In that cohort as a whole,

Figure 1

Sibling placements as against current plan in the British cohort

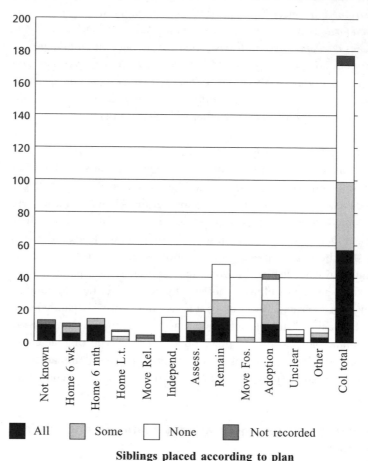

Siblings placed according to plan

siblings were more likely to be placed together when the current plan involved a return home within the short or long term. Thus, in 75 per cent of cases, children remained with all of their siblings when the current plan was to return them home within six months.

In stark contrast, in approximately 50 per cent of cases where the current plan was to remain placed, children were separated from their entire sibling group. Disturbingly, for example, children were separated from all of their siblings in 11 out of 13 cases where the current plan was for long-term foster care. Similarly, 66 per cent of children with a current plan involving adoption were separated from some or all of their siblings. There may, of course, be a range of individual or combined reasons for separation but the issues raised by this finding are brought into particularly sharp focus by the finality of adoption. If a view of continuity is held which relates attachment in stable relationships to the development of a concept of self and the promotion of well-being, and if relationships are seen as being based on a continuous stream of shared experiences, then pre-adoption planning becomes an area of strategic importance in social work practice. The potential for more sibling group placements, the importance of contact, and the use of therapy or other intervention where needed to improve sibling relationships may be seen as related matters needing urgent attention.

The meanings, perceptions and feelings that form the fabric of children's lives are built upon previous experiences, emotional attachments, fears, desires and defences (Ferguson, 1981; Ward, 1984; Hoopes, 1990; Silber and Dorner, 1990). Sibling relationships are woven into this and, for older children, represent a cumulative history that is likely to have played an important part in the development of essential parts of the self (Bee, 1992) and to be implicit to a child's sense of well-being. Siblings represent the past to each other, as well as the present and the future. Permanency planning continues to sever too many of these shared life histories.

It is worth asking whether the degree of inclusivity achieved reflects differences in current legal status (Pruzan, 1997; Hestbaek, 1998). As Figure 2 demonstrates, however, patterns of sibling placement in this study did not seem to vary much according to legal status. Approximately 30 per cent of all accommodated children in the survey were separated from all of their siblings, while another 30 per cent or so of all cases designated as care orders involved children so separated. In this cohort at least, it would appear that purpose of placement, current plan and type of placement, particularly in relation to whether the placement was perceived as short-term or long-term, had more bearing on sibling placement than legal status.

Figure 2

Sibling placements as against current plan in the British cohort

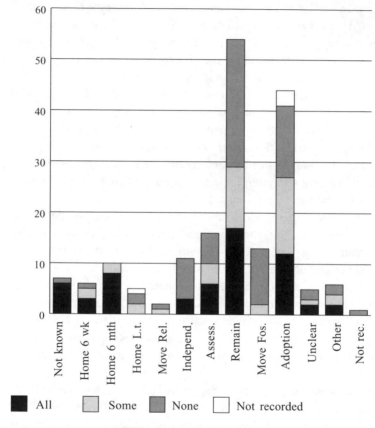

■ All	▢ Some	▨ None	▢ Not recorded

Siblings placed according to plan

Where separation does occur, continuity may be preserved by maintaining contact between siblings. Here, legal status did seem to have an effect. In this cohort, while there was no contact at all between siblings in ten per cent of the cases designated as care orders and only 35 per cent of this group were in contact on at least a monthly basis, all of those designated as accommodated had contact at least four times a year, with the majority (65 per cent) in contact at least monthly.

The small sample size inevitably renders the emergence of clear messages for practice problematic. The complexity of the variables involved must also be taken into account. Differences in approach in relation to continuity (e.g. the vigour with which permanency planning is pursued and the degree of openness within it), as well as variations in case histories, in presenting problems, and in placement availability all restrict the possibility of making definite practice prescriptions.

Clearly, though, continuity as a principle of practice can be seen to relate to conceptualisations of permanency, and particularly to the finality of adoption without contact. The patterns reported above raise important issues in this regard. Furthermore, the concept of inclusivity in care planning is connected with notions of partnership. This concept is problematic because it operates at different levels and may be interpreted in different ways.

Discussion

This research has demonstrated that sustaining continuity in sibling relationships for looked after children requires very careful planning and that the availability of a range of placement types able to meet the varying needs of siblings as individuals and as groups is integral to this planning. Critically, children in long-term and especially pre-adoptive situations appear to require a more proactive and planned approach to continuity planning. Studies relating to child development and social work practice in adoption (Triseliotis, 1984; Schaffer, 1990; Silber and Dorner, 1990) have emphasised the increased vulnerability of children who are looked after in terms of the fragility of self-concept, compounded over time, and the importance to them of attachment. A more inclusive approach to sibling continuity planning is urgently needed.

The study reported here provides some evidence that continuity planning which centres upon the use of short-term or respite care within a current rehabilitative plan seems to carry with it more likelihood of siblings being placed together. The placement of siblings together in adoptive and other permanent placements should assume the same priority. The lack of suitable adoptive placements for sibling groups would appear to be impeding the ability of social work professionals to plan effectively for sibling continuity. The research also revealed a lack of short-term, respite and specialist provision for looked after children which raises broader issues in relation to the spread of placements.

The impact of this lack of preventative and respite provision was evident in wider strategies of prevention and protection. Significantly, the case study research found that the needs of sibling groups were more intense when looked after children entered care as a result of a family crisis, particularly where child protection issues were present. In some cases it was demonstrably apparent that such crises might not have occurred had prevention strategies been in place.

Conclusion

Issues relating to the timing, level and purpose of social work intervention were found in this research to have had a significant impact upon sibling placement and contact. Of equal significance were the scope and range of placements available. Underlying strategies in relation to prevention and protection may perhaps owe much of their rationale to the relationship between these two key elements within care planning. What is very clear is that sibling continuity planning requires more tangible and prescriptive policy and practice guidelines. In this study, patterns relating to the purpose of placement where current planning related to adoption, pre-adoption, long-term placement and remaining placed were identified in this sample as not beneficial to sibling continuity. On the other hand, when short-term and respite placements were utilised as part of rehabilitative planning, siblings were more likely to remain together and sibling continuity benefited from this.

The availability of placements able to take sibling groups and siblings with special needs within both long-term and short-term provision clearly impacts upon the ability of social work professionals to plan effectively for sibling continuity. What emerges from this study is that permanency planning for looked after sibling groups requires a more proactive and integrated approach through policy, practice and resourcing.

References

Bagnell K (1980) *The Little Immigrants: The orphans who came to Canada*, Toronto: Macmillan.

Bilson A and Barker R (1992) *Parental Contact Research Project: A study of looked after children following the 1989 Children Act*. Research report: University of Northumbria at Newcastle upon Tyne.

Beardsall L and Dunn J (1992) 'Adversities in childhood: Siblings' experiences and their relations to self-esteem', *Journal of Child Psychology & Psychiatry*, 33, pp 349–359.

Bee H (1992) *The Growing Child: An applied approach*, Harlow: Longman.

Berridge D and Cleaver H (1987) *Foster Home Breakdown*, Oxford: Basil Blackwell.

Biehal N, Fisher M, Marsh P and Sainsbury E (1996) 'Rights and social work' in Coote, A (ed.) *The Welfare of Citizens*, London: Rivers Oram Press.

Department of Health (1989) *The Children Act 1989: Principles and Practice in Regulations and Guidance*, London: HMSO.

Dunn J and Kendrick C (1982) *Siblings: Love, envy and understanding*, Cambridge, Mass: Harvard University Press.

Ellison M (1999) 'European siblings in care: comparative policy and practice in Denmark and Britain'. Unpublished Ph.D thesis, University of Northumbria at, Newcastle upon Tyne.

Ferguson H K, (1981) 'Open adoption', *Adoption & Fostering*, 104, pp 45–46.

Fisher D, Marsh P, Phillips and Sainsbury E (1986) *Children In and Out of Care*, London: Batsford.

Fratter J, Rowe J, Thorburn J and Sapsford D (1991) *Permanent Family Placement: A decade of experience*, London: BAAF.

Gustafsson P (1993) 'Siblings in family therapy', *Journal of Family Therapy*, 17, pp 317–327.

Hamlin E (1979) 'A Comparison of perceived sibling role relationships between problem and non-problem sibling groups: an exploratory study'. Unpublished

D.S.W. dissertation, Chicago: The Catholic University of America.

Harrison D (ed.) (1979) *The Home Children: Their personal stories*, Winnipeg: Watson & Dwyer.

Hestbaek A (1998) *Out-of-Home Care in Denmark: The translation of legal principles into practice*, Copenhagen: Danish National Institute of Social Research.

Hoopes J L (1990) 'Adoption and identity formation', in Brodzinsky D M and Schechter M D (eds), *The Psychology of Adoption*, New York: Oxford University Press.

Kahan B (1994) *Growing Up in Groups – Great Britain: Review of recent trends in residential and extrafamilial care of children and young people*, London: HMSO.

Lewis K and Karen G (1990) 'Siblings: a hidden resource in therapy', *Journal of Strategic and Systemic Therapies*, 9, pp 39–49.

Pruzan V B (1997) 'Denmark: voluntary placements as a family support', in Gilbert N (ed), *Combating Child Abuse: International perspectives and trends*, New York: Oxford University Press.

Quinn V N (1990) *Applying Psychology*, New York: Harper Collins College Publishers.

Rowe J, Hundleby M and Garnett L (1984) *Child Care Now: A survey of placement patterns*, London: BAAF.

Schaffer H R (1990) *Making Decisions about Children: Pyschological questions*, Oxford: Blackwell.

Silber K and Dorner P M (1990) *Children of Open Adoption and their Families*, San Antonio: Corona Publishing Company.

Stone J (1995) *Making Positive Moves: Developing short-term fostering services*, London: BAAF.

Timberlake E and Hamlin E (1982) 'The Sibling Group: a neglected dimension of practice', in *Child Welfare*, 61:8, pp 46–71.

Triseliotis J and Russell J (1984) *Hard to Place: The outcome of adoption and residential care,* London: Heinemann.

Ward M (1984) 'Sibling ties in foster care and adoption planning, *Child Welfare*, 63:4, pp 321–332.

Wedge P and Mantle G (1991) *Sibling Groups and Social Work: A study of children referred for permanent substitute family placement*, Aldershot: Avebury.

10 A 'for ever and ever family'
Siblings' views as represented in reports for adoption hearings

Julie Selwyn

Julie Selwyn is a lecturer in the School for Policy Studies and a member of the Family Policy and Child Welfare Research Centre at the University of Bristol.

Adoption is no longer primarily concerned with finding homes for babies. As the social construction of adoption has changed to encompass all children, irrespective of their age, ethnicity, or level of disability, the number of sibling groups needing placement has grown. These children have often experienced many moves, had changes of carer and may be displaying challenging behaviour as a result of previous life events. Finding placements for siblings raises many issues: Should the children be placed together? How will their individual needs be met? With whom should the children have contact? This chapter examines whether the views of siblings were recorded in documents submitted at adoption hearings. What did the children think about their placements and their contact with family members, and what were their concerns?

From a larger random sample of 62 adoption case files (for a fuller discussion see Selwyn, 1996), 15 sibling files were examined to look in detail at siblings' views as recorded by the social worker and guardian *ad litem*. The adoption hearings had taken place between 1990–1996 at the Principal Registry (Family Division) London and the Bristol County Court. Not all the children had their own case file number so some sibling groups were filed together. The total number of children was 32 children; three family groups of four children and the other siblings in pairs.

The child's voice

Over the last twenty years there has been an increased awareness of the importance of listening to the voice of the child. The Adoption Act (1975) states that, so far as is practicable, the wishes and feelings of the child should be ascertained and consideration should be given to those views, taking into account the child's age and level of understanding. The key document prepared by the social worker for the adoption hearing is the Schedule 2 report that asks that the following be recorded in Section O:

> ... the wishes and feelings (of the child) in relation to the adoption and the application including any wishes in respect of religious and cultural upbringing.

The signing of the UN Convention on the Rights of the Child (1989) by the UK in 1991 confirmed the right of children to be heard either directly or through a representative in any proceedings that affect them (Article 12).

In addition to the legal requirements to record children's views, psychological research has found that children's abilities should not be underestimated. Brown and Dunn (1992) found that children are able to talk about their feelings and those of others from a very young age. From the age of two, children have conversations which evaluate their environments.

An examination of the Schedule 2 reports found few contained direct quotations from the children. Just a few words filled in Section O appeared. A typical example was: 'Both children stated that they wished to be adopted and live with their present mum and dad for ever and ever.' Social workers used the section to record other information such as the foster carers' views, the history of the child's care career, or the history of any therapeutic intervention. All the reports examined lacked an analysis of how the cultural, religious and language needs of the children would be met. There was no discussion at all on this topic.

> Since the failure of rehabilitation attempts in Summer 1990, Saeed has known the LA plan is for adoption of himself and his brother. Saeed was involved in the LA attempts to find an adoptive family for himself and his brother. When I saw him on ... Saeed stated his clear

wish to stay with the Fs [adoptive family] and be adopted by them. Saeed has no expressed views as to his religious or cultural upbringing. However, very much by his own choice Saeed is known by the name of John (Section O of a Schedule 2).

This was the only comment on the file of two children with a Moroccan father and a Scottish mother who were placed with an English mother and an Asian father. The guardian did not comment at all. There seemed to be an assumption by social workers and guardians that children's cultural needs would be met in their adoptive placements. Six of the children were of dual heritage and were placed where one adoptive carer was black. However, the ethnicity of the carer was not the same as that of the child. The assumption again seemed to be that if one carer was black then the child's needs would be met.

Other Schedule 2 reports left Section O completely blank. Many of the sibling groups had had multiple experiences of abuse but were not given any opportunity in the Schedule 2 to voice their views. Two children (aged eight and ten years) had spent their early lives in women's refuges, escaping from domestic violence. Following their mother's inability to continue caring for the children, they were placed with two successive foster carers, both of whom abused the children. They were then placed for adoption. One can only guess at how these children might have felt about being placed in another home, their insecurities and their hopes, but the section was left blank. As a guardian had not been appointed, the children had no representation.

When guardians were not appointed, problems often began to emerge. Two sisters, placed with an adoptive family, had almost identical Schedule 2 reports. The section for the children's views read: 'Sarah and Sandy appear to have a clear understanding of the meaning of adoption and have stated to me that they wish to be adopted as soon as possible and find it hard to understand why this cannot be achieved immediately.' It came to the court's attention via a General Practitioner that the adoptive parents were having marital difficulties and, as a guardian had not been appointed, a child psychiatrist was asked to interview the children and ascertain their wishes. Each child was interviewed individually with the youngest skillfully interviewed with the help of a glove puppet. The interviews were recorded verbatim and filled 17 pages. Here is an excerpt.

Do you know why I've come to see you?

No, not really.

Do you know what it's about? (A big smile and shaking head no) *it's about being adopted* (an even bigger smile). *What do you understand by being adopted, what does that mean?*

It just means you go somewhere else and stay with them, that's all really.

How do you feel about that?

I don't mind really.

Tell me about your life here, what's it like?

It's alright.

What's the nicest thing about it?

I don't know.

What's the worst thing about it.

Well, the worst thing is mum and dad; they're always shouting; they're always telling me off; most of the time they're not but recently they keep on telling me off...

A picture emerged of a very unhappy little girl, scapegoated by the prospective adopters who were having major marital problems. The adoption hearing was halted.

The appointment of guardians was important as they were more likely to record the child's voice. A group of four siblings were very concerned that no one would listen to them. They had been returned to their father's care on four separate occasions, each time despite their protestations. The children were afraid they would once again be returned, in spite of being in adoptive placements. The eldest child's Schedule 2 report read:

Deborah understands the need for an adoptive family to be sought for her and was anxious for this to happen. She has settled well with the prospective adopter and has always been clear that she wished to stay with them. Her religious and cultural needs are well met.

The guardian saw the children individually and separately. The children had discussed what they wanted to say and had written down the points for the judge to see in a letter:
1. He [father] pulled teeth out with pliers.
2. They pushed bed in front of door to stop old dad from getting in.
3. He [father] hit with sticks – everywhere face and body.
4. He threw dog down landing.
5. He took . . . and . . . out stealing.
6. He squirted blood on . . . and wiped knife on her.
7. What he did to . . . and heard her screaming. He broke down . . . door when she locked it.
8. He got drunk a lot and came home angry.
9. Weetabix every breakfast and beans every supper.
10. Punched old mum and gave her black eyes.

The letter continued detailing other abuse and is a powerful testimony to the children's determination that they did want to have their say in the process.

Social workers were also far more likely than guardians to underestimate the abilities and competence of the children. Two brothers, John aged ten and James aged nine, had very little written about their wishes and feelings. The youngest child had mild learning difficulties and the social worker wrote: 'In view of James's limited intellectual capacity and likely weaker attachment to and memory of his birth mother and early life experiences the concept of adoption and what it means is beyond his understanding.' The guardian, however, interviewed both boys:

Both boys present as lively, polite, sociable and interesting children . . . James does not appear to have many memories of his past or at least he mentions none. He was unwilling to work on his life story, although he shows interest in John's. He's expressed no interest in seeing his family again although he, like John, was interested in the

information I was able to give about my contact with his family...
John has a tendency to answer for James but, on the subject of the
adoption application, James was quick to answer for himself without
waiting to hear his brother's answer.

The guardian's report does not give the impression of a child who cannot
understand the concept of adoption.

Relationships

The relationship between siblings has been described in many ways:
hostile, intimate, ambivalent and loving. The network of relationships in
which children grow up is complex and can lead to supportive or hostile
sibling relationships. Their intensity means that conflict is common in
all sibling relationships (Strauss *et al*, 1980). However, siblings growing
up in homes where there are marital difficulties, where the adults
relationship is hostile, and with frequent quarrels may be more likely to
have sibling relationships which are in conflict and aggressive (Jenkins,
1992, pp 125–139). Conversely siblings can also be a great source of
comfort and support to each other during stressful times. When parents
are psychologically unavailable, siblings offer and receive comfort
(Bryant and Litman, 1987).

The importance of relationships seemed to come out by chance in the
Schedule 2 reports. Social workers did not seem to consider whom the
children wanted to see or who were the key people in their lives. Siblings
were written about as though they were a unit without individual
experiences and needs. Guardians did ask questions about relationships,
but the relevance for the child was not expanded upon in other parts of
the reports. For example, 'When I spoke to Billy about his feelings
regarding his adoptive family he commented that one of the *best things*
[my italics] was that his baby sister sleeps in the next room.' In
comparison the social worker wrote: 'Billy wishes to remain forever in
his present placement.' The importance to Billy of the relationship with
his sister was not discussed by the social worker or the guardian.

Neither guardians nor social workers asked any of the children
specifically about their wishes and feelings about the siblings left at

home with birth parents. One group where the Schedule 2 report was left blank were placed separately, with the baby still at home with the birth parents. The guardian recorded how agitated one of the children became and stated the child had real concerns: 'He still has strong feelings about R [the father] and got quite distraught when we talked about the baby still being in that household. His words were, "it is a very dangerous place to be".'

One of the most striking recent research findings is that siblings from the same family tend to be almost as different from each other as children from different families. Why is this? The reason is complex. Siblings appear to have the same experiences but they *perceive* them differently. For example, the death of a grandparent will be perceived differently by a four-year-old and a ten-year-old. The death will have a different impact on each child. As well as perceiving the same or shared environments differently, siblings also experience different environments. For example, different schools, teachers, friends they may have, hobbies and activities. Each sibling's development is also affected by their genes, which interact with the shared and non-shared environment (Dunn and Plomin, 1990). These findings highlight the importance of treating each sibling as an individual person with their own thoughts and feelings. However, several of the Schedule 2 reports were identical. The recording for each child read word for word the same. This occurred even when the children were in different adoptive placements.

When children had been made subject of a Freeing Order, the reports were often submitted again for the adoption hearing. There was often a gap of a year between the two court hearings. A year in the life of a child is a long time and many events would have occurred during that time. For a particular family of four in different placements, there had been many changes since the Freeing Order, not least the birth parents moving to a house opposite the eldest child's prospective adopters' home. Yet the section on wishes and feelings was left blank for all four children. On her birthday the eldest child had visited her parents and had refused to leave. A clinical psychologist had been appointed by the court and had reported: '[the child] believes she has no choice about being adopted. Her *perception* is that she had to agree ("the As wanted to adopt me, I had to say yeah to everything").' The girl had remained with her birth mother as the court had accepted the psychologist's view that the child had never separated psychologically from her. It was interesting to see the girl's papers lodged with the court for a second time after the situation at home had broken down and she had returned to live with the prospective adopters again. There was no evidence on any of the four children's files that they had been asked for their views. If the children had been able to feel they were being treated as individuals and genuine participants, it might have enabled the eldest child to have been given more time, rather than being railroaded into an adoption because her younger siblings were ready. It might also have prevented another rejection by her birth mother and allowed her to talk through her ambivalent feelings.

Adoption is a complex process. Any older child being adopted will have a whole raft of past life experiences, ambivalent or confused feelings about adoption and hopes and fears for the future. Siblings who are placed for adoption have an additional set of wishes and feelings about their relationships with each other, their history of past strategies for survival, and future hopes for each other. The complexities of sibling relationships were omitted from this sample of Schedule 2 reports. The support and/or conflict that often characterises sibling relationships was not even raised in the reports. Children's views rarely appeared. There was no discussion of how each child felt about their adoptive placements or whether the children wanted contact with each other when in different placements. The children were lumped together as if they had identical wishes and feelings. It was symbolic that some siblings did not even have their own case file number.

There was no evidence on any of the social work reports that the children had seen how their wishes and feelings had been recorded. This only seemed to be common practice for the official solicitor where it gave the children the opportunity to agree or disagree with written statements and to feel they did have a role in the process.

When children *were* given a voice, their wishes and feelings came through powerfully. These siblings had a great many fears: fears of being found by birth relatives, fears for those siblings left behind and a fear that it was not possible to go against social work plans. The children felt helpless. There should be a great deal of concern about why there was so

147

little recorded of the child's wishes and feelings in the Schedule 2 reports and concern for children who were not represented by a guardian. Although having a guardian did not guarantee that the child's wishes and feelings would be recorded, there was a far greater likelihood if one was appointed. For too many of these children the section on wishes and feelings had been left blank. Even when it had been completed it was filled in with a few words which filled the space, but said little about what the child thought or felt. The children were excluded from presenting their views in a matter which would have enormous impact on them for the rest of their lives.

Allowing children genuinely to participate in the adoption process might threaten the social workers' position of power, or disturb paternalistic views of children: the 'we know best' approach. It might also threaten decisions taken because of dogma or ideological views. Social workers are often seen by other professionals as the champions for children, as the profession which does have the child's interests as paramount. To live up to this, social work must recognise that each child is an individual, with their own thoughts, experiences and feelings and that these are valid. Shemmings (1996) has argued that the most effective way of involving children in conferences is when each individual's child's needs, wishes and feelings are identified by working in partnership with the child. During the adoption process, too, social workers need to work in partnership with the child, combining their professional judgement with the needs of children to be active participants. For adoption to be a service *for children* as the last Adoption White Paper's (1993) title suggested, children's right to be heard in matters which affect them has to be taken seriously.

References

Bryant B and Litman C (1987) 'Siblings as teachers and therapists', *Journal of Children in Contemporary Society*, 19, pp 185–205.

Brown J and Dunn J (1992) 'Talk with your mother or your sibling? Developmental changes in early family conversations about feelings', *Child Development*, 63, pp 336–349.

Dunn J and Plomin R (1990) *Separate Lives: Why are siblings so different?*, New York: Basic Books.

Jenkins J (1992) 'Sibling relationships in disharmonious homes' in Boer F and Dunn J (ed) *Children's Sibling Relationships: Development and clinical issues*, Hove and London: Lawrence Erlbaum.

Selwyn J (1996) 'Ascertaining children's wishes and feelings in relation to adoption', *Adoption & Fostering*, 20:3, pp 14–20.

Shemmings D (1996) *Involving Children in Child Protection Conferences*, Norwich: University of East Anglia, Social Work Monographs 152.

Strauss M A, Gelles R J and Steinmetz S K (1980) *Behind Closed Doors: Violence in the American family*, Garden City, NY: Anchor Books.

United Nations (1989) *Convention on the Rights of the Child: Adopted by the General Assembly of the United Nations, 1989*, London: Stationery Office. (This edition published 1996.)

11 Mein tumhari didi hun (I am your sister)

Shobha and *Marylin*

Marylin feels that writing about her experience of reunion may be useful for other people either within the Asian community or for those involved in a sibling reunion where the birth mother is deceased. Shobha and Marylin have chosen not to identify themselves by their real names.

Shobha ki kahani (Shobha's story)

'ANITA is an attractive and intelligent four-year-old of Indian parents. She seeks a loving and secure foster home with view to adoption. If you would like to offer a home to this child, please apply to the Children's Officer' (*New Statesman*, 1970). A year later, I moved from the children's home to my adoptive family, a white family with three birth children living in the Cotswolds.

One evening, on 4 July 1983, my mum told me that my birth father had been in England searching for me. This information brought with it a burst of happiness and a resurgence of my childhood dream of finding my mother. Also surfaced pain, sadness and tears that I had kept carefully hidden away in recent years. Through my birth father I hoped I would find my mother.

Weeks later, the day my mum and dad returned from North America where they had visited my birth father, my mum told me that my mother had died of breast cancer just three years earlier. Days later, on 15 August, I flew out to meet and stay with my birth father, my Papaji. I was introduced to a large and warm extended family where I became a Didi (sister) among my many cousin brothers and sisters.

It was to be three years later that I first laid eyes on my sister. Of course, at this time I did not even know that I had a sister. My Papaji had only mentioned two younger brothers whom he had said he might point out to me at church. On 22 March 1986, while searching for my mother's grave, I went into the church and a young woman in the youth group said in a loud voice, 'Who's that?'. This was my first unknowing glimpse of my sister. Two days later, I located my mother's unmarked grave. Two days after that, I was at St.Catherine's House ordering my mother's death certificate and looking through the birth indexes over a ten-year period. I located my two brothers in the indexes, Michael born in 1975 and Mark born in 1976, and someone born in 1972 who could possibly be a sister. As no one had mentioned a sister, I kept the reference but discounted it. On 13 April, a family friend told me that I had a sister, aged about 12, who closely resembled my mother. The same day I discovered that my sister's name was Marylin.

On 8 June 1986, I went to a church service at my mother's church with my friend Shanti. We looked for the six-foot man with a wife and three young children that I had been told about. To our luck and amazement they sat in the pew directly in front of us, just inches away. The boys, aged nine and eleven, looked so small and were dressed in matching burgundy jumpers. Later that afternoon, we walked by the council house (the address on the death certificate). The same two boys were playing outside – one on a skateboard, the other on a swing – while my sister walked across the road, tall and slim in a lemon skirt, her long brown hair clipped back at each side. Her face was just like my mother's. There could be no doubt – these three children were clearly my sister and brothers. Shanti even asked Mark the way over to the canal, while I stood speechless!

Despite my agnosticism, over the next few years I regularly attended the morning church service to catch a glimpse of my sister and brothers' lives and to watch them grow up from a distance. After church, I would visit the grave and then sit in an Indian café thinking about my sister and brothers.

On one occasion a friend and I, while selectively leafleting my sister's road about a video course at the community centre, deliberately knocked on her front door. Marylin answered the door and my friend provided the sales pitch as I looked on, speechless yet again! Being both the eldest and female, my sister became my focus. To begin with, she represented a concrete and tangible link with my mother. Yet I also knew that she was a person in her own right, with her own needs and experiences, and that she was too young to be "tainted" by the knowledge of my existence. I wondered if Marylin would ever accept me as her sister. I asked myself how I could ever explain to her and whether I should even try.

By 1991, Marylin was 18 years old. I now decided to develop a friendship with Marylin and to tell her who I was after her A level examinations, to minimise disruption to her life. At church a young lad befriended me and introduced me to everyone except the one person I wanted to be introduced to! I was so nervous that even smiling and saying hello to Marylin seemed difficult. Several church services later, I finally spoke to Marylin and we exchanged names and addresses. On each subsequent visit we would talk. I even went to an Easter lunch and, of course, Marylin introduced me to Michael and Mark. Our growing friendship, in the context of my hidden identity and the possible complications at a later stage, now led me to limit my visits.

One Sunday in July 1991, I decided that today was THE DAY to tell Marylin that I was her sister. Mind you, I had decided this on my previous visit too! This time, however, I was determined. After the church service, I invited Marylin to join me for lunch. Unfortunately for me, she now had a boyfriend, Sanjeev. I found myself sitting in an Indian restaurant with Marylin and Sanjeev. My carefully planned revelation over lunch could not take place.

Afterwards they dropped me off by the railway station and Marylin walked with me up the road. This was my last and only chance that Sunday (even if it was in the middle of the street!). So I did. I do not remember quite what I said (although I am sure I had rehearsed for days, even years!!). I do remember that she burst into tears and hugged me, and told me that she had always wanted a big sister. There was no disbelief, no questions, just acceptance of what I was saying. I gave Marylin an envelope to take with her containing a copy of my original birth certificate, two photographs of myself with our mother, a copy of a letter our mother had written, and a Post Adoption Centre leaflet. A few minutes later Marylin walked back to the car.

Marylin ki kahani (Marylin's story)

Shobha introduced herself to me at the end of the church service and sounded keen on making friends. I was unused to having strangers approach me like this – but I thought nothing of it since I had seen her before in church. (Later, I was to realise the reason for this enthusiasm.) As we talked, it became apparent that Shobha was at a loose end that afternoon, and she wanted me to go to lunch with her so I could tell her about the area.

I felt quite awkward with the invitation, not only because I already had plans with my boyfriend, but also due to the fact that this sort of thing never happened to me. However, I accepted on the condition that Sanjeev came with us – this way I felt more at ease and I could continue my afternoon with him afterwards. Shobha's persistence astounded me, but I felt that, if I were a stranger in a new church, I would want someone to be nice to me too.

At the point in time that I met Shobha my life was very rocky. Although it was a positive stage in my life, it was also emotionally difficult. The A level exams were over and I had a place at university waiting for me, which would mean leaving home for the first time. My boyfriend (now my husband) and I had a very serious relationship and we were coming to terms with the imminent but temporary separation. On top of that, my (step) mum was awaiting a kidney transplant in India and had been there for the last two years. The shock of the coming revelation was to be quite a score chalked up beside everything else.

Lunch was civil, but awkward at times and the conversation didn't really flow that well. I sensed Shobha didn't want Sanjeev to be present, but I didn't know her well enough to have gone alone, so I was glad when it was over.

When we got back to the train station Shobha asked me to get out of the car for a minute, saying she wanted to tell me something. As I got out I wondered what it could be – I had formed the opinion that I would avoid this girl if I could as I felt awkward around her and I didn't like that. We walked for a few seconds in silence; I noticed it was a lovely bright day, leaves scattered on the ground and a cool breeze blowing, and it was very calm. Shobha said she had been wanting to tell me something for ages and didn't know how to break it to me. There was another silence and by now I just wanted to know. She looked dead straight at me, and fixed her eyes on mine and said, 'I'm your sister'.

She continued looking at me and waited, anxious for a reaction I think. I was not prepared for those words; it was as if I hadn't heard them at all. My mind was spinning with all sorts of questions – how could this be? Is it true? Why? How? But almost simultaneously I threw my arms around her, my heart filled with emotion, and there were tears in my eyes. I remember her saying, 'You and I have the same mother', which meant she was a secret part of my mother's life, but she was essentially family. All the negative thoughts flew out of my mind, after all blood was blood. It was at this point everything else made sense – the persistence over lunch, the resistance to Sanjeev's presence and the enthusiasm of befriending me. Shobha gave me an envelope containing various documents that proved our relationship and verified we shared the same mother.

This changed everything in my life forever – but I didn't really come to terms with the announcement until many years later. At first, I tried not to think about Shobha much because then I would have to deal with the other questions in my mind. This one truth had turned my whole world upside down and changed all my views and thoughts about my life, family and, most importantly, about my mother.

I began to question my mother's reputation; she had had a child out of wedlock, by another man, and then gave her child up. I wondered if my dad knew about Shobha, or if my mother had taken this secret with her to her grave. Initially, I was angry at my mum for allowing herself to get pregnant, especially since she was a Christian. I could not come to terms with the situation for many years because everything I had believed in and been taught had fallen apart around me. After some time, I felt immense pain for her, and for the torment she must have gone through with the adoption. In the 60s, the Asian community was very close knit so something like this would have been difficult to hide, and there was no way that it would have been accepted. The worst thing was not knowing the circumstances under which Shobha came to be, but it was out of my hands.

I kept this secret from my dad, brothers and stepmother, almost on pain of death – and having to carry that was a burden. I knew I had to tell my brothers at some stage, because they had a right to know – but I didn't feel they would be able to cope with it just yet. I was in turmoil emotionally, and I didn't like the feeling of being pushed down from the "eldest" child spot; for some reason I thought the boys would stop loving me and give my respect to Shobha.

I must admit for a while I resented Shobha and the fact that she had tracked me down. However, if I was in her shoes I would have done exactly the same thing; if I knew I had family out there I would have traced them all too. My husband helped me deal with the fact that I had a half-sister, and made me realise that it was not Shobha's fault at all. She was only looking to belong and didn't want to take anything away from me. She was quite happy to let things go the way they were and didn't push for anything more than I could give.

Shobha is still a secret – and everyone knows her as a friend of mine. I will never do or say anything that would tarnish my mother's name in the eyes of the world, and especially not for my dad who still misses her. That would break him.

Apni kahani (our story)

Today we are able to talk and laugh about the things we said and did in those early years. We recall the awkward moments that passed in silence on the day of the "revelation" when finally Shobha was able to disclose her birth identity, marking a new stage in her quest for the recognition she had been seeking for many years. On the other hand, a new chapter was opened in Marylin's life with a long-lost sister (who, as a child, she had always imagined she had). For both of us, this day affirmed our relationship as sisters, a previously hidden bond, where now each sister knew who the other was!

As we reminisce, those early meetings come to mind, before Marylin went to University, and we remember how we would write letters to each other and occasionally speak on the telephone. Shobha was always sure to send Marylin a birthday card, and maintained steady but unobtrusive contact. There were also a couple of visits arranged at the University digs, in the later years, where we began to get to know each other better.

For me (Marylin), the relationship only really took off a few years after my graduation, once I had married and life had become more settled for me. Those early days were largely data-gathering sessions, where I tried to complete the missing links in my family story. I wanted as much information as I could lay my hands on and, through Shobha, I found the perfect solution.

Not surprisingly, I (Shobha) felt overwhelmed after each meeting, by the quantity of information that we discussed and exchanged. It was as if a dozen evenings had been crammed into one, with our parting comments raising even more questions for both of us.

We realise now that we each had very different needs and, therefore, approached the reunion from different positions. Since our mother was dead, the story was incomplete and we endeavoured to resolve some of the issues that concerned us. The focus remained initially on our mother – we talked about her life, illness and her death. However, both of us wanted to reach a point of friendship and to start to look to the future, but this was to take time – more for Marylin than for Shobha.

Shobha helped me (Marylin) come to terms with our mother's death. With my dad's remarriage that chapter in my life had been firmly closed, and unfortunately I had not been given the chance to grieve openly. We pieced together the historical detail through knowledge, photographs, documents, certificates, names and addresses that Shobha had accumulated over the years. We discussed her visit to India, to our mother's parents and younger sister. She even told me where the grave was since I had never been taken there. I was able to share many thoughts with Shobha that I otherwise would never have spoken about. This played an extremely important role in the process of coming to terms with the loss, and also built great bonds in the relationship between me and my sister.

I have been fortunate that Marylin has accepted me (Shobha) as her sister. I knew that revealing my birth identity would shock Marylin. However, I had not anticipated the issues that she was to struggle with for many years. Also I had not realised that I would provide a great release to Marylin's emotions regarding our mother. Yet this has assisted in building the friendship we have. In those early years I tried not to pressure Marylin in any way. Perhaps allowing the relationship to develop at a pace that felt comfortable to Marylin allowed her the time to adjust to this new reality whilst I had time to reflect on our future.

We have discussed transracial adoption, the practice that removes black children from their community, culture and language, placing them in white families with a foreign culture. I (Marylin) cannot imagine being removed from the Indian Christian community and being unable to live my culture or speak Hindi. I cannot accept that Shobha could ever fit into a white family, or why a white family was chosen, given the consequent estrangement of Shobha from our mother's culture and language. Some things can never be justified.

In every aspect of Shobha's life, Marylin is acknowledged and accepted as Shobha's sister: from Shobha's friends, and her adoptive sister to her Papaji, who remembers Marylin as a child. In Marylin's life, though, this sisterhood is hidden: Marilyn's need for secrecy, to protect our mother's name and her life within the Indian Christian community, influences our relationship, rendering it invisible.

Two years ago I (Marylin) told Michael and Mark about Shobha. A week later, we finally all met together as two big sisters and two younger brothers. We telephone each other regularly and meet when we can. Last year, together on the anniversary of our mother's death, we planted rose bushes on her grave. Over the years our relationship has developed through different stages to arrive at the understanding, trust and friendship that we feel towards each other today.

12 **Adopting siblings:** my experience

Joy Wilkings

Joy Wilkings has both a personal and professional interest in adoption. She and her partner adopted four children between 1985 and 1990 and their lives have been well and truly changed by this. Joy has been active as a member of various adoption support groups, and co-ordinator of ACCORD for multiracial families. Joy is also a social worker and, after ten years working with an emergency duty team, has recently moved into education social work.

I am writing about my experiences as an adoptive parent. I hope this will be of interest to other adoptive or would-be adoptive parents, but primarily I hope that social workers, by reading this, will find information and ideas to help them when arranging and supporting placements of siblings. I have used pseudonyms for all persons mentioned in this account.

I am writing this article shortly after Aaron's (our younger son's) 18th birthday. This event reminded me of one of the peculiar aspects of adopting older children, in that he is 18 but we have only been parents for 13 years. In that time we adopted four children. Initially, we adopted two boys (Aaron and his older half-brother Karl) who were aged five and six when they joined us. Two years later we adopted Toni, then aged two, and three years after that, we adopted Amber, aged four months. Thus we have experience of a variety of sibling relationships, as have our children. Now they are all legally brothers and sisters but two were previously related, although in terms of appearance people often assume the youngest three are biologically related which, of course, is not the case. I should explain that Karl and Aaron had the same white birth mother but Karl's biological father is white (Irish) and Aaron's black (Jamaican). Toni and Amber also each had a white birth mother and African-Caribbean father. My partner and I are both white. Another article could and perhaps should be written specifically about transracial adoption; however, the point to make here is that we were asked by social services to provide a home to half-brothers for whom staying together meant one would be placed transracially. When we decided to extend our family we were already a multiracial family and felt that Aaron should not be the only black person in our family. We specifically looked for a black girl, hence Toni joined us and subsequently Amber.

The first question to be addressed is why does anyone choose to adopt siblings? In our case there was a mixture of motives but, primarily, we wanted more than one child. We had discovered that we were unable to have birth children, but it had taken years to reach this conclusion due to undergoing new developments in the treatment of infertility – by which time, had things turned out differently, we might well have had more than one child. Secondly, the adoption process is lengthy and intrusive, and so the possibility of getting two children together had considerable appeal. We were also conscious that sibling groups are harder to place and thus we felt that offering this would increase our chances not only of being approved but also of avoiding another lengthy wait for an actual placement. We also felt altruistically it would be a "good thing" to help keep brothers and sisters together and that we were in a position (both economically and emotionally) to be able to offer a home to more than one child. Thus the reasons for applying to adopt siblings were quite mixed but, at best, we hoped it would help meet both our needs as a childless couple and the needs of waiting children.

Looking back, we did not really consider the different implications of adopting related and unrelated children. We simply felt we were more than ready to become parents and should "go for it". Our family and friends accepted our aims, and, if they expressed any worries, it was more about taking children of school age rather than taking more than one child. We thought it might make the situation easier in that the children would have each other to play with, and we also thought it could help them emotionally by having each other. Another consideration was also that we were so eager to become parents we might almost have overwhelmed one child.

Thus we actively sought and were approved to adopt two siblings of either sex. Although it seemed an interminable wait between approval in April and hearing about "our" children in August, I now realise it was not that long. We were excited to learn about Karl and Aaron, who were half-brothers then aged six and five, and the process began.

Meeting siblings is complicated because you may react very differently to each of the children. The first meeting is always difficult. We had gone with a more positive impression of Aaron, the younger boy, from the photographs, but on the first meeting Karl impressed us most, being more easy to understand and easier to relate to. We played with them at the children's home and left, eager to see them again for an outing at the weekend. The eight weeks of introductions were demanding and exciting. We only ever saw the boys together, although within that we would take turns to do things with them individually. Karl certainly led the way in terms of explanations and showed more emotional reactions to the proposed move. The comments from social workers were that they knew Karl wanted to move but they were less sure how Aaron felt, and they were worried he was just going along with things to please his brother. Looking back now, I would say Aaron was more closely attached to staff at the home and did not have the same desperate need to move that his older brother had. Far from being so worried, the staff should have been pleased at Aaron's response and we should all have been more worried by Karl's readiness to move.

The timing of any move depends on various factors and, in our case, the autumn half-term week seemed a good idea. The boys therefore moved in permanently eight weeks after we first met them. Although many people talk about a "honeymoon period" we did not experience this, except perhaps in the introductions and overnight stays when, looking back, everyone had been on their best behaviour. Immediately upon moving in, both boys launched into a great deal of testing-out behaviour, especially Karl who certainly knew this bit of the script. Despite all the preparations, we were also learning on our feet about how to look after children – meals, clothes, toys, books . . . All those adjustments must be made by any new adopters but the sheer quantity of food, washing, tidying up, took us by surprise. Indeed, it is true to say that our initial adjustment to parenthood was probably the most exhausting experience of our lives. Years later, our fourth child joined us as a baby and friends wondered how we would cope – but by that time we could take new demands in our stride.

There are a few issues which I feel are particularly significant about adopting siblings. One of the challenges facing parents adopting siblings is that the children have known each other prior to meeting the new parents. That also means, as Karl pointed out to us several years after they had joined us, that he had known Aaron longer than we had, with the implication that he knew him better than we did. This is a hard reality for parents to live with.

Another factor is that meeting new children and developing relationships with them simultaneously would normally only happen with twins. The older child did not have time alone with us prior to sharing us with his brother, nor did the younger child have the attention devoted to him in the way that, later on, the two girls did when they arrived individually. However, to cope with the demands of instant parenting, my partner and I both worked part-time for the first year and we were able to devote an enormous amount of time to the boys both together and individually.

Clearly siblings will have a shared past, and we rather naively hoped that being placed together would help the boys in terms of dealing with the impact of past losses in their lives, especially the deaths of their mother and grandmother. Also sibling placements are arguably a potent form of open adoption with built-in contact daily with a birth relative, thus removing one of the losses inherent in adoption. Furthermore, there was some contact planned for our sons with a maternal aunt. However, Karl and Aaron had experienced the losses of the past differently and, even up to the present day (with both of them now adults), they have not actually been able to help each other. There may also be an unconscious element of blame of each other that they were unable to remain with birth relatives; the explanation given was that these relatives either had other children to care for or had their own difficulties, which meant that none of the boys' many aunts or uncles could offer them a home. However, it is also true that some might have been able to cope with one but not both of them. I would say, however, that growing up in a family with several adopted children, and being part of a social network with other adoptive families, has helped all of them deal better with being adopted, and has lessened the feeling that it must somehow be their fault.

One of the most important issues for siblings dealing with the impact of the past is that, invariably, the older child has protected the younger one, at some personal cost to him/herself. This aspect of the older sibling parenting the younger was also part of our experience. Aaron had underdeveloped speech and Karl tended to act as an interpreter for him. Clearly we sought to help Aaron, which resulted in the unintended (but nevertheless essential) consequence of disempowering Karl of an important role in his life. Similarly, at school, Karl protected Aaron, but, as Aaron's confidence increased, Karl was left without that role too. Karl had provided emotional security for his younger brother and an anchor for him, and this was one of the reasons Aaron was less damaged and more easily able to develop his relationship with us. To some extent, this caused yet more problems for Karl who struggled with giving up his erstwhile control of Aaron. That, in turn, was one of the factors that hampered Karl in developing a rewarding relationship with us. This aspect of (in Karl's eyes) loss of his brother's loyalty became even more of an issue when our next child, Toni, joined the family for, although both boys at times resented the demands she made on our time, it was ultimately only the younger lad who really developed a relationship with her, and it was clear that the older one was jealous of this. Karl was good with our youngest child, Amber, when she was a baby, but as she got older his own difficulties continued and he had nothing left to give her. As time passed, Amber was developing strong and hopefully enduring links with Toni and Aaron, and her relationship with Karl withered away. Karl no longer lives at home and when he asked Amber by phone, just after her eighth birthday, how old she was, she was outraged that he did not know, but sadly that remark symbolised the state of their relationship.

However, I have jumped ahead in the story, and I need to return to the time when it was just the two boys living with us. We began to notice something which other adoptive parents have recognised, which I call the "see-saw" experience. What I mean by this is that a pattern emerged that one of the boys would be in trouble and the other would be good, and then they would swap roles. It was like an invisible see-saw. For example, Karl might be in trouble for damaging something, which he would deny, and we would be cross about the lies more than the damage (this was before we understood about the effects of attachment disorder on behaviour) and, while this was going on, Aaron would be co-operative and helpful. However, as soon as the situation with Karl had been resolved and we were all friends again, Aaron would begin to act up in a difficult way. This was exhausting to live with, and I would sometimes wish that they would both misbehave together if that also meant they could occasionally both be co-operative with each other and with us for a while. However, I did realise that part of what was going on was that the one who was not in trouble was in fact behaving well in order to try and hold the placement together for himself and also for his brother. It was as if the "good" one could not risk behaving badly while his brother acted out, through fear of us not being able to cope . . . and ending the placement. I know that many other adoptive parents have experienced this and it is hard to live with for all concerned. We tried endlessly to reassure both boys that they were with us permanently, but I realise now how frightened each boy must have been to see us getting frustrated at his brother's behaviour, and fearing we might ask for them to leave.

This see-saw effect lessened over the years, but not in a very positive way. From being fairly up and down between the lads the trend developed of Karl being more often in difficulties than Aaron; hence, eventually, Karl did become labelled as being more difficult (or equally we could say that, as time passed, we recognised that Karl was in fact more emotionally damaged than Aaron). Thus a stability of sorts emerged in the family as we all developed strategies to cope with Karl's ever-present difficult behaviour and, as his teenage years passed, this somewhat unhealthy equilibrium became the norm, with Aaron, Toni and Amber all achieving in their own very different ways, and Karl more or less stagnating. And yet, still, at those rare times when Karl did make an effort to achieve something, Aaron's behaviour quickly deteriorated.

Alongside the dynamic between Karl and Aaron, it has been very interesting to see the relationship develop between our two (unrelated by birth) daughters. Although I have not told this to Toni and Amber, I actually feel relieved when at times they are both stroppy together and feel safe enough to unite against me; equally, I can enjoy the many times they are both relaxed and getting on with life. They do get cross with each other and us, but they are not on an invisible see-saw!

Dealing with the many aspects of sibling rivalry is part of the experience of parenting siblings. Your ability to deal with this as a parent depends partly on your own experience as a child, and I think it is relevant that I grew up as an only child while my partner had a younger sister. Not having had the experience of arguing and making up with siblings, or of having to share your parents' time, means that I have at times struggled with these sorts of issues more than parents who have grown up with siblings themselves might. Social workers should discuss this more with people applying to adopt during the assessment and preparation stages.

It is true, of course, that some placements do break down and, although it probably did not seem like it to our lads, it was, at times, our commitment to them as siblings which kept the placement going. We might have given up with Karl, but we felt we could not because of Aaron. Indeed, this feeling intensified when the girls joined the family; we wanted them to feel secure and to realise that adoption is permanent, and we felt that unless we did hang on with Karl their sense of security could be undermined.

There is only a 16-month age gap between the boys, and they were in consecutive school years. This made for particular problems about treating them the same while seeing them as individuals. This has been an ongoing problem over the years. For example, because they are very different in appearance and personality, at times I felt it was important to emphasise their family connection by dressing them in matching or similar clothes, a practice which had commenced at the children's home where they lived before moving to us. Yet, one of the first things I bought for them was different clothes of their own choosing.

We felt it was very important to help the boys develop their individuality and yet also enjoy being together. They started a few activities together, such as cubs and jujitsu, but Aaron was far more into group activities, hence he stayed when Karl left. Aaron was also able to join new groups successfully without Karl's presence, and this was an important part of his social life. Karl was far more talented at sport, and we encouraged him in this, but sadly he could not commit himself to anything, even to things he was good at.

The boys started off attending the same school. Education is another topic which deserves an article to itself, but suffice it to say here that there were many problems stemming from the fact that they were in the same school, with Aaron in the year immediately below Karl. So, when they moved to senior school, we felt it was a good idea for them to go to different schools, which was not easy to achieve because of the education authority's (understandable) policy of placing siblings together. As the boys carried on through the education system, we felt that we had done the right thing in terms of giving them each a chance to do the best they could without the complication of being at the same school, although this was an extra strain for us, having to deal simultaneously at one time with four schools. This also meant they had different friends. When they were younger, they were both friends with a brother and sister living locally whose parents also became close friends of ours and this was a good time for all of us. Apart from that, they have had hardly any joint friends and now inhabit totally different social networks.

I will return to the time when we had already adopted Karl and Aaron (they were then aged eight and six) and we began to think about adding to the family. With typical naïvety, Karl enthused about the idea of a sister and told everyone he was getting one immediately. Aaron seemed less certain whether he wanted one or not. We were reapproved easily for a preschool-aged girl of mixed heritage. When we heard about Toni we did not initially tell the boys for fear of disappointing them, and we also felt we had to meet her first to be sure it felt right for us as the parents to proceed. However, once told, they were excited, and a very hectic period of introductions began since she lived in another area, and Toni's social workers had the exhausting idea that we should see her daily in this two-week period before she moved in. We kept the boys off school on the day Toni moved in, and we all went to collect her. The arrival of Toni, who, at two years and three months, already knew her own mind, transformed the household. Shortly after Toni moved in, we talked to the boys when she was in bed about how they felt, and Karl interestingly answered for both of them saying, 'We haven't made up our minds about Toni, me and Aaron. Mum and Dad like her but before she came it was our house – now she's taken over'.

Toni's arrival had, in fact, acted as a defining moment for many hitherto unrecognised aspects of all our personalities. For Karl, Toni demonstrated by her ready grasp of ideas and her problem-solving ability the extent of his intellectual limitations. This was even more true when she started school and the euphemisms the school had used about Karl's progress became more obvious. Years later, when he was 13 years old, Karl noted sadly when Toni was reading her cards aloud on her seventh birthday that he had hardly been able to read anything at that age. For Aaron, Toni's arrival made him confront his blackness in a different way because, henceforth, he was seeing and living with another black person everyday. This bond between them strengthened as time passed, especially when Toni became old enough to join Aaron at the Saturday School run by the local African-Caribbean community association. For me, Toni gave me the opportunity to parent a preschool-aged child and a daughter, and thus fulfilled needs I had which were deeper than I had been aware of. Toni recently told me we are "kindred spirits" and I certainly feel this. For my partner, also, her articulateness and love of debating ideas has been very rewarding and he, too, was pleased to have a daughter.

We had not intended to adopt four children when we started out, and when we thought about a fourth child we said to our social worker we did not want to be seen as being greedy; we were quite surprised by her favourable reaction to the idea. We were conscious that Toni held a favoured position in the family and felt that it would do her good no longer to be the only girl and the youngest. We also had enjoyed parenting her and wanted to repeat the experience. As I write this, I feel I am having to defend and explain why we had another child. But why should I? At the end of the day, like most people who want a large family, we just did it. We did feel that it was important for a new child to be the youngest, and our existing three children all agreed with the idea of adopting a baby. Social services again re-approved us.

When we heard about Amber, she was four months old. At that time Karl was 11, Aaron nine, and Toni five. We had a very different intro-ductory experience this time. After the previous protracted arrangements we prepared ourselves for several visits (Amber's foster home was in another part of the country) and planned for myself and my partner to go first to meet her. The social worker expressed surprise we were not taking the other children and pointed out that having met her on the Thursday we could stay in the area for the weekend and bring her home on the Monday! So we took her at her word. We all went to the foster home and my partner and I went upstairs to see Amber first because we felt this was the right thing to do, and we then brought her down to meet the others who all wanted to hold and feed her. The journey back home on Monday was memorable as we had to keep stopping and moving round inside the car to allow everyone a turn of sitting next to Amber.

At the time of her adoption, a friend drew a card with Amber in the centre of a wheel and us all surrounding her, giving the impression of her both as the focus of attention and also holding us together which was at that time quite true. In terms of jealousy – yes, Toni did at times, and still does, resent the time given to Amber, and this feeling is mutual. However, the age gap is such that both can have their different needs met in different ways and yet also at times enjoy activities together. They have, I think, a very "normal" relationship. Karl, as mentioned above, was very good with Amber when she was a baby but, as he became a teenager, he spent less time at home and less time with her. Unfortunately, I could not trust him to look after the younger ones in the way that I later asked Aaron to. Aaron is good with younger children and spends a lot of time at the homes of his friends whose younger siblings view him as a hero. He has not been happy, however, to spend as much time with Toni and Amber as we might have hoped.

Time for everyone is a real issue. At times, I have felt as if I am being pulled in pieces trying to meet everyone's needs. I also wonder if I have created problems for myself by encouraging everyone to pursue individual interests. At one time our calendar, covered with everyone's commitments, was amazing and to this day my partner and I sit down on Sunday evening to 'start the week' by checking who is doing what in terms of transport and childcare. For the girls, the age gap means that different bedtimes give them both one-to-one attention. But, as ages change so do needs, and recently with Toni I have developed a system of 'our Wednesday', when once a fortnight I meet her direct from school and take her shopping, or to the cinema, or out for a meal, since on that same day Amber visits one of her friends after school. This has helped a lot at an age where Toni, as a 13-year-old, wants to spend more time with friends but needs time with a parent too.

Another complexity of adoption is that the children have differing degrees of contact with birth relatives. I mentioned that Karl and Aaron had ongoing contact with an aunt, Cathy, and, through her, occasional links with other relatives. When we adopted Toni, Aunty Cathy treated her as a niece in terms of presents as well as genuine interest. In turn, my partner and I treated her child as our niece. The boys occasionally went to stay with Cathy, particularly Karl, and we hoped this would help him feel more comfortable about his identity. Within the family we all refer to her now as Aunty Cathy.

A few years ago, there was a brief reunion with some of the boys' older birth cousins but that has not been sustained. Several years ago, Aaron became preoccupied with his father, Mr W, and fantasised that he could go and live with him. With the help of a social worker, we were able to arrange for Aaron to meet him. In fact, we took all the children and it was a memorable evening. I think we wanted Aaron's father to meet the other children to know what sort of a life Aaron was experiencing. Although we knew that Karl had lived with Mr W, too, we did not appreciate that they would have such vivid memories of each other, and Mr W was interested to learn of Karl's progress and, indeed, to tell us of some of Karl's difficulties when he had been small. Mr W had only seen Aaron as a baby, and, while it helped Aaron to meet him, it was difficult, too, as Mr W did not want any sort of ongoing contact. This was a hard message for Aaron to hear but, importantly, he heard it from his birth father – not from a social worker or anyone else – hence he was able to accept it, which did curb his wild assertions about what 'my real Dad will do one day'. The other main benefit was that all the family gained a positive impression of Mr W.

The other person to have some contact (albeit indirect) with a birth relative is Toni. Toni writes and exchanges photos with her birth mother twice a year. This is helpful for her, but it is also a more private activity and I don't think she talks to the others about it. Although, by the time Amber joined us, contact in adoption was seen as good practice, she actually has less contact than any of the others – not even a photo of her birth mother. This is not easy for her and perhaps is one reason why Toni does not mention her contact with her birth mother to Amber. At Amber's request, we did write to the authority where she came from to try and make a link, but so far without success. Returning to Karl, we have from time to time asked if he wants help to trace his birth father who we believe still lives in the same city as us, but he does not want to do this.

Thus, they all have quite different degrees of contact with birth relatives. They also have differing numbers of half-siblings that we know about. Karl has two older half-siblings, Aaron several half-siblings (but Mr W would not be specific), Toni has one younger half-sibling on her mother's side who was born after she came to us and to whom she sends occasional cards. (The other girl does not live with her birth mother either.) We have no information about half-siblings for Amber but we know she was her teenage parents' first child. These half-siblings are hardly ever referred to in our family life and, if asked how many brothers and sisters they have, Karl, Aaron, Toni and Amber would all simply list each other. They would also, I think, stick up for each other outside the home, despite their disagreements within it. Indeed, it is one of Aaron's disappointments that, since Toni started at a school he previously attended, no one has bullied her, as he would like an excuse to step in on her behalf!

There are many factors influencing how children see themselves within a family, and, for us, race, gender and age at placement are intertwined. In our family it is perhaps unfortunate that the two oldest children are boys and the two younger ones girls because, inevitably, the younger children have had a more secure start in life with us, and this leads to a self-fulfilling prophecy that the girls are easier to live with, get told off less, are happier and are more rewarding. It is like a virtuous as opposed to a vicious circle. This has led to resentment, especially from Karl. He has also, as the eldest, felt the younger children were treated more favourably, and as they are all black and he is white, he has at times accused us of showing preference to his siblings simply because they are black. In most families, the youngest child is seen as being indulged and there is some truth in that, if only because, by this time, parents have realised how short childhood is and they have perhaps learned to relax more and worry less. Perversely, the youngest child does not see it like this, and Amber often suggests we should adopt someone younger than her (but that is not our intention).

This is, of course, by no means the end of the story, and other stories could be told about our experiences. Karl is now 19, Aaron 18, Toni 13 and Amber eight years old. I sometimes wonder what their relationships will be with each other as adults. Only time will tell. I also sometimes wonder whether Karl and Aaron would have coped better if they had been placed separately – my feeling is it was right to keep them together but it was far harder than I could have imagined.

I have been reassured to talk to other parents and to hear them admit in moments of honesty that they do not always feel the same about all their children – love is in some ways too narrow a word to encompass the multitude of emotions I have felt about all my adopted children. It has not been easy for any of us, and yet it is an experience I would not have missed and through which I hope we have all ultimately gained.

13 The achievement and sustainability of sibling contact
Why the reality falls short of the ideal

Anne M Jones

Anne M Jones has worked with children since 1965 in a variety of roles which she has enjoyed – as a probation officer to the old-style juvenile courts, as a child care officer, as a playworker with children in refuges, as a youth worker, also in a child psychiatric clinic and currently in a children and families team.

Her academic and professional qualifications include the Advanced Award in Social Work, MA in Social Work (Bradford University), Certificate in Child Protection (Warwick), the Diploma in Child Care Analytic Studies from the Tavistock Clinic with the University of East London, and an Honours degree in Literature from the Open University. However, she feels that she owes most of her learning experience to children themselves, especially her own.

Sibling rivalry: a normal part of growing up

'Sisters, sisters,
There were never such devoted sisters . . .'

These words were the refrain of a song by The Beverley Sisters, frequently heard on the radio during the mid-50s when I was growing up. This refrain was sung by my own sisters, or my brother, usually in a heavily ironic tone, whenever the minor inter-sibling warfares broke out that mark everyday family life. The domestic details ranged from who had "pinched" whose hairbrush to more overt rivalries for parental attention: 'She's got more on her plate than I have.' I recall the intensity of these feelings as very powerful; fortunately, I can also recall the attitudes of my parents. In spite of their own worries, they succeeded in making it clear not only that they were not going to tolerate petty squabbles, but also that each one of us was precious enough in our own different ways to render those rivalries meaningless in the wider pattern of our family life, focused as it was upon education and service to the wider community.

The complex discussion by Melanie Klein (1990) on envy and gratitude is a forcible argument for the initial power of the mother's successful nurturing of a baby in turning away feelings of envy between siblings and, in doing so, leading to a creative way of living.

Whereas envy is a source of great unhappiness, a relative freedom from it is felt to underlie contented and peaceful states of mind – ultimately sanity... the basis of inner resources and resilience (which) can be observed in people who, even after a great deal of adversity and mental pain, regain their peace of mind (Klein, 1990, p 203).

Studies on attachment theory bear this out. Older siblings with secure attachments to their mother are not only more inclined to comfort a distressed younger sibling but also to engage in less conflict with them in joint play (Belsky and Cassidy, 1994).

Rivalry between siblings in itself does not necessarily imply a problematic relationship. On the contrary, the opportunities for it to be expressed and to be resolved are a normal part of development.

Removal from home: then and now

When a child is removed from his/her parent(s)' care, for whatever reasons, a continuum in their relationship with their family is disrupted or lost. Even where removal seems to be in the child's best interests, that disruption inevitably affects all other family and subsequent relationships, and placements elsewhere introduce further complications into the child's life. Consequently, there are fewer possibilities for resolution of sibling rivalries.

Until the mid-1970s, it was easier to keep sibling groups together than it is now because of the widespread use of children's homes. I clearly recall in the early 70s working with groups of four and even five siblings, whose parents could no longer care for them and who had been in group homes all together. The strength of the bonds that developed between them compensated to some extent for their grief and loss. I have since witnessed similar bonds between the children in Romanian orphanages who know they are related to each other, either as siblings or cousins. These bonds may be manifested as much by intense fighting as by companionship or concern, so rivalry, of itself, does not imply a problematic relationship. In "group homes", fights between related children seemed somehow more accepted by both staff and children than those between non-related children.

In Romania, I saw a graphic example of companionship and concern when a girl led me to her younger sister, in great distress with stomach pain that later turned out to be appendicitis. The younger girl had hidden herself away from everyone else and it was only through her sister's intervention that she eventually received treatment. These girls will remain together until they leave the orphanage when, at a stage in life where others may have no adult support, they will at least have each other.

Since the mid-1970s, the emphasis in the UK upon foster care as a preferable alternative to institutional care (when parents are unable to look after their children) has led to the separate establishment of family placement sections within social services departments. Strenuous efforts have been made within these sections to recruit, train and support families who have the potential to care for another family's child(ren). These sections may share many of the common objectives and values of their colleagues in other teams, but have also developed a whole new body of theory and practice.

Agendas influencing the separation of sibling groups

Although it seems a truism to state that siblings are likely to have one another long after their parents are no longer in their lives, this vital fact is frequently overlooked when children are removed from parental care. The placing of a child away from his or her family of origin is not a simple act of moving him/her from one place to another, but an entire process which might have commenced long before the child(ren) left the parent(s). A multiplicity of factors – practical, emotional and historical – come to bear upon this process of placement decision-making, often resulting in sibling groups being split and family ties disregarded. There may be many reasons which may include:

1. An awareness in both teams of the child's history and of efforts made by the child's social worker to keep the family together. When this work is seen to have failed, the feelings of both sets of social workers may feature in the complex interplay of considerations.
2. Few, if any, placements being available.
3. The fact that no placement is "tailor-made". Options are restricted by the child's age, sex, stage of development, history, cultural and religious considerations, accessibility to education (especially where a need for special education exists) and the reasons for removal.
4. Carers' own abilities, circumstances and history, which may mean they themselves might collapse under the strain of taking more than one child.
5. Placement workers feeling protective towards their "own" carers and partners, resulting in resisting a placement request (when this occurs, the worker might be over-ruled by a manager, but often only as a very short-term expedient).
6. Timing – rarely do requests for placement occur at a time when careful, considered planning can take place and furthermore, many placement officers resist efforts at forward planning out of the necessity to retain emergency places.
7. Parents themselves being perhaps too distressed to be able to contribute in a valid and relevant way to the course of planning. In certain circumstances, factors emerge at a later date about a child's family history which might have been contra-indications to the placement.

All the above factors may be inter-linked but, ultimately, one set of considerations will take precedence over another, despite the most careful and lengthy discussions. In my experience, it is rarely possible to balance all the above considerations even-handedly, combining, as they do, factors about the child, the birth family, the carers and the social workers, together with their organisation.

Systems operating against systems

Each of the above systems – the child and family of origin, the carers, the social workers in their team contexts – is likely to have its own rivalries and tensions. Within social services departments, the separation of teams between placement work and fieldwork means that each has its own individual hierarchy and management structure. Most placement teams have their own systems for receiving referrals from fieldworkers, whose teams, again, have their own systems for referral. In some local authorities, placement teams exert a greater amount of power in decision-making, although, in other authorities, the reverse might prevail. Furthermore, within placement teams, individual workers may exert influence on behalf of "their" carers, and influence decisions accordingly.

At the same time, the very nature of both teams having in common the shared social work concern for children and families frequently means that there may exist bonds between social workers across teams which at times resemble the complexities of sibling relationships. Mutual concern as colleagues can co-exist with resentment, even hostility, and might operate in a context of highly charged emotion. This emotion might be brought about, for example, by a mixture of both a tacit recognition of the pain inherent in working with damaged children (Boston, 1990; Hoxter, 1990; Crompton, 1992) and the agreed value base that children need their own family, but that the task has proved impossible (Kerr, 1995).

As far as the child(ren)'s family system is concerned, circumstances and emotional states are crucial but are rarely given the priority needed – beyond the bare facts of age, gender and cultural requirements – because all too frequently the determining factor in placement is space, sometimes any space. Efforts might be made to place the child within the extended family for reasons which might have as much to do with softening the blow as with their ostensible grounding in the principle of the Children Act 1989 that a child is best brought up within his/her own family, but such placements might conveniently overlook chronic family problems such as long-standing feuds which, in time, further complicate matters.

Case examples

Case 1

A social worker had been working with the parents of two children aged four and six for almost a year, in an attempt to address issues of emotional abuse and suspected sexual abuse. Because of the reluctance of the parents to work together with the social worker, it was recommended that legal sanction should be resorted to in order to accommodate the children. However, at that point, the parents agreed to co-operate, on the understanding that joint work was still a possibility and that the sibling pair would remain together – the social worker recognising the parents' desire to hold their family intact and ultimately to be reunited with them. In spite of the social worker having forewarned the placement section about these children, in the event, the only placements that could be found were at opposite ends of the county. The child with special needs remained closer to home, but still not close enough to remain in the catchment area to be collected and taken to special school. The parents and their social worker felt betrayed by these arrangements and, of course, the parents turned their anger upon the social worker who, in their eyes, had not told them the truth. Although contact arrangements were organised, the logistics for both parties were such that these were limited to twice weekly and later once weekly meetings. The complexities of organising these involved:

a) a social worker having time available for driving and supervising;

b) fitting in with school hours;

c) the foster carer's time and agreement to host contact visits (some carers dislike contact at their homes, often with good reasons);

d) the time involved in collecting one child to be taken on a 50-mile journey across a country area and back again;

e) organising all the above to fit in with the parents' own travel arrangements, which might be extremely difficult by public transport, and arranging payment of fares.

In the above situation, where there were many unknown elements, it was nevertheless clear from the outset that contact would be a major consideration, calling upon large amounts of time commitment by personnel within the department. The travel time for the child who was conveyed to the venue was in itself exhausting. Within a few weeks, the host foster carer was commenting that the child 'doesn't seem too bothered . . . always dead tired and doesn't play . . .'

Comments such as these can be used powerfully, to detract from the ongoing importance of the consistency of sibling contact. Such comments also overlook the fact that grief reactions in children frequently mean a masking of real feelings (Bowlby, 1980; Compton, 1992).

Over the weeks, sufficient evidence emerged to commence care proceedings, resulting in the original plans to rehabilitate the family being rethought within an altogether different timeframe. There were now many more professionals involved in these children's lives including a guardian *ad litem*. All the professionals and the carers could claim to be giving 'paramount consideration to the best interests of the children'. However, underneath the complex interplay of personalities, the ultimate determinant was the fact of the lack of suitable placements where the children could be together, coupled with the carer's powerful words about the children 'not seeming bothered about seeing each other'. Over the months, contact fell off and became non-existent for some years.

Case 2

The elder of two brothers, aged three and 18 months, had been placed as a baby with paternal grandparents who had never liked the mother from the moment their son had brought her to meet them. When the second child was born, the mother was offered considerably more support than with her first child and succeeded in sustaining care of him. All attempts at contact were blocked by these grandparents who considered the mother should never have been allowed to keep the boy. When contact was arranged, they and their son (the father of both boys) sabotaged it in ways which were emotionally harmful to the children, who in turn became very antagonistic. This proved so distressing to the mother that she felt impotent in her attempts to help her sons resolve their differences. Undermined, she opted to cease contact.

Case 3

The younger of two sisters, aged three and one, was gradually rejected by her mother to the point at which a placement away from home became inevitable (and was requested by the mother). Eventually, an adoption placement became a possibility and was welcomed by the mother. Although some contact was offered, she refused it initially. Meanwhile, in the placement, insufficient attention was paid to the significance of the relationship between the children. In time, on the adopters' request, contact lapsed; however, immediately before the adoption hearing was due, the mother refused to consent unless the children saw each other for 'one last time'. The judge agreed to this. The older child was taken to see her sister and, as the social worker involved, I was immediately struck by the bond that still existed between them. Also, I shall never forget how, on the journey home, the older sister, now aged six, sank back into me saying, 'I'm happy now I've seen her at last'.

Discussion

Each of these cases provides examples of the considerations which feature at the time of placement and how, in time, for a variety of reasons one set of considerations recedes in favour of others. As Obholzer writes:

> *In order to manage oneself in role the fundamental question is 'How can I mobilise my resources to contribute to the task?' This requires recognition of where one's role ends and another's begins . . . rivalry, jealousy and envy often interfere with the process of taking up either a leadership or a followership role* (Obholzer, 1994, p 45).

In the examples given, the parents of the children were effectively disempowered at the point of their children being accommodated and were unable to regain a voice, except in Case 3 and then only because the social worker felt able to push her case hard enough to ensure that she was heard. Feeling powerless is concomitant with the 'confusion and helplessness parents feel particularly at the early stages of separation from their offspring' (Little and Millhaus, 1993, p 10). The family social worker in each instance retained, as the main consideration, the safety and protection of the child(ren) being accommodated. As her role in this regard decreased, the role of the foster carer, placement worker, and, in Case 3, the new agency worker, increased in significance, even though the social worker remained an important part of the decision-making process.

In such complex situations as I have described, a large number of people participate in planning and decision-making for children who are separated on a long-term basis from their parents. In each case, as the prospect of rehabilitation recedes, the placement itself and the child's daily and growing security within it, become pressing considerations; consequently, when foster carers speak out loudly and eloquently, as in Cases 2 and 3, it is not difficult to understand why the unseen factors, such as the general child care knowledge of the theoretical importance of sibling contact, might be overlooked. As Obholzer points out (1994, p 46), we are all prey to 'the presence of irrational and unconscious processes that interfere with attempts to manage oneself, the group, task and roles in a conscious and rational way'.

All too frequently, the child's social worker is aware that the choices are stark. A placement which may seem outwardly "safe" could be jeopardised by too much conflict, engendered through issues about which the child him/herself has been unable to express any viewpoint, doubtless because children at a young age do not have the vocabulary or the means to express the notions of siblingness. I know that, as a worker in such a situation, one puts the child's outward show of stability above all else because one knows what the child has been through and what is at stake if that apparent new-found serenity is lost. Furthermore, in the climate of blame in which many social workers find themselves, as 'society's scapegoats for its own failings' (Valentine, 1992), there are expectations of being seen to do the right thing by "rescuing" children, as the representatives of 'society's institutions . . . which serve to contain anxieties for society as a whole' (Obholzer, 1994, p 170).

Conclusion

I have tried to show how it comes about that siblings become separated, on the face of it for sound adult reasons. It is my belief that children who lose contact with siblings suffer a further emotional loss over and above those already suffered through the loss of parents and extended family, and that their grief is rarely acknowledged or allowed to heal.

Without the opportunity to act out childlike dramas of love, hate and rivalry, the child's personality development can also suffer. The bitter-sweet love/hate tensions which I recall so vividly from my own childhood were an essential part of my development; now, in my later years, these relationships help sustain me, as they do millions of other people. To allow these vital but unseen growth opportunities to be missed by children looked after by the local authority is to deny them an inalienable aspect of themselves, and to deprive them possibly of support in their later years when the adults who influenced the earlier decisions are no longer there to help emotionally sustain them.

References

Belsky J and Cassidy J (1994) 'Attachment : theory and evidence', in Rutter M and Hay D, *Development Through Life*, Oxford: Blackwell Scientific.

Boston M (1983) 'Introduction', in Boston M and Szur R, *Psychotherapy with Severely Deprived Children*', London: Routledge & Kegan Paul.

Bowlby J (1980) *Loss*, London: Hogarth.

Crompton M (1992) *Children and Counselling*, London: Edward Arnold/Hodder & Stoughton.

Hoxter S (1983) 'Some feelings aroused in working with severely deprived children', in Boston M and Szur R, *Psychotherapy with Severely Deprived Children, op. cit.*

Kerr A (1995) 'A psychoanalytic approach to the work of the guardian *ad litem*', in Trowell J and Bower M (eds), *The Emotional Needs of Young Children and their Families*, London/New York: Routledge.

Klein M (1990) 'Envy and gratitude', in Klein M, *Envy and Gratitude: Collected works 1945–1963*, Volume 3, London: Virago.

Marsh P and Triseliotis J (1993) *Prevention and Reunification in Child Care*, London: Batsford.

Obholzer A (ed) (1994) *The Unconscious at Work*, London: Routledge.

Valentine M (1994) 'The social worker as bad object', *British Journal of Social Work*, 24, pp 71–86.

14 **Siblings together:** myth or reality?

Judy Tomlinson

Since qualifying as a social worker, Judy Tomlinson has worked for more than ten years in local authority social work teams, mainly with children and families. For the past six years she has worked independently: as a guardian ad litem, providing independent social work assessments for courts, and carrying out Form F assessments in the fields of foster care, respite and adoption. She has recently completed an MA in Children, Policy, Practice and the Law at Liverpool University.

Whatever the quality of the relationships people have with their siblings, their existence can rarely be overlooked. Even in their absence, they retain a significance beyond that of friends, colleagues or acquaintances. As Judy Dunn has pointed out, the time siblings spend together is often greater than the time they spend with either of their parents:

It is the beginning of a relationship which lasts a lifetime – longer, indeed, than that of a marriage or of parent and child (Dunn, 1984, p 14).

My professional interest in the subject comes from my experiences as a local authority social worker in children and family teams, and as a guardian *ad litem*. The material for this chapter is based on a combination of that experience and research I carried out while studying for an MA in Children, Policy, Practice and the Law. As part of that degree I investigated the issues relating to the placements of siblings in care from the perspective of team managers in three different local authorities in the North West of England and looked at local authority policies in that region.

When referring to siblings, I include not just those who share the same birth parents (full siblings), but half- and step-siblings. From the child's perspective, the importance is not only whether they share the same genes – though this is important – but whether there has been a shared experience. Children may have no parent in common but yet have significant attachments to each other. In one example, I worked with three children whose mothers were sisters. The family ties with the maternal grandmother were so strong that often the cousins had lived together for periods of time. They had a good "sibling" attachment.

The significance of siblings

An estimate for the percentage of people in Europe and the USA who have siblings is 80 per cent (Dunn, 1983, p 787). Wedge and Mantle added that 60 per cent have two or more siblings (1991, p 30). It is difficult to determine whether these statistics are replicated in the care population. The Department of Health holds statistics on individual children in care but the information they receive is anonymised, and no questions are asked about the existence of siblings. Hence they have no information about siblings. General statistics about siblings were not being collected in any of the three local authorities where my interviews took place.

A number of individual studies have sought to provide some information. Kosonen (1996) and Bilson and Barker (1992/3) found that the number of children in care who had siblings was 82 per cent and 86.5 per cent respectively. Using these figures as indicators, it would be reasonable to deduce that the majority of children in the care system have siblings who may also be in care or with the birth family or adopted.

Children in care have, by definition, suffered loss by virtue of a separation from one or both parents. Have these children also lost relationships with siblings? Again, there is a lack of information directly available nationally or from local authorities. In the studies mentioned above, Kosonen found that only between a quarter and one-third of children were living with one or more of their siblings (1996, p 811) while Bilson and Barker found that 26 per cent were placed with all their siblings and a further 21 per cent with some but not all siblings. Bilson and Barker also found that, of those children who were separated from one or more siblings, only 37 per cent had regular face-to-face contact. Using the figures they had gathered from six local authorities, they calculated that, if applied to the whole of the UK, there would be

26,000 children in care with siblings and, of these, nearly 20,000 would be separated from some or all of them.

These figures are consistent with my perceptions of the situation in the areas where I have worked. The team managers I interviewed confirmed that work with siblings was for them 'highly significant'.

Separating and separated siblings in practice

The separation of siblings is an aspect of the placement of children which, if the above figures are only approximately accurate, must feature in most social workers' caseloads. In this section I discuss the situations I have met and the dilemmas these posed. I illustrate the situations with comments from the team managers I interviewed.

The point of entry into the care system

When children are first looked after, it is often at a point of crisis, and decisions have to be made on limited information. Even if it has been possible to plan for the placement, the lack of resources can dictate how children are placed. In my experience it is most unlikely that a group of three or more siblings would be placed together, and it is often difficult to find a placement for two.

I was guardian *ad litem* for three children – Kate, Fiona and Danny, aged four years, three years and 18 months respectively – who were removed from their mother on an emergency protection order and needed an immediate placement. No foster home was available to take all three, and so one child had to be placed separately from the other two. The social worker's decision was that Kate and Danny should stay together. The repercussions of this decision, taken in haste, were significant. Fiona found herself isolated in a placement where she competed directly with a foster child the same age as her, who was well established in the foster home. Danny was eventually placed with an aunt, along with a baby born during the proceedings, and Kate and Fiona continued in their separate placements for a further year until they were eventually reunited.

Another sibling group where this was avoided was again one of three children. The older two, Jane and Jenny, aged eight and six years, were placed in an emergency foster home while their younger brother, John, went to a short-term placement where he could have remained for the duration of the proceedings. Jane and Jenny had to move, and the social worker insisted on a placement for all three together. This was found by allowing the placement to go above numbers. Four years later, the children remain in this placement which has now become permanent.

Information from team managers showed that there could be no doubting their commitment to placing siblings together, but that they were not always or even often successful:

The number of times we have vacancies for sibling groups is the exception to the rule.

I think there would be elation in the team if we can keep siblings together.

An indication of the level of commitment was the practice of placing more children in a foster home than it was approved for.

You're aware that it's a very crowded foster home. On paper it often looks very scary.

While in one authority separated siblings were kept 'on referral' with a view to re-uniting them if a placement became available, in practice the separation usually continued until permanency plans were being considered and implemented.

I think the decision is often made the day the child comes in. If we separate the children at that stage sometimes we've separated them for life.

Placement breakdown

One of the most difficult decisions is what to do when a joint placement is breaking down for one of the siblings. This was a situation I faced with two children, Ruth, aged seven, and Richard, aged six. The foster carers found Ruth's challenging behaviour unacceptable and asked for her to be removed, but they wanted to continue to care for her brother. In order to decide whether to remove Ruth or both children, I carried out an assessment of the sibling attachment, using the framework provided in *Patterns and Outcomes* (Department of Health, 1991). My conclusion was that the sibling relationship was very significant to both children and that they should be kept together. The foster carers' rejection of the older child meant that they would be unable to sustain the sibling relationship if the children were separated. The strength of the sibling relationship was a major factor in the decision but other aspects, including the foster carers' abilities and the likely response of Richard to the separation, were all put into the equation.

The process of reaching the decision to remove both children proved stressful, for me as the social worker, for the family placement worker supporting the carers, and for the agency. I benefited from being given time to carry out the work, and from the support of an experienced professional within the authority not involved in the case. Even so, at times, it felt as though I was charting new waters as there was a lack of written procedures or guidelines to follow.

The literature describing the relevant decision-making processes highlights the need for good information about sibling relationships, alongside assessments of the children and families (Hegar, 1993; Hindle, 1995; O'Leary and Schofield, 1995). This was echoed by the team managers:

> I'd need to be shown evidence which is based on an extremely good assessment of the levels of attachment, levels of need, a picture of each child in relation to each other. . .

At the same time, there was a recognition that such evidence was not always available. Where assessments were carried out, they were based on the *Patterns and Outcomes* material referred to earlier. But there was also a recognition of the current pressures for social workers:

> I don't mean this as a criticism of social workers. I think their role has changed. The skills developed in . . . working with children, doing assessments . . . are not necessarily part of the social worker's everyday role now.

As a guardian *ad litem*, I have come across cases where there has been no assessment of the sibling relationship. The work of Dance (1997) may throw valuable light on the extent to which sibling assessments are carried out, and how effective they are.

Planning for permanency

The question of whether siblings should be placed together or not appears to become a focus at the point when long-term plans for children are being considered. This was confirmed in my interviews with team managers. It was at this point that checks would be done to ensure that, if the plan was to separate siblings, the proper steps had been followed in reaching the decision.

There were differences in the ways in which the three local authorities approached this decision. In one, it had to be referred to the Assistant Director of Social Services; in another, when the policy had been first implemented the Director was involved, but later this was devolved to a third-tier manager. In the third authority, such decisions were taken to the fostering or adoption panel before any families were identified.

It is when formal decisions are being made that the dilemmas begin to emerge. If siblings have been split, should they be reunited or placed separately? If they have been kept together, perhaps by the opening of a small residential unit on a short-term basis, how should the sibling relationship be sustained if no family is available to take all the children? In many cases, the individual children have particular needs which might be better met in a separate placement. How can these needs be balanced against those of the other child/ren and against the long-term needs of supporting the sibling relationship so that it is still meaningful when the children reach adulthood?

In the case of Kate and Fiona, who were referred to earlier, the care plan prepared for the final hearing of the care proceedings stated that the local authority wanted to look for a placement for both children together. However, it was acknowledged that this would delay their move into a permanent family, because they would each make significant demands on future carers. The plan focused on the children's need for a sibling relationship. I was most concerned that, during the proceedings themselves, there had been no attempt to sustain or improve this relationship. What contact had taken place had been for all the children of the family, when they saw their mother, and did not allow for developing and improving the sibling links.

The implementation of the Children Act 1989 brought a welcome emphasis on the wishes and feelings of the child, and on the importance of his or her individual needs. The Act also places a duty on the local authority to place siblings together where possible (see below). But it largely focuses on the individual child in relation to the parents. It is unfortunate that, in the guidelines issued at the time of the Act's implementation, the significance of siblings is not made more explicit. For example, in discussing the areas to be considered when reviewing children's cases, no mention is made of siblings (Department of Health, 1991b, p 84). A section covering the placements of siblings and arrangements for contact would have prevented these issues being overlooked in practice.

There is not a comprehensive body of research on which to base practice when considering the separation or reuniting of siblings. My interviews with team managers showed that they had a thoughtful approach to what would work, but that they based ideas on their personal experience and that practice was therefore not uniform throughout the local authority. One approach identified was to stagger the introductions to the permanent home:

You'd need to be clear and identify which ones came in first . . . I would say get the eldest in and on your side, and you'd have a reasonable chance.

An alternative was to use a bridging placement:

We knew there was going to be a long-term placement for three children together. . . so we reunited in a short-term home to get a picture of how these three children functioned together for the long-term match.

However, if children have been in separate placements for an extended period before a placement is available in which they can be reunited, there are then difficult decisions to make about the impact of a further change of placement for some or all of the siblings. The relationship with the short-term carer was a factor to be taken into account, as well as the sibling relationship, the level of contact which has been sustained and the attitude of the birth family.

What happens to the sibling relationship in care?
There is research evidence to support the view that the quality of the sibling relationship is linked to the quality of care received in the family, as well as to the individual natures of the children concerned (see for example Brody and Stoneman, 1987; Jenkins, 1992). It should not therefore be expected that, at a time of family breakdown, siblings will necessarily have an optimal relationship. Helping children improve this relationship should be one of the tasks of the local authority when providing services for children in care. Examples include situations where an older child has taken on a parenting role in respect of the younger children and no longer needs to carry this responsibility, or where children are reflecting in aggressive behaviour the impact of living with violence against a parent.

In my experience, this relationship work is not a high priority and, indeed, may not even be identified as a need. Where there is clear evidence of sibling rivalry, for example, this may often be given as a reason for the separation of siblings instead of their receiving appropriate help to improve the relationship.

A further area where the sibling relationship is not given the emphasis it deserves is in the arrangements for contact. There has been a significant improvement in the commitment given to sustaining contact with birth parents, involving a great deal of staff time and complex arrangements. With this background, it is perhaps not surprising that there is a reluctance to consider separate contact for siblings in addition to contact with the birth parents. Yet the sibling relationship may have greater potential in these circumstances. Sustaining sibling contact can be reassuring to the children concerned, can help limit the sense of loss involved in the separation, and can maintain a relationship which may have life-long meaning for those concerned.

Where siblings have to be separated, initial placement decisions can have an impact on the development of contact arrangements. One team manager informed me that she looked for foster placements geographically close to one another, where the children could attend the same school – and preferably the same school as when living at home – and where there was a similar lifestyle.

A case example involved three brothers, one of whom had been placed in a separate foster home in order to meet his individual needs. The sibling contact was of a high level, with a staying contact at the foster home of the other two boys on alternate weekends, and contact during the week. This type of arrangement demands an enormous commitment from carers. An additional problem is the formality of the arrangements. Ideally, the contact should move to becoming flexible, where the children are able to suggest seeing their sibling when they would like to. Not all foster carers are able to progress to this situation.

I was told about three girls who had been placed separately, all of them adopted. The adoptive mother of the oldest child, who is now 18 years old, recognised the value of her maintaining links with her sisters and was instrumental in keeping them in touch, through some periods where the level of commitment of the children concerned waned. These children now have an awareness of each other which can last through adulthood.

I worked with another family of three children, Mary, Graham and David. Graham suffered serious physical injuries while at home and came into care at the age of two. His behaviour was such that he experienced four foster homes within the period of the care proceedings. The other two children were eventually removed from home, but they had fewer problems and were quickly placed in a permanent home. Their carer, a very experienced foster mother, recognised the importance of Graham to Mary and David, but regretfully said that she could not manage Graham's difficulties. She did support and encourage contact, including taking Graham on holiday with her family. After a year, and with a permanent placement for Graham no nearer, she felt that Mary and David had settled sufficiently for her to offer to have Graham as well. He moved to her family, and all three are now successfully adopted. I agreed with the foster carer that, had she taken all three together, this would have stretched the family to breaking point, with the risk of all three children having to be removed. The way it turned out, Mary and David were able to welcome Graham to their home and, even though the process took nearly three years, the end result is very positive. Lessons which can be learnt from this are that it is not necessary to place all siblings in a placement at the same time, that ongoing contact for siblings whatever the plan is invaluable, and that there needs to be flexibility in responding to changing circumstances.

When siblings have differing needs

Often, the plans that are made for children in care, and especially sibling groups, are linked to the resources available. This may be explicit, in that there may be no families coming forward to take groups of three or more. But it can also be less overt, as when it appears that the individual needs of the children are such that no family could be found to meet them. In this situation, a decision to separate the children may be defended as due to the children's needs, whereas it may largely reflect the social worker's perception of whether a family can be found and the local authority's commitment to supporting such families.

Parents willing to take into their home a ready-made family, especially of more than two children, are making a significant undertaking. Support with the practical side, for example, providing large enough vehicles so that all the family can go out together, extensions to the family home, or washing machines and help with ironing, could enable more people to come forward to offer themselves as carers.

However, there are situations where the individual needs of the children would be difficult to meet within one placement. One of these which is not uncommon is where there are older children – who have a significant attachment to the birth parents, and for whom adoption is unlikely to be appropriate – and younger children, perhaps including a baby who was born during proceedings, whose needs would best be met by an adoption placement. This leads to the scenario of some siblings placed for adoption, and the others placed in long-term foster homes having ongoing contact with the birth family. How can sibling contact be sustained in these circumstances? Would it be better to place all the children in a long-term foster placement, with the likelihood of an extended wait for such a placement to become available?

There are no easy answers, and the team managers' response to being asked what would improve the situation most was 'more placements'. Without adequate resources the task of making these finely balanced decisions becomes more difficult.

Local authority policies

Decisions that social workers, team managers and others in the organisation make in respect of siblings are a reflection of local authority policy, and of the degree of commitment there is to implementing that policy. I wrote to the 21 local authorities in the North West of England asking if they had a written policy regarding the placement of siblings in care. I obtained information from 15.

Many of the authorities were clearly aware of the thinking behind section 23(7)(b) of the Children Act and were committed to the idea of placing siblings together where possible. But 11 said that they had no written policy, one indicated that all the policies were in the process of being reviewed, and two stated that their policy was contained in broader policy statements. Only one authority had an explicit policy which included comprehensive guidelines and a clear acknowledgement that the sibling relationship was significant.

In my interviews with team managers, I discovered that there was no systematic collection of data with regard to siblings. Hence it was not possible to determine: how many children in care had siblings placed elsewhere in the care system, how many referrals were received for siblings, the reasons for separation where this had occurred, the number of children with siblings not in care, or in what cases sibling attachment assessments had been carried out. Without accurate data no one can know if policies are being implemented successfully. When the policies themselves are unwritten, or subsumed in broader policies, their interpretation is left to individuals. Decisions about what resources are needed to be effective in placing sibling groups have to be made in a vacuum. It is not surprising then that the team managers expressed considerable dissatisfaction with the current situation.

Conclusion

All the professionals to whom I have spoken have stated that siblings should be placed together where possible. However, the lack of information surrounding the subject allows for a considerable variation in interpretation of what is possible. Accordingly, there is little consistency about what emphasis should be given to the sibling relationship compared to the other factors which come into play when planning for children. Without clear guidance from local authorities, social workers and team managers are left to make value judgements.

Of equal concern is the indication from both my professional experience and my research that active pursuit of good outcomes for sibling groups is not common. When siblings have been placed together, or encouraged to develop meaningful relationships, this has often been the result of chance rather than purposeful planning – the availability of a foster home for all the siblings together, or, for example, a foster carer who has made a commitment to maintaining the links.

It is my view that there should be a greater recognition of the importance of sibling relationships, reflecting their long-term potential and the significance of siblings' common experiences. This should be demonstrated through clearer policy guidelines, and supported by suitable resources and effective monitoring. There would then be:

- a stronger commitment to finding families for sibling groups;
- a willingness to consider more imaginative options, such as small residential units or respite support;
- practical support to encourage families to come forward; and
- a proactive stance towards improving damaged sibling relationships, resulting in more sibling groups being placed together.

Separation of sibling groups should become the exception rather than the norm. But until the necessary changes have been implemented, many children will continue to face the anguish of separation from siblings as well as from parents.

References

Bilson A and Barker R (1992/3) 'Siblings of children in care or accommodation: a neglected area of practice', *Practice*, 6:4, pp 307–18.

Brody G H and Stoneman Z (1987) 'Sibling conflict: contributions of the siblings themselves, the parent–child relationship, and the broader family system', in Schachter F and Stone R (eds), *Practical Concerns about Siblings: Bridging the research-practice gap*, Binghamton, New York: Haworth Press.

Dance C (1997) 'To split or not to split: decision-making in sibling group placement'. Paper presented at BAAF Research Symposium, 26 November 1997.

Department of Health (1991a) *Patterns and Outcomes in Child Placement*, London: HMSO.

Department of Health (1991b) *The Children Act 1989 Guidance and Regulations, Volume 3 – Family Placement*, London: HMSO.

Dunn J (1983) 'Sibling relationships in early childhood', *Child Development*, 54:4, pp 787–811.

Dunn J (1984) *Sisters and Brothers*, London: Fontana.

Hegar R L (1993) 'Assessing attachment, permanence, and kinship in choosing permanent homes', *Child Welfare*, 72:4, pp 367–78.

Hindle D (1995) 'Thinking about siblings who are fostered together', *Adoption & Fostering*, 19:1, pp 14–20.

Jenkins J (1992) 'Sibling relationships in disharmonious homes: potential difficulties and protective effects', in Boer F and Dunn J (eds), *Children's Sibling Relationships: Developmental and clinical issues*, Hillsdale, NJ: Lawrence Erlbaum.

Kosonen M (1996) 'Maintaining sibling relationships: neglected dimension in child care practice', *British Journal of Social Work*, 26, pp 809–22.

O'Leary S and Schofield F (1995) 'The right of siblings to live together', *Practice*, 7:1, pp 31–43.

Wedge P and Mantle G (1991) *Sibling Groups and Social Work*, Aldershot: Avebury.

15 **Black siblings**
A relationship for life

Beverley Prevatt Goldstein

Beverley Prevatt Goldstein is a black lecturer in the Centre for Applied Social Studies at the University of Durham. She currently directs the DipSW/MA programme and is also active in the management of Kemet, the Black Practice Learning Centre. Her major social work experience is in child care, particularly in adoption and fostering. Her teaching, research interests and publications centre on identity, anti-oppressive practice, social work education, and the professional development of black students as well as the above.

This chapter focuses on black siblings 'simply as actors in the social world' (Waksler, 1991). It should not be inferred from this focus that there is anything abnormal, special or pathological about black siblings. Rather, there are issues in the social world which have impacted upon, and continue to impact upon, black families, leading to their developing particular ways of understanding and structuring sibling relationships. This chapter, in exploring the nature of black sibling relationships, traditionally and currently, reflects an awareness of the diversity within "black" and also considers relationships where one sibling identifies/is identified as black and another as white. It acknowledges continuity and change, strengths and difficulties, and places black sibling relationships within the broad band of sibling relationships. It considers, first, the sibling relationship in the birth family since this is the principal context for siblings and since adequate support here is of direct benefit and likely to reduce the need for placement. It subsequently builds on this in suggesting appropriate assessment and support in placement. Thus it strives to contribute to good practice in a range of social work interventions with black siblings (and black and white siblings).

It may be a cause for celebration that there has, to date, been little research on black siblings. This lack may signify that this group has, to some extent, avoided the pathologisation which underpins much social work and social policy research. This chapter will therefore use other sources: story, biography, language and conversation, supplemented by the few references to these groups found in the limited research, and by the wider academic literature on siblings.

"Sibling" is an academic term that does not easily fit into everyday experience. The language of "sisterhood" and "brotherhood" is more usual in black traditions and is used to cover a wide range of relationships (see Early Years Trainers Anti-Racist Network [EYTARN] 1994, p 41). Kosonen's research indicates that this wide range is not limited to black families (1998). For the purposes of this paper, the widest interpretation of this relationship will be used, i.e. having one or more parent in common, or residing or having resided together and being or having been "parented" together.

The black sibling tradition

The black sibling tradition arises from a variety of sources. Some of the African family structures, where the family of origin remains significant throughout life (see Sudarkasa, 1996), have contributed to the continuing importance of the family of origin in current African/African-Caribbean/ African-American families (Billingsley, 1968; Hill, 1971). This is not uniformly true; there is some evidence that class and community are important variables and that the way closeness is expressed ranges from co-residence, to exchange of goods and services, to emotional support (Reidmann and White, 1996). The language of sisterhood and brother-hood comes not only from these African roots but is reinforced by a strong religious tradition (Gilkes, 1985) and by the political language of sisterhood and brotherhood, expressed, for example, by a Jamaican Theatre Group (Sistren, 1986) and by the Black Power Movement:

> We must strive to lift as we climb. We must strive in such a way as to guarantee that all our sisters, regardless of social class, and indeed all our brothers, climb with us (Angela Davis, 1989, p 158).

The literature displays, in a very everyday way, the significance of the relationship across childhood and into adulthood:

Hi, my name is Sister. My other name is Shirley Anne, but everybody calls me Sister. This is my little brother, Mike. Everybody calls him Brother just like they call me Sister (Yarnborough, 1979, p 1).

The languages of the Asian sub-continent similarly demonstrate the importance of the sibling relationship. Siblings are usually addressed by the relationship rather than their name, e.g. aapa, baaji, bujjo, bijji for sister (Urdu) and bhaiya and dada for brother (Hindi). Other words (jaan, sahab) may be added to denote respect, and cousins are usually addressed by words signifying sister or brother in combination with their name. This notion of respect for older siblings, together with the responsibility of older siblings for younger siblings and a relationship of exchange beginning in childhood, unequal at a point in time but balanced in the long term, has underpinned the black sibling relationship. Sudarkasa describes it thus:

Responsibility is the value that required African extended families to be their brothers' and sisters' keepers (1996, p 68).

There is evidence that the notion of responsibility in childhood has been retained in many black communities in the Caribbean (Wiliams, 1987), in Britain (Williams, 1987; Modood *et al*, 1994), and in the United States of America:

My older brother was responsible for getting my sister and me our evening meal. He read everything and retained everything but in those hours together, we read everything too. I still love to read (Manns, 1997, p 206).

The emphasis of Barnardo's Positive Options*, in prioritising the wider family unit, including siblings, in their work largely with sub-Saharan African communities, attests to the importance of the sibling relationship as a responsible one at a young age in many communities with African connections (Matovu *et al*, 1998). Co-residence among African-Americans (Reidmann and White, 1996) and among South Asian adult siblings

---

*Positive Options supports children and families who are affected by HIV/AIDS, and facilitates their planning for the future.

in Britain (Peach, 1996), and the sharing of responsibility which enabled individuals in the Caribbean and South Asia to leave their children with their siblings and migrate to Britain (Williams, 1987), and subsequently to finance the education of their siblings, nieces and nephews overseas from Britain (see Modood *et al*, 1994) all demonstrate that the relationship of responsibility and reciprocity begun in childhood often sets the pattern for life.

The sibling relationship is a complex one, with attachment, responsibility and respect co-existing with rivalry and aggression. This has been true of black sibling relationships as of any other. These negative aspects are clearly demonstrated by the relentless teasing between bell hooks and her sisters and brother (hooks, 1993, p 32), and the pain expressed by Audre Lorde:

> *I have never gotten over the anger that you did not want me as a sister, nor an ally, nor even a diversion one cut above the cat. You never got over the anger that I appeared at all* (1984, p 155).

Yet it is clear that these relationships were sufficiently significant for the siblings to strive to get over their differences, particularly as they grew older (hooks, 1991, p 173) and that parents strongly encouraged this:

> *Often Mama would "preach" on the subject of sisterhood . . . Envy and little hatreds would surface but for the most part we learned how to bond as sisters across our differences* (hooks, 1991, p 91).

Factors that facilitate black sibling relationships

Current research suggests that positive (rather than negative or indifferent) sibling relationships are influenced by: a warm emotional climate in the home (Brody and Stoneman, 1987); some shared adversity (Jenkins, 1992); a shared environment (Dunn, 1996); positive parental communication about each child to the other (Dunn and Kendrick, 1982); opportunities for interaction without parents (Dunn and Kendrick, 1982); receiving support and help from each other (Kosonen, 1998); same-sex siblings (Dunn and Kendrick, 1982); and female older siblings (Dunn, 1996), to which I would add parents who model interaction and support with their own siblings. Two common factors in many black sibling relationships – responsibility and reciprocity – are conducive to the above and these will be explored first, before identifying the factors which may contribute to a lessening of sibling attachment.

Responsibility and reciprocity

The black sibling relationship continues to incorporate aspects of responsibility and reciprocity. Dosanjh and Ghuman's (1998) research on Punjabi families indicates that 80 per cent of the children are expected to help in the house and 42.5 per cent to help with younger children (22.5 per cent did not have any siblings). The practical implication of this is that the siblings are seen not only as partners in play but also as caretakers of each other. This is not uniform and each family adopts a different balance which takes into account the traditional perspective, the norms of the wider society, and their own current situation. The relative ages, abilities and disabilities of the children will influence who adopts the giver and the taker role and the nature of the exchange, which may include play. The nature of the exchange, while often gender specific, is not always so, for example, 'a high positive value is placed on "mothering" whether the person doing so is male or female' (Lewis, 1975).

Responsibility is seen as appropriate sibling behaviour that is the foundation of a life-long reciprocal relationship, rather than as co-parenting or substitute parenting. This is radically different from the English/North American theories where siblings taking responsibility can be viewed as asymmetrical (Boer, 1990) or complementary (Dunn, 1983). Traditionally, this role is seen as: educational to the giver as they learn skills for life; necessary for family functioning as parents shoulder wide economic and social responsibilities; and integral to an interdependent style of family life. This positive perspective is supported by the inclusion of "responsibility" in Pringle's four basic needs of children (1975) and by the literature on "resilience" (Fonagy, 1994; Gruesc et al, 1996; Gilligan, 1998).

This level of responsibility, often carried by older girls, is not confined to black siblings. Morrow indicates that 50 per cent of girls and 30 per cent of boys took some domestic responsibility and that sibling caretaking was widespread (1994, p 134). Both Morrow (1994) and Jones (1999) challenge the refusal in British professional and academic circles to acknowledge the level of work carried out by children and young people in the domestic sphere, suggesting that this refusal maintains a construction of childhood as one of dependence rather than interdependence. At a professional level, any responsibility is, if not overlooked, frequently pathologised as antithecal to Western mores of child development (Morrow, 1994). This pathologisation of responsibility within the sibling relationship has perhaps been most focused on black families and working-class families as both have been vulnerable to professional scrutiny, with aspects of their family life likely to be deemed deviant (Lawrence, 1982). Children and young people are apt to be influenced by this negative view of sibling responsibility and may resent a level of responsibility for siblings, or of authority by siblings, particularly if this is not experienced by their peers. Parents therefore need to incorporate sensitivity to the individuality and rights of the child while also seeking the social networks which reinforce their positive traditions.

Shared adversity

Families with black siblings will experience the minor and major stresses that are common. They may also be vulnerable to a higher incidence of poverty, poor housing and ill-health (Butt and Mirza, 1996), though this will be extremely variable (Modood *et al*, 1997). Additionally, there will be the context of racism. The impact of racism should not be underestimated (EYTARN, 1994) though, again, it will be very varied. Nevertheless, the common experience of interpersonal racism (Barter, 1998) can be the shared adversity which promotes attachment within black sibling relationships. Much of the literature on siblings suggests that, 'In the face of adversity, the children grew closer together with an increase in friendly affectionate behaviour' (Dunn, 1996).

This is supported by Fahlberg's illustration of the significance of the meeting of need in facilitating attachment (1991). But a common experience of adversity does not automatically lead to attachment (Kosonen, 1998). In order to facilitate sibling bonding and attachment it requires:

- a common naming of that experience of racism by parents (Wilson, 1987);
- siblings having the opportunity to share these common experiences (Dunn, 1996);
- siblings being given the opportunity by parents to meet each other's needs (Dunn and Kendrick, 1982) and providing support and help to each other in the adversity they encounter (Kosonen, 1998).

Research indicates that many black parents provide opportunities for interaction (Dosanjh and Ghuman, 1998), attempt to reduce the impact of racism (Jackson *et al*, 1997; Peters, 1997), and strive to build high self-esteem in their children (Peters, 1997; Dosanjh and Ghuman, 1998). They often demonstrate an awareness and challenging of racism, though they may not always explicitly discuss this with their children (Wilson, 1987; Peters, 1997).

Factors which impede black sibling relationships

There are also a number of factors which may adversely affect the relationship between black siblings. They reflect some commonality of experience – racism, disadvantage, emigration – even though they are not experienced by every black family nor are they exclusive to black families.

Overwhelmed parents

The experience of adversity can negatively impact on sibling relationships (as well as life chances) if overwhelmed parents are unable, in these circumstances, to offer emotional warmth, positive communication, and so on (Kosonen, 1994). Dunn suggests that daily minor hassles experienced by the mother (or main carer) do impede the sibling relationship (1996). Black parents are vulnerable to economic adversity and racism and are often unsupported by family support services (Smith, 1992; Butt and Box, 1998). Some literature on diverse black experiences (Williams, 1987; hooks, 1991) suggests that the wider family and local community have been used to supplement emotional warmth and this may still be a bonus in some families (Modood *et al*, 1994). Many other black families, regardless of circumstances, offer this warmth (Peters, 1997; Dosanjh and Ghuman, 1998) and, in striving to challenge adversity, become closer. Nevertheless, there will be some individual children and siblings who will be damaged by a negative home life and hence a positive sibling relationship may be made more difficult for them to achieve (hooks, 1993).

Physical distance

Physical distance can impede the sibling relationship in diverse ways. Physical distance from wider family due to emigration and re-emigration, economics and immigration restrictions may reduce the emotional resources of the parents and consequently those available to their children. Distance from the wider family may make it more difficult for parents to easily model sibling interaction and support. Physical separation between the child siblings may also limit their relationship by preventing interaction and a shared environment. This separation may happen for many reasons including economic factors, better opportunities for schooling and supportive communities in different continents, parental separation and placement in the 'looked after system'. There is literary evidence of what this can mean, for example, in the following poem by Lemn Sissay (1992):

My Brother

We laughed, played draughts

under a sweeping, sleeping sun

by the coconut tree
and the smell of lemon grass.
He had returned from Paris.

It took us half an hour
to get the right coconut
and two minutes to mix the juice
with raspberry cordial.

That night I cried
how alike we could have been.

Many black families, with traditions of separation, are able to surmount these difficulties. However, it does require a sustained effort to engender a family feeling, particularly when the surrounding norms restrict the concept of family to nuclear families or those sharing a household.

Shadism (preferential treatment based on light skin colour)

Perceived or actual parental preferences for each child based on gender, age, disposition and so on, may impact on the sibling relationship for black siblings, as for others (Vandell and Bailey, 1992). Differences in shade among black siblings are commonplace and is often accepted as such within black families and communities (hooks, 1991). However, the experience of racism outside the home may be slightly different because of shadism and this may be brought into the family dynamics; for example, 'We grew up with the inherent contradictions in the colour spectrum right inside those homes: the lighter sister, the mixed-blood cousin, the darkest in the family' (Moraga and Anzaldua, 1981, p 5).

This may mitigate against the shared experience of belonging and of adversity between the siblings, though many parents challenge this shadism by the use of the inclusive concepts of "black", "Asian", "Muslim".

Implications for practice

Family support

The levels of responsibility and reciprocity commonly found in black sibling relationships facilitate a shared environment, opportunities for interaction without parents, and opportunities for siblings to receive help from each other. A black political perspective, which encourages the framing of racism as a shared rather than an individual experience, and which also encourages the challenging of shadism by inclusive concepts such as black, Asian and Muslim can also contribute to to the perception of a shared experience among siblings. A sense of family (Modood *et al*, 1994) provides the motivation to support and interact with adult siblings which, in turn, provides role modelling for child siblings. All these factors, as well as maintaining a black tradition, can foster sibling attachment if combined with a warm emotional climate, positive communication about each child to the other, and sensitivity to the individuality and rights of the child.

These need to be valued and supported by those working to support families at every level: at primary prevention, e.g. community development, universal services; at secondary level, e.g. services for children in need; and at tertiary level, e.g. child protection and placement. Strategies for supporting families at all these levels also need to be directed to reducing the stresses on black families that may result from poverty and racism, and which impact on the emotional climate and sibling relationships. There are indications that white birth parents of black children may feel inadequately supported (Alibhai-Brown and Montague, 1992; Banks, 1992) and that they may refer their children to social services more readily (Barn, 1997). Support for these parents needs to be combined with appropriately valuing the advantages black parents may have to offer (Wilson, 1987; Rachid, 1998).

While black sibling relationships, like any others, are likely to contain elements of jealousy, rivalry and aggression (see Dunn and Kendrick, 1982) as well as abuse (Wiehe, 1990) there is no evidence that the different level of responsibility which is common to many black families worldwide enables higher levels of abuse. Therefore, it cannot be assumed that sibling responsibility facilitates abuse or is itself exploitative. Rather, if any level of responsibility above the eurocentric stereotype is assumed to be abusive, this may contribute to black children being vulnerable to negative enquiries and to being inappropriately taken into the "looked after" system.

Placement considerations

If it is considered essential to receive children into the "looked after" system, placing black siblings together should be the preferred choice. Black siblings accustomed to responsibility and reciprocity and to shared adversity are likely to have developed that 'supportive base camp' (Gilligan, 1997, p 88) which promotes resilience. Placement together helps maintain these relationships, for example, 'The things that I missed most were . . . the responsibility for younger brothers and sisters . . . My reality was . . . plaiting my little sister's hair' (Joy in Islington Social Services' Video, 1987). This may be a crucial buffer against the adversities likely to be experienced in the "looked after" system and in a racist world (Modood *et al*, 1994).

Placement together, however, is insufficient by itself. Placements need to be chosen which replicate the positive black traditions of responsibility and reciprocity between siblings, as well as opportunities for interaction without parents/carers, a political understanding of racism, the challenging of racism and shadism, interaction and support between parents/ carers and their siblings, and the maintenance of a warm emotional climate. Such placements need to be supported both financially and by positive social work intervention. If placement together is not deemed to be in the interests of the children, then BAAF's Black Perspectives Advisory Committee suggests that the following should be considered: placement in two branches of the same family, or with families living nearby, or in a small children's home with appropriate staffing, or with siblings overseas, with proper planning and support. Where children are separated, Kosonen's advice (1998) is relevant: 'children should be enabled to maintain sibling contact without the emotional influence of parents . . . [and siblings] should be offered positive joint activities' (pp 38–9). Contact with relatives becomes even more important if siblings are split and Barn (1997) and Rachid (1998) both suggest that contact is more likely to take place if placements are with black foster or adoptive families.

Parenting black and white siblings

The basics of good parenting for black and white siblings to assist them in forging a relationship for life are little different from those identified in the body of this chapter. However, the reality that, in the majority of parenting situations, the person with the main parental role, i.e. the mother, will be white (Peach, 1996) is likely to engender a different dynamic. The white parent may find it easier to connect to the white child:

I used to tell him far more than the others how lovely he was, perhaps because all parents want their children to look like them and when Terry [who is light skinned] and I were together we didn't look like a mismatch, different coloured socks that should not be together (Alibhai-Brown and Montague, 1992, p 222–3).

This is likely to mitigate against the warm emotional climate, positive communication about each child and shared environment that were advocated earlier, all of which, in turn, are likely to impact on the child's self-esteem as well as on the sibling relationships. But this is not inevitable. Black children are valued by many white parents:

I support my daughters by examining my own inherent racism constantly and challenging this, helping them to feel good about being black and making sure that they are proud and positive about their roots . . . Have to be especially supportive about being black as [there is the] possibility of more confusion than in an all black household (EYTARN, 1994, p 34).

Similarly many black and white siblings do go on to develop close sibling relationships:

My childhood and adulthood have been extremely positive. The few negative experiences I had regarding racism drew me closer to my family as it was them I turned to. Within my family I don't think I have been treated differently than my sister. There was the usual sibling rivalry, but on the whole we got on pretty well. We have always been a close family. My upbringing was one filled with love. Both parents have always been very open about me exploring my ethnicity and to tell me whatever I would like to know about my natural father (Black sibling, personal communication, 1998).

Although we argued from time to time we never seemed to argue as much as most sisters and brothers and I feel I was extremely lucky to have a sister [so] patient and understanding. Although we had a great childhood, I know this was mostly due to the fact that we had fantastic parents (White sibling, personal communication, 1998).

The children, while having much in common with one another, will not be similarly positioned as regards racism and may have different experiences and perspectives. White parents of black siblings may also have difficulty in understanding the experience of racism and may use negative strategies in preparing their children:

> *When I was younger, on occasion my Dad used to tell mildly racist jokes or mention names. It used to confuse me, as he didn't usually use terms like that and he always used to look uncomfortable using them. I found out a few years ago that that was his way of preparing me for "the outside world"* (Black sibling, personal communication, 1998).

> *I did in fact treat her differently. I attempted to make her aware of the problems she may encounter due to her colour. . . 'Coon', 'Sambo', 'Rubber Lips', etc., would have been sprinkled into conversations to make her aware of both the words and the possibilities of them being used against her* (White father, personal communication, 1998).

This may affect the self-esteem of the black child(ren). When only some of the children experience racism, or this negative parental communication, the sibling relationship may also be affected. In every case, the task of parenting black and white siblings is a complex one centring on managing difference in a context where those differences, e.g. black and white, are given competing values by society (Brah, 1992, p 140). A parent needs to counteract society's negative evaluation that white is best (Ginsburg, 1992) while giving positive messages to each child that 'being yourself is the best you can be' (Cummings, 1994, p 56). Moreover, there will be other differences and many other commonalties between the children. A parent needs to find the balance between focusing on the commonalities and on the differences (see Brodzinsky and Schechter, 1990). This tension of parenting for difference in the context of inequality can be done, e.g. when parenting male and female siblings (see also Lorde, 1988).

Additional implications for practice

Family support

Parents of black and white siblings need to be validated and supported in their parenting to:

- tell each child that 'being yourself is the best you can be';
- counteract society's evaluation that white is better than black, while giving positive messages to each child;
- understand the world they are preparing each child for and use appropriate strategies;
- find the balance between focusing on the commonalities and the differences; and
- provide the environment outlined earlier.

Placement considerations

In most instances, black and white siblings will establish a relationship that deserves recognition and continuity. Placement decisions need to value this and keep the siblings together, if at all possible. There is some evidence that further work is needed in understanding the needs of the siblings to be together and in valuing black carers appropriately:

> The children were placed with a white family, while search for a 'mixed parentage' family for T [mixed parentage] only... went on without much success. White foster parents and child psychologists argued against splitting T from other [white] siblings and social work assessment argued in favour of removing T from the white family. A suggestion of placing all children with a black family was commented on as being 'problematic' (Ahmad, 1990, p 24).

Assessment and support need to move forward to include a focus on the competence of the carer to provide the positive environment identified above. These competencies may be met by any parent/carer and are a challenge to every parent/carer. They may be more readily met, however, by a black parent/carer (Wilson, 1987; Prevatt Goldstein, 1995; Rachid, 1998). As with other sibling groups, there may be reasons why placement together is not in the interests of the children. The recommendations of BAAF's Black Perspectives Advisory Group and of

Kosonen (1998) which facilitate positive interaction between siblings should again be considered.

Conclusion

This chapter has explored the significance of the sibling relationship within black communities and has identified, with reference to wider research, the traditional factors which facilitate sibling attachment. These are seen as being responsibility and reciprocity, opportunities for inter-action without parents, a shared environment, and shared adversity. Appropriate professional intervention in family support and placement, which could reinforce the positive factors and enable the experience of adversity to be perceived as shared, has been suggested. Negative influences, including overwhelming adversity, separation and shadism which impinge both on the well-being of the children and on the sibling relationship, have also been listed. Appropriate family support and choice of placement in the context of wider community and social action have been suggested to ameliorate these.

All these positive and negative factors and all the professional inter-ventions advocated are equally relevant to black siblings and black and white siblings. However, parenting black and white siblings together, particularly by a white principal carer, adds an extra dimension of difference and the additional implications of this both for parenting and placement have been outlined.

Throughout, this chapter has suggested strategies of parenting in placement that will enable siblings to lay the foundation of a responsible and reciprocal relationship for life and to develop a "supportive base camp" that will help them cope with racism and other adversities.

Acknowledgements
I am indebted to Marcia Spencer and Sylvia Barker of BAAF, Justine King of Kemet and Shahida Ali of the University of Sunderland for their enthusiasm, support, research and editing skills. Thank you.

References

Ahmad B (1990) *Black Perspectives in Social Work*, Birmingham: Venture Press.

Alibhai-Brown Y and Montague A (1992) *The Colour of Love: Mixed race relationships*, London: Virago Press.

Banks N (1992) 'Some considerations of "racial" identification and self-esteem when working with mixed ethnicity children and their mothers as social services clients', *Social Services Research*, 3, pp 32–41.

Barn R, Sinclair R and Ferdinand D (1997) *Acting on Principle*, London: BAAF.

Barter C (1998) *Protecting Children from Racism and Racial Abuse*, London: NSPCC.

Billingsley A (1968) *Black Families in White America*, Englewood Cliffs, NJ: Prentice Hall.

Boer F (1990) *Sibling Relationships in Middle Childhood*, Leiden: University of Leiden, DWSO Press.

Brah A (1992) 'Difference, diversity and differentiation', in Donald J and Rattansi A (eds), *Culture and Difference*, London: Sage.

Brody G H and Stoneman Z (1987) 'Sibling conflict: contribution of siblings themselves in parent–sibling relationships and the broader family', *Journal of Children in Contemporary Society*, 19, pp 1939–53.

Brodzinsky D M and Schechter D (eds) *The Psychology of Adoption*, New York: Oxford University Press.

Butt J and Mirza K (1996) *Social Care and Black Communities*, London: HMSO.

Butt J and Box L (1998) *Family Centred*, London: REU.

Cummings J (1994) 'A child's daydream', in Featherston E (ed), *Skin Deep*, Freedom, CA: The Crossing Press.

Davis A (1989) *Women, Culture and Politics*, New York: Random House.

Dosanjh J S and Ghuman P A S (1998) 'Child-rearing practices of two generations of Punjabis: development of personality and independence', *Children & Society*, 12, pp 25–37.

Dunn J and Kendrick C (1982) *Siblings: Love, envy and understanding*, Cambridge: Harvard University Press.

Dunn J (1983) *Sisters and Brothers*, London: Fontana.

Dunn J (1996) 'Brothers and sisters in middle childhood and early adolescence: continuity and change in individual differences, in G H Brody (ed), *Sibling Relationships: Their causes and consequences*, New Jersey: Ablex.

Early Years Trainers Anti-Racist Network (EYTARN) (1994) *The Best of Both Worlds: Celebrating mixed parentage*, London: EYTARN.

Fahlberg V (1994) *A Child's Journey through Placement*, London: BAAF.

Fonagy P, Steele M, Higgit H and Target M (1994) 'The theory and practice of resilience', *Journal of Child Psychology & Psychiatry*, 35:2, pp 231–57.

Gilkes C T (1985) 'Together and in harness: women's traditions in the Sanctified Church' *Signs*, 10:4, pp 69–9.

Gilligan R (1998) 'Beyond Permanence? The importance of resilience in child permanency planning', in Hill M and Shaw M (eds), *Signposts in Adoption*, London: BAAF.

Ginsburg N (1992) 'Racism and housing: concepts and reality', in Braham P, Rattansi A and Skelington R (eds), *Racism and Anti-Racism*, London: Sage.

Gruesc J, Goodnew J and Cohen L (1996) 'Household work and the development of the concern for others', *Developmental Psychology*, 32:6, pp 999–1007.

Hill R H (1971) *The Strengths of Black Families*, New York: Emerson Hall.

hooks b (1991) *Yearning*, London: Turnaround.

hooks b (1993) *Sisters of the Yam*, London: Turnaround.

Islington Social Services Department (1987) *Networks Video*, London: Islington Social Services.

Jackson J S, McCulloch W R and Gurin G (1997) 'Family, socialisation, environment and identity development', in McAdoo H P (ed), *Black Families*, London: Sage.

Jenkins J (1992) 'Sibling relationships in disharmonious homes: potential difficulties and protective effects', in Boer F and Dunn J (eds.) *Children's Sibling Relationships: Development and clinical issues*, Hillside, NJ: Lawrence Earlbaum.

Jones G (1999) 'Barriers to adulthood: dependency and resistance in youth', in Cunningham-Burley S and Jamieson L (eds), *Families and the State: Changing relationships*, Basingstoke: Macmillan.

Kosonen M (1994) 'Sibling relationships for children in the care system', *Adoption & Fostering*, 18:3, pp 30–5.

Kosonen M (1998) 'Foster children's sibling relationships: compensation and/ or reflection of adversity,' in BAAF (ed), *Exchanging Visions*, London: BAAF.

Lawrence E (1982) 'In the midst of plenty the fool is hungry', in Centre for Contemporary Social Studies (ed), *The Empire Strikes Back*, London: Hutchinson.

Lewis D K (1975) 'The black family: socialisation and sex roles', *Phyllon*, 36, pp 221–37.

Lorde A (1984) *Sister Outsider*, Freedom, CA: Crossing Press.

Lorde A (1988) *A Burst of Light*, London: Sheba Feminist Publishers.

Manns W (1997) 'Supportive roles of significant others in African-American families', in McAdoo H P (ed), *Black Families*, London: Sage.

Matovu L, Mwatsama M and Ndagire B (1998) 'Family patterns in East African communities: implications for children affected by HIV/Aids', *Adoption & Fostering*, 22:1, pp 17–24.

Modood T, Beishon S and Virdee S (1994) *Changing Ethnic Identities*, London: Policy Studies Institute.

Modood T, Berthould R, Lakey J, Nazroo J, Smith P, Virdee S and Beishon S (1997) *Ethnic Minorities in Britain: Diversity and disadvantage*, London: Policy Studies Institute.

Moraga C and Anzaldua G (eds) (1981) *This Bridge Called My Back*, Massachusetts: Persephone Press.

Morrow V (1994) 'Responsible children? Aspects of children's work and employment outside school in the contemporary UK,' in Mayall B (ed), *Children's Childhoods Observed and Experienced*, London: Falmer Press.

Peach C (ed) *Ethnicity in the 1991 Census 2*, London: OPCS.

Peters M F (1997) 'Historical note: Parenting of young children in black families', in McAdoo H P (ed), *Black Families*, London: Sage.

Prevatt Goldstein B (1995) Review on Phoenix A and Tizard B, *Black, White or Mixed Race, Issues in Social Work Education*, 14:2, pp 98–105.

Pringle M L K (1975) *The Needs of Children: A personal perspective prepared for the Department of Health*, London: Hutchinson.

Rachid S P (1998) 'Diverse realities,' *Community Care*, 15–21 October, pp 28–9.

Reidmann A and White L (1996) 'Adult sibling relationships: racial and ethnic comparisons', in G H Brody (ed), *Sibling Relationships: Their causes and consequences*, New Jersey: Ablex.

Sissay L (1992) *Rebel Without Applause*, Newcastle upon Tyne: Bloodaxe.

Sistren (1986) *Lionheart Gal*, London: The Women's Press.

Smith T (1990) 'Family centres, children in need and the Children Act 1989,' in Gibbons J (ed), *The Children Act 1989 and Family Support*, London: HMSO.

Sudarkasa N (1996) *The Strength of our Mothers*, Trenton, NJ: Africa World Press.

Vandell D L and Bailey M D (1992) 'Conflicts between siblings,' in Shantz C U and Hartup W W (eds), *Conflict in Child and Adolescence Development*, Cambridge: Cambridge University Press.

Waksler F C (1991) *Studying the Social Worlds of Children: Sociological readings*, London: Falmer Press.

Wiehe V R (1990) *Sibling Abuse: Hidden physical, emotional and sexual trauma*, Lexington, Mass.: Lexington Books.

Williams C (1988) 'Gal . . . you come from foreign', in Grewal S, Kay J, Landor L, Lewis G and Parmar P (eds), *Charting the Journey*, London: Sheba Feminist Publishers.

Wilson A (1987) *A Study of Identity*, London: Allen & Unwin.

Yarnborough C (1979) *Cornrows*, New York: Coward McCann.

16 The placement of sexually abused and abusing siblings

Ann Head and *Marian Elgar*

Ann Head is a guardian ad litem and independent researcher.

Marian Elgar is Senior Lecturer, School of Social Sciences and Law, at Oxford Brookes University. She is also a guardian ad litem.

The authors' study (Elgar and Head, 1997) considered the progress of 85 children from 35 families who had been the subject of care proceedings, during which sexual abuse within the family had been a factor in the application for an order. Of the 85 children, 51 were girls (60 per cent) and 34 were boys (40 per cent). The largest group in the study were girls, aged five to ten years, of whom there were 18 (21 per cent). There was a particular preponderance of girls over boys in the 11–16 age group, in which there were 11 girls and only three boys. Seventy-two per cent of this sample of children had been separated from at least one sibling following the court proceedings. At a later stage, 51 children from 24 families were followed up in more detail and a total of 53 carers (foster carers, adoptive parents, residential staff and some parents and relatives) were interviewed. All findings on the views of carers, reported below, relate to the second stage sample of 51 children.

The family situations in the study fell into three distinct groups:

Type A: families where one child disclosed sexual abuse and where that child was the only child removed from the family (the scapegoat model);

Type B: families where all the children in the family were sexually abused and all were removed from home (the serial abuse model);

Type C: families where one child was sexually abused, the others were probably not but all the children were nevertheless removed from home (the selective model).

The families in the study were divided as follows:

Type A: 11 families

Type B: five families

Type C: five families

Type B/C: three families. These were families where it was difficult to tell whether all the children had been sexually abused or not.

There was no discernible difference in age or gender which could have suggested why particular children were singled out for sexual abuse. A total of 15 children were the oldest child in their family and the one who disclosed abuse; in the majority of cases this was the only child removed from the family; but it was impossible to gauge, in these cases, on the information available, whether others had also been abused or were at high risk of being abused.

A very high proportion of children were described by their carers as having special needs. Forty-seven (92 per cent) children were said by at least one carer to have special emotional needs. A high proportion of the children were described as having special educational needs (30 children; 63 per cent) and, of these, 24 children had a statement of educational need. Pre-school children were not included in the questions about educational need and therefore these figures may be an under-estimate. It is impossible to say whether the high number of children with special needs reflects the potential for such children to be selected for abuse or whether it represents the after-effects of the experience of abuse itself; clearly both factors could be operating.

Separation

There was a high level of separations in the sample. Given the importance attached to sibling relationships in the literature (e.g. Ward, 1984; Wedge and Mantle, 1991) and in government guidelines (Department of Health, 1991), it was an unexpected finding that 72 per cent of the children had been separated from at least one sibling, although Kosonen's (1996) findings in this respect are similarly worrying. (Half-siblings are included in this figure where they were part of the family group.) The reasons given for the separation by the guardians *ad litem* who were interviewed at the first stage of the research are shown in Table 1. The picture is, however, more complex than this. At the stage of permanent placement of the children, the situation showed in Table 2 applied.

Table 1

Reasons for separation

	Number	*%*
Child's needs differed from siblings	19	22
Differential risk assessment	19	22
Lack of appropriate resources	20	23.5
Scapegoating of the child by family	1	1
Combination of the first two reasons	2	2

(N=85)

Table 2

Changes in placement or separation status by time of permanent placement

	Number	*%*
Children placed with at least one sibling	38	74
Children moved to be with at least one sibling	9	18
Children moved to separate them from a sibling	4	8
Children separated because of lack of resources	10	29

(N=51)

Note: some children appear in both the first two categories

Caring for siblings together

Thus, although the majority of children became separated from at least one sibling, there was also considerable success in placing children with at least one brother or sister. Many carers felt that particularly damaged children should have been placed alone, partly because of their need for a lot of individual attention and partly because of the stress involved in caring for more than one very difficult child. Sixteen children in the second stage of the study (31 per cent), in the opinion of their carers, should have been placed alone. In the cases of a further nine children (18 per cent) the carers were unsure as to whether they should have been placed alone. Some comments of carers illustrate this point:

P's individual needs were not being met. She did not necessarily need one-to-one attention but needed to be away from the other two. She seemed frightened. She was unable to talk about her experiences and she wanted to.

I briefly had both boys together. It was horrific. *They were in and out of each other's beds. R was walking all night long.*

In the beginning I felt that the girls hated each other. T would have been better placed with no siblings but it's out of the question now (After 2½ years in the same foster home).

Sexualised behaviour was a major factor in the breakdown of foster placements. A total of ten children at the second stage (20 per cent) were moved prematurely from their placements and, of these ten children, three had had to move twice. Sexualised behaviour was given as a reason for requesting removal by six carers.

There were more placement breakdowns for children placed singly in foster homes than for children placed with at least one sibling. There were nine disruptions of care for children placed singly (including two disruptions for two children) and two sibling groups of two were also moved prematurely: one group because of sexualised behaviour and the second because carers lost faith that social services were trying to secure a long-term placement. Thus the study, although dealing with small numbers of children, supported findings reported elsewhere that the placement of siblings together tends to aid placement stability (see, for example, Thoburn and Rowe, 1988; Wedge and Mantle, 1991).

Sexually abusive behaviour among the children

Prominent amongst the difficulties faced by carers in the study was the propensity of the study children to invite further sexual abuse or to perpetrate abuse on other children. Many children were described as being inappropriately affectionate to adults, even total strangers, and carers were very concerned about their vulnerability in this respect. Carers often had to take precautions in relation to members of their own family, for example, never leaving a partner or son, or any young children, alone with the child in their charge. As many as 30 children (59 per cent) were described by their carers as demonstrating sexualised behaviour towards adults and 28 children (55 per cent) were sexually abusive towards other children – either their siblings, other children, or both.

Many of the children in the second-stage sample had been sexually abused by more that one adult (18 children, 35 per cent) and some had suffered sickening cruelty and degradation. There was a strong correlation between children who had been seriously sexually abused and those who were considered to be a sexual risk to other children; of the 17 children who, carers were sure, had suffered penetration, all but one were found to have been sexually abusive to other children.

For some children, the sexually abusive behaviour they displayed seemed to diminish as they settled into their placement. On the other hand, some children were not thought to be abusive initially, but the behaviour emerged in a later placement or later in the same placement. One hypothesis to explain the latter phenomenon is that some carers were not initially aware of the possibility of children sexually abusing other children; alternatively, some children, who had not been abused in their family of origin, may have begun to display sexualised behaviour following abuse perpetrated on them by a sibling. Bank and Kahn (1982) suggest that siblings may become involved sexually with each other when they are caught up in frightening situations and the children in the study had almost all had the frightening experience of removal from home. It was difficult to substantiate either of these hypotheses but, in several cases, there was good reason to believe that one or the other did apply. It was clear that some carers were alive to the issues and went to great lengths to bring the subject into the open and to protect children from abuse. This good practice needed to be extended to carers who were less experienced or well informed.

Sexualised behaviour was one of the problems carers found hardest to deal with, particularly if it affected the welfare of other children. One carer found that her grandchild had been sexually abused by her foster child and other carers were told that they must choose between their foster son, who had been sexually abusive to other children, and a younger foster daughter, whom they hoped to adopt. These situations caused enormous anguish to the families concerned.

Equally concerning for carers were discoveries that there was ongoing sexualised behaviour between siblings in the same placement. Occasionally such a discovery led to the separation of the siblings. In other cases, carers worked very hard to address the issues and protect children from each other. It was clear in some cases that children were re-enacting the roles they had learned in their family of origin; for example, with one child assuming a passive, victim role and the other the role of aggressor. Carers generally found it easier to identify with the victim and the researchers were not sanguine about the future prospects for children who were seen by their carers as abusive and aggressive. Many carers may have been helped to cope better with the children in their care if they had had information about the dysfunctional birth family and guidance as to how to discourage unhelpful and conflicted relationships reforming within their own family.

Sibling placement: concurrent planning

Some carers were able to cope with extreme behavioural difficulties and highly sexualised behaviour where others found the task too much. There were great discrepancies in age and experience between foster carers and adopters; foster carers and, in particular, short-term foster carers were generally older and more experienced while adopters were usually much younger and often lacking in any experience of caring for children. This latter group, in the sample, was often coping with sibling pairs or with groups who presented considerable difficulties, including sexualised behaviour. Their commitment to the children was not in doubt, but they did not seem to be the best placed carers to help the siblings with their premature sexuality or with their set roles vis-à-vis one another. Nor did they generally find it easy to promote and encourage contact with other members of the children's birth family. Of eight adoptive families, only one felt that they had had adequate help post adoption.

There were a few cases where children had remained with their initial carer, even though this was originally intended to be a short-term placement. Three sets of carers were outstanding in coping with the most extreme testing behaviour, including sexualised behaviour, from their foster children. The success of these placements, against all the odds, suggested to the researchers that the concept of concurrent planning might be particularly helpful in such cases (Katz, 1994). Concurrent planning involves the placement of children with carers who are prepared and trained to work with the local authority towards rehabilitation of the children to their birth family, but who will become permanent carers if rehabilitation proves impossible to achieve. The carers in the sample were experienced and committed, coped with birth family contact, and gave the children confidence to talk, perhaps for the first time, about their experiences of abuse. They were used to working in partnership with social services and perhaps flexible enough to work with them towards rehabilitation or to continue as long-term carers, according to which was the more suitable plan for the children. The success of adoption placements of sibling groups where the adopters were also the children's first carers has been noted elsewhere (Barth *et al*, 1988; Rushton and Mayes, 1997).

Sibling placement: staggered placements

For long-term placement to work well it seems clear that there needs to be a degree of mutual attachment between child and carers. Rushton and Mayes (1997, p 122) have identified attachment as a key prerequisite of placement success:

> *The development of a close, affectionate tie between new parents and their children appeared to be crucial in enabling the parents to cope with behavioural or educational difficulties in the children.*

In the research study reported here, there was sometimes a conflict between a child's need to attach to a caring adult and his or her possibility of being with a sibling. Children who have been sexually abused within their family often have difficulties in making attachments (see, for example, Steele and Alexander, 1987).

These children, as described above, may come from backgrounds where there is a poverty and confusion of relationships within a sexually abusive family. For some of the most dreadfully abused and neglected children in the sample, the making of at least one attachment to a caring adult was regarded as the first priority if the children were to have any hope of leading anything like a normal life in the future. This was pointed up by the correlation in the study between the children who had been seriously sexually abused (involving penetration) and those children whom carers found difficult to like. Of the 17 children who had suffered severe abuse, eight were described by at least one carer as not being 'easy to take to'.

It was sometimes very difficult for carers to look after more than one child from such an extreme background and this was reflected in the carers' views, referred to earlier, that some children needed the kind of nurturing which would only be possible in a one-to-one relationship. In such extreme cases there could be an argument for placing siblings at different times, allowing one particularly deprived child a chance to begin to make an important attachment before being joined by a sibling or siblings. The timing of sibling placements is an issue which has been raised in an American study which concludes that there is merit in considering 'staggered placements' (Lepere et al, 1986).

Contact

Where children in care had been separated from siblings at placement, there was generally some contact organised between them. There were only six children who had had no contact organised with a sibling or siblings and this resulted, for all but one child, from placement for adoption. The contact varied in frequency between weekly and twice per year. For the majority of children in long-term care, there was a reduction over time in the frequency of contact with siblings, so that those children who were in adoptive or long-term foster homes commonly saw brothers and sisters placed elsewhere only two or three times each year. Approximately two-thirds of the carers thought that sibling contact was beneficial to the children in their care.

Contact was more problematic for children who had been removed from home, leaving siblings behind. Such a situation meant that contact with siblings always also involved a parent or parents. Both children and carers seemed to find this situation more difficult. Some carers expressed the view that their foster child was constantly reminded of his or her exclusion from the family and was unable to maintain a relationship with siblings who were expected to take sides either with parents or with the excluded child. It was not surprising that, in the cases of seven such children, all contact with siblings ceased after a period. Quotations from carers illustrate these difficulties for children in the "scapegoat" group (see above):

L feels singled out and that it is all her fault. [We] . . . feel anger at her rejection; the parents are just using L.

Contact was difficult. S was abused by B's father. There was no question of him leaving home, but S missed B . . . mother was very protective of B. Mother wouldn't leave them alone. S needed reassurance that B was all right.

(In this case S was in foster care and B was still at home. Contact dwindled.)

There was very little indirect contact (letters, telephone calls) between siblings in our study. This seemed to be a neglected area. Nor was there much indication that sibling contact was designed to promote important, meaningful or memorable access between siblings, for example, aiding siblings to share birthdays, Christmas or important events in each others' lives.

The dwindling of sibling contact, its low profile and the neglect of opportunities for indirect contact are of considerable concern, particularly in the light of the regrets of adults looking back on their upbringing in care and the indications from literature that the closeness of sibling bonds relates to high access (Festinger, 1983). Begun (1995, p 239) makes this point:

The character of the sibling bond is determined, to a large extent, by the nature of the interactions which are permitted between siblings. Foster care placements that do not permit significant opportunities for regular contact between siblings fail to support their development of a meaningful relationship over time.

Assessment

Good early assessment of the needs of children who have been removed from sexually abusive homes is essential. The key elements of such an assessment, in the light of our study of children post-care proceedings, are:

- the maximum information about the sexual abuse – who the perpetrators were (intra or extra familial, parent or child) and the severity of the abuse;
- as clear a picture as possible of the ways in which each child has been treated by the parents and therefore of the implications of the family interactions;
- using key substitute carers in assessment;
- the relationships between the siblings. Some key questions which could be asked are:
  – How much and in what way do the siblings influence each other's development?
  – Do siblings have disabling or reinforcing views of each other?
  – Do siblings react to life events by closing ranks or accelerating rivalry?
- an assessment of each child's attachment needs.

As well as a thorough assessment of the needs of the siblings, thought also needs to be given to the preparation and support of the substitute carers. Reference has already been made to the work of Rushton and Mayes (1997) in identifying the need for carers to promote attachment behaviour in the children. Continuing support is likely to be needed by carers taking on the care of needy sibling groups and this appears to be particularly lacking post adoption.

Conclusions

General
1. The decision to split siblings may have lifelong implications; there is a potential loss of a relationship or relationships which can offer important support throughout life.
2. The separation of siblings may cause mourning and depression.

3. A judgement about the relative unimportance of a sibling tie should be made only with considerable caution. Emotional closeness between siblings varies according to age and developmental stage and any decision about separation should take this into account.

4. Conflict, animosity and competitiveness are sometimes given as reasons for the separation of siblings. This should be seen in the light of findings that rivalry and even some violence are present in most relationships between young siblings.

5. There is no support in the literature for separating siblings because one has a caretaking role towards the other. This is a normal part of many sibling relationships.

6. Siblings in placement are reassured by the presence of a sibling, even one who is too young to provide parenting (Heinicke and Westheimer, 1965). This is consistent with Bank and Kahn's (1982) hypothesis that strong sibling bonds develop, not out of caretaking, but out of high levels of access.

Siblings in abusive families

1. Destructive levels of conflict between siblings may arise when disparities between siblings (in intelligence, for example, or other socially desirable traits) are clear and given emphasis by parents. If one child is consistently the loser for adult affection and approval, then a separate placement for that child may develop self-esteem. However, the consequent separation will prevent dysfunctional family relationships from being addressed; thus Begun (1995, p 244) states: 'Separated siblings will have no opportunity to resolve the pre-existing conflicts or restructure the roles which may have made separation seem desirable.'

2. Foster carers and adoptive parents need help to identify the family systems which have made it advantageous for children to assume particular roles towards each other and they need help in working towards healthier relationships for the children.

3. Sometimes the demands of sibling groups from abusive families are too much for carers to manage and some separations are inevitable. In these circumstances, contact between the siblings is of paramount importance. Faced with evidence that sibling contact, although felt to

be beneficial by carers, falls off over time, it seems essential that more thought be given to the encouragement of contact at times of significance for the children and for the maintenance of indirect contact, so that feelings of closeness are engendered.

4. There are often conflicts between satisfying a child's need for attachment to an adult carer and placing the child with a sibling or siblings. There is no clear-cut answer to this problem but it may be that, sometimes, placement of children at different times in the same substitute family should be considered. There is also room for the promotion of attachment behaviour by substitute carers, as suggested by Rushton and Mayes (1997).

Siblings from sexually abusive families

1. The dynamics of a sibling group which has experienced intrafamilial sexual abuse may prevent children from:
   – recovering from their experiences of sexual abuse (because of constant reminders by siblings); and
   – making healthy attachments to adults who can offer a good experience of parenting.
2. Gerrilyn Smith (1996) argues against the placement together of children who have been sexually abused within their family of origin.
3. There is a risk that sexually abused children will abuse others. This risk increases with the severity of the abuse and the experience of the child.
4. It may be that some very seriously sexually abused children cannot safely be cared for in homes where there are other young children, at least not until their abusive behaviour has been addressed.
5. Some carers have become very expert at helping children recover from experiences of sexual abuse and their expertise needs to be better disseminated. There is considerable discrepancy in experience between carers, with adopters being generally the least experienced and yet often being asked to care for groups of siblings who have experienced sexual abuse. There seems to be room for a better use of resources to help the most damaged children.
6. Children who are removed from their family as a result of an allegation of sexual abuse, leaving other siblings behind with parents,

are a particularly disadvantaged group, finding it hard to cope with feelings of guilt and exclusion and unable to establish satisfactory relationships with the siblings left behind. If such a damaging separation is deemed to be inevitable, it seems important that social workers and others strive to make arrangements for sibling contact which will not be sabotaged by parents or by carers or professionals who fear contact between the children and their parents. As Jones (1991, p 60) has noted:

. . . removal of the child from the family in the aftermath of discovery acts to underscore for the victim his/her sense of guilt and responsibility for the family break-up just at the time when the child's psychological state is at its most precarious.

References

Bank S P and Kahn M D (1982) *The Sibling Bond*, New York: Basic Books.

Barth R P, Berry M, Yoshikami R, Goodfield R K and Carson M L (1988) 'Predicting adoption disruption', *Social Work*, 33, pp 227–33.

Begun A (1995) 'Sibling relationships and foster care placements for young children', *Early Child Development and Care*, 106, pp 237–50.

Department of Health (1991) *Children Act 1989, Guidance and Regulations, Volume 3, Family Placements*, London: HMSO.

Elgar M and Head A (1997) *From Court Process to Care Plan: An empirical study of the placement of sexually abused children*, Oxford: Centre for Socio-Legal Studies, Wolfson College, University of Oxford.

Festinger T (1983) *No One Ever Asked us . . . A postscript to foster care*, New York: Columbia University Press.

Heinicke C M and Westheimer I J (1965) *Brief Separations*, New York: International University Press.

Jones D P H (1991) 'Professional and clinical challenges to the protection of children', *Child Abuse and Neglect* 15, Supplement 1, pp 57–66.

Katz L (1996) 'Permanency action through concurrent planning', *Adoption & Fostering*, 20:2, pp 8–13.

Kosonen M (1996) 'Maintaining sibling relationships – neglected dimension in child care practice', *British Journal of Social Work*, 26, pp 809–22.

Lepere D W, Davis L E, Couve J and MacDonald M (1986) *Large Sibling Groups: Adoption experience*, Washington DC: Child Welfare League of America.

Rushton A and Mayes D (1997) 'Forming fresh attachments in childhood: a research update', *Child & Family Social Work*, 2:2, pp 121–7.

Smith G (1996) 'Reassessing protectiveness', in Batty D and Cullen D (eds), *Child Protection: The therapeutic option*, London: BAAF.

Steele B and Alexander H (1990) 'Long-term effects of sexual abuse in childhood', in Sulloway F, *Orthodoxy and Innovation in Science: The influence of birth order in a multivariate context*. Paper presented to the American Association for the Advance of Science, New Orleans, 1990.

Thoburn J and Rowe J (1988) 'A snapshot of permanent family placement', *Adoption & Fostering*, 12:3, pp 29–34.

Ward M (1984) 'Sibling ties in foster care and adoption planning', *Child Welfare*, 63:4, pp 321–2.

Wedge P and Mantle G (1991) *Sibling Groups and Social Work*, Aldershot: Avebury.

17 Sexually abused and abusing children
Their impact on "foster siblings" and other looked after children

Elaine Farmer and *Sue Pollock*

Elaine Farmer is a Senior Research Fellow in the School for Policy Studies at Bristol University where she also teaches on the Diploma in Social Work, the degree in Early Childhood Studies and is Programme Director for the Masters Degree in Child Welfare. She spent several years as a social worker in the UK and Australia before moving into research and teaching. Her research interests include the reunification of separated children with their families, child protection, residential and foster care. She undertook research in the Department of Health programme of research on child protection and the subsequent programme on residential care. Her latest study is on the fostering task with behaviourally difficult adolescents and is part of a new research programme on family support.

Sue Pollock is a Research Fellow in the School for Policy Studies at the University of Bristol where she combines teaching on the Diploma in Social Work with research interests in parenting and child care. She has undertaken research in the recent Department of Health initiative on residential child care and is currently working on a study of young men's transition to fatherhood as part of a new Economic and Social Research Council research programme on youth, citizenship and social change.

Until recently, the issue of sibling relationships had been neglected in research. The emphasis in both research and social work practice has been on the parent–child relationship rather than on relations between children (Farmer and Parker, 1991). However, during the 1980s, a number of writers emphasised the particular qualities of sibling relationships and Dunn (1984) argued that sibling relationships are often the most enduring of all. In spite of the lack of detailed attention to children's relationships with each other, there has been a general assumption in social work practice that siblings should be placed together wherever possible (Wedge and Mantle, 1991), particularly in the light of research findings suggesting that placement of a child with one or more siblings increases the stability of placements in care (Berridge and Cleaver, 1987; Fratter *et al*, 1991) and of subsequent restoration to the birth family (Farmer and Parker, 1991).

However, it would appear timely for thinking in this area to be developed further. Although research findings have suggested that, in aggregate, there are advantages in placing siblings together, it does not follow that this will be true in all cases. In a review of the literature on the sibling relationships of children in the care system, Kosonen (1994) notes that 'much more needs to be known about the complexity of sibling relationships for children separated from their families'. Wedge and Mantle (1991) concluded that sibling placements can be beneficial, but that they carry a risk of additional problems and can put undue stress on foster carers. At the moment there is little evidence to guide practitioners as to when placement with siblings is or is not likely to be beneficial. One group of children who require particular attention are siblings who have been sexually abused or who have shown sexually abusing behaviour.

This chapter will draw in particular on the evidence from two recent research studies (Elgar and Head, 1997; Farmer and Pollock, 1998), one of which was conducted by the authors in order to explore the placements of sexually abused and/or abusing children in substitute care. It will examine: first, how often sibling groups are placed together and with what consequences; second, contact issues between separated abused siblings; and third, the impact of sexually abused and/or abusing children on their "foster siblings" or on other children with whom they share placements. Since the risk of sexual abuse to other children extends not only to "foster siblings", referring to the foster carers' own children, but also to other looked after children in foster and residential care, the impact on both groups of children will be included.

The placement of sexually abused children with their siblings

Practitioners and clinicians have for some time commented on the particular difficulties of sibling placements when a sibling group has been sexually abused (McFadden *et al*, 1984; Smith, 1989; Macaskill, 1991). How far have such difficulties led to sibling placements being avoided? In a study of 85 children who had been involved in care proceedings where sexual abuse was a ground, Elgar and Head (1997) found that 72 per cent (62) children had been separated from at least one sibling. Similar figures were revealed in a scrutiny of the case files of 250 children who were newly looked after in 1993 and 1994 (Farmer and Pollock, 1998). In this latter study, 79 per cent of children who at some stage had experienced sexual abuse or shown abusing behaviour were not placed with siblings on admission to care, as compared with 64 per cent of non-abused children. However, this difference was not statistically significant. It appears, therefore, that siblings who have been sexually abused are only slightly more often separated from their siblings when placements are made than is the case with other children. Of course, there are a number of reasons for siblings being separated. Sometimes only one child is known to have suffered abuse and this child alone is removed from the family, while at other times sexual abuse by one sibling of another will lead to separation.

What do we know about the consequences of placing sexually abused siblings together? Macaskill (1991), in a study of 80 foster and adoptive placements of children of all ages, found that sexual activity occurred in eight out of the 14 sibling groups in her study (57 per cent). Sexual behaviour between siblings was reported as a problem in respect of more than a quarter (26 per cent) of the sexually abused siblings who were placed together in Elgar and Head's study (1997) and this caused great strain on carers. As many as a third of the carers in Elgar and Head's study felt that the abused children in their care would have been better placed alone. This was because, in some cases, siblings were considered to be harmful to each other and, in others, a disturbed child placed in a sibling group had been unable to get enough individual attention. At times, one child's recovery from their abuse was clearly being jeopardised by a sibling's continuing sexual behaviour or abuse.

It was also noted in the Elgar and Head study that, in some placements, sexual activity between siblings was considered to be a problem where it had not been reported by the carers in a previous setting. This disparity appeared to relate to differences in awareness between different caregivers rather than to variations in the levels of sexual activity across placements. The authors considered that residential workers and foster carers with little previous experience had the lowest awareness of sexual activity between children in placement or minimised these behaviours. Farmer and Pollock (1998) also found that information about sibling sexual activity in substitute care was rarely recorded on the case file, even when it was well established and long-standing. A lack of verbal or written reports about such sexual behaviour cannot therefore be taken to mean that none has taken place.

This evidence suggests that, in many cases, sexually abused and abusing children are not placed with their siblings but that, when they are, very high levels of vigilance are needed if further sexual activity between the siblings is to be avoided (see also Smith, 1995; Smith, 1996). The presence of a sibling may act as a trigger for further sexual activity whilst some children have derived comfort from sexual contact with their siblings and this may be a considerable motivating force. Smith (1996) also notes that, when a sibling group has been manipulated to establish abusive hierarchies in which they abuse each other, this behaviour is likely to continue. When there is known to have been sibling sexual activity, it is clearly important to look at the power differential and the degree of risk to the younger or weaker sibling when decisions about placement are made (McFadden *et al*, 1984).

Contact with siblings

When sexually abused children are separated from their siblings, contact with them raises a range of issues, apart from the possibility that sexual activity will occur during contact visits. In some cases parents simply forbid contact with siblings in order to maintain the fiction that the abuse did not take place (Elgar and Head, 1997; Farmer and Pollock, 1998). Smith (1995a) suggests that sometimes the law should be used to secure continued contact with siblings in these situations, as otherwise the only way in which some abused children can continue the relationships is if they retract the allegation. However, another scenario is that pressure may be put on a child to retract through the siblings who see the perpetrator and, for this reason, Jones and Parkinson (1995) suggest that access to all siblings may need to be denied. Another aspect of contact which requires attention is that some children have been involved in exploitative sexual relationships as a result of people they have met through family members like siblings and parents. These links therefore need careful monitoring.

Contact for sexually abusing children raises further issues. Farmer and Pollock (1998) found that, while all the sexually abused adolescents in their study had some contact with siblings, 40 per cent of the abusing children never saw their brothers or sisters. Children who had abused others also had less contact with their mothers than other children. Since only a minority of the young people's victims had been siblings, this suggests that young people who have shown abusing behaviour to any child are at risk of losing contact with their siblings and of seeing their mothers rarely. Clearly, these issues require further attention (see also previous chapter).

Sexually abused or abusing children: their impact on other children

Whether children with a background of sexual abuse or of abusing behaviour are placed with siblings or are separated from them will be decided at an early stage of planning. For all children, decisions then have to be made about the kind of placement which will be sought and about the suitability of any particular mix of children in that setting, taking into account any risks from or to the placed child. In practice, when a new admission is under consideration, there is rarely any mechanism which will ensure that full attention is given to the match of the child with others already in residence. The placing social worker will rarely have completed a full assessment of the child and will often not know very much about other children already in the placement. It will then be up to the head of the residential unit or the foster carers to

231

say if they think that the suggested placement is unsuitable.

However, in practice, heads of home are often not given the discretion to refuse admissions and foster carers may feel that their choice is constrained, for example, by a desire to please the social worker or the need for payment. Routine screening of the suitability of new referrals for admission, in contrast, is in place in a number of more specialised settings, such as some independent living units and residential schools. At admission, attention was paid to how the child would fit in with the existing child group in only 30 per cent of the placements made in Farmer and Pollock's study of sexually abused and abusing adolescents (1998), and this reduced to 20 per cent when specialised settings were excluded.

In practice, it appears that social services departments place the majority of sexually abused adolescents in residential care and most teenagers with a background of abusing behaviour either in foster care or in residential schools or secure units (Farmer and Pollock, 1998). What then do we know about the risks that these young people present to other children? Farmer and Pollock found that, in a sample of 40 young people aged ten or over, almost one in five of those who had been sexually abused went on to abuse another child in the one placement in residential or foster care which was the focus of the study. A similar proportion of adolescents with a background of sexually abusing behaviour abused a child in their placement. Those they abused were younger siblings, either in a shared foster placement or on contact visits, the younger children of the foster carers, and other children in residential and foster care. In Elgar and Head's sample (1997) of sexually abused children of all ages on care orders, 39 per cent sexually abused other children in residential or foster care. Those children who had suffered penetrative abuse were especially likely to abuse others in placement. Macaskill (1991) reported that, in 51 per cent of her sample of 80 foster and adoptive placements of sexually abused children of all ages, some type of sexual activity was directed towards other children in the family.

Although the figures from these studies vary quite widely, they do suggest that children who have suffered sexual abuse at any stage may present very real risks to their "foster siblings" and to other children with whom they are placed. Indeed, when the whole histories of the young people with backgrounds of sexual abuse in Farmer and Pollock's study (1998) were checked, it was found that as many as half of them had gone on to sexually abuse another child at some stage, either at home, at school, or more often in substitute care. It is clear then that, at the time of placement, full consideration needs to be given to the age and vulnerability of other children in a placement in order to ensure that the caregivers can offer sufficiently tight supervision to ensure their safety. In some cases it may be necessary to seek a placement where there are no other children, or at least no others younger than or close in age to the placed child. A few young people who have committed acts of aggressive and coercive sexual assault will require secure residential settings.

If caregivers are to be able to provide high levels of supervision, they need full information about children's histories before placements are made. However, there is evidence to suggest that practice falls far short of providing such information. In one study (Farmer and Pollock, 1998), information about sexual abuse or abusing behaviour was not passed on to caregivers in approaching half the placements (45 per cent) and, in another (Macaskill, 1991), 32 per cent of foster or adoptive parents had not known about the sexual abuse in the child's background prior to placement. Sometimes this was because the placing social worker had not known about the child's history and, it must be said that, without the systematic use of case summaries, information on file is easily "lost" after a change of social worker. Similarly, Monck and New (1996), in their study of sexually abused children in treatment facilities, found that social workers did not know about the previous sexual abuse experiences of 40 per cent of the children for whom they held responsibility. Other reasons for information about abuse histories not being passed on to caregivers may include mistaken views about confidentiality, minimisation of the significance of these abuse incidents, and a desire to avoid labelling children while, occasionally, information is withheld in order to secure a placement where it is thought that with full knowledge carers might refuse to take a child.

Whatever the reason, a failure to share information about children's backgrounds of sexual abuse or abusing behaviour can have very serious consequences. In the absence of this information, caregivers cannot plan to provide the high levels of supervision which can sometimes avert further abuse and so other children are placed at unnecessary risk. In Farmer and Pollock's study (1998), a number of young people sexually abused their "foster siblings" or their own siblings soon after they joined foster families in which the foster carers had not even been told about the children's backgrounds. As one foster mother said:

I was just shell-shocked . . . I was in shock for about a day. I just couldn't get over it . . . I would have tackled the sexual behaviour side completely different if I was aware of it, but at the time I wasn't.

It is likely that, in future, social services departments will face legal challenges from aggrieved foster carers and other parents if they have failed to share such vital information.

There are other risks. In the absence of adequate information about the abuse, caregivers may find that they have unwittingly recreated aspects of the context of the original abuse (McFadden, 1987; Davis *et al*, 1991; Macaskill, 1991). For example, in Farmer and Pollock's study, ten-year-old Sharon was terrified when her foster carers' son came into the bathroom to use the toilet as she was getting into the bath. This family practice with their younger children had to be quickly altered as it seemed to have revived memories of Sharon's original abuse. The foster carers had not been told that Sharon had been sexually abused in the first place. As well as being bad experiences in their own right, situations of this kind can lead to allegations of abuse from frightened children who misinterpret situations which are similar to their earlier experience of abuse (McFadden and Stovall, 1984; McFadden and Ryan, 1986; McFadden, 1987).

Children, including "foster siblings", may encounter other difficulties when sexually abused or abusing children are placed with them. They are often the recipients of a child's disclosure because many looked after children have lost trust in adults (Macaskill, 1991; Martin, 1993). Other children should therefore be told to tell their carers if a placed child tries to involve them in sexual activities (Nobbs and Jones, 1989) or if a child discloses abuse to them. It has also been argued that children need information about the abusive behaviour of other children with whom they share placements in order to protect themselves against abuse (National Children's Home, 1992).

"Foster siblings" and others who share placements with abused or abusing adolescents may be put at risk outside of, as well as within, the care setting. One in five of the young people in Farmer and Pollock's study (1998) had been working as prostitutes or were on the fringes of this world, either during their placements, while absconding, or after discharge from care. Half of these children procured other residents from their placements for the purposes of prostitution and some involved others in the making of pornographic videos. Children who shared placements with younger people who worked as prostitutes therefore ran the risk of being drawn into prostitution. For some, initiating others seemed to be a compulsive activity – a replay of their own experience of being initiated – and, on occasions, young people procured others for their clients at the request of those adults. This was one way in which paedophiles could gain access to new children and it is known that some pimps target particular children's homes (Shaw et al, 1996).

Conclusion

This evidence shows that children with backgrounds of sexual abuse and/or abusing behaviour require careful consideration at the time of placement. Placements with siblings carry particular burdens for caregivers because of the risk of sexual activity between siblings. Each sibling group needs to be carefully assessed for the individual needs of each child and the degree of risk to each. Plans for the placement of sexually abused and/or abusing children also need to give full attention to the other children already in the setting and to the levels of supervision which caregivers can provide. Foster carers and residential workers require full information about the children's histories prior to placement. This should, if possible, include details about: the abuse, such as the time of day and circumstances in which it took place; the age, gender and identity of the perpetrator; the child's age when it started and stopped; how the abuser gained compliance and silenced the child; and whether sibling sexual activity, other abusing behaviour or prostitution have been evident (McFadden, 1986; Macaskill, 1991; Farmer and Pollock, 1998). Such information would help carers to make plans to protect all the children in their care, to understand how children's behaviour in placement might link with their past experiences, and to avoid situations which replicate the context of the original abuse. It would also assist in gauging the children's need for counselling or other specialist help, and in more carefully planning and monitoring contact arrangements with siblings and other family members. Over and above this, caregivers need enhanced levels of support and training, and ready access to specialist consultation in order to manage children with such high levels of exploitation and disruption in their backgrounds.

References

Berridge D and Cleaver H (1987) *Foster Home Breakdown*, Oxford: Blackwell.

Davis E, McKay B, McStae L, Pringle K and Scott S (1991) 'Fostering young people who have been sexually abused', in Batty D (ed) *Sexually Abused Children: Making their placements work*, London: BAAF.

Dunn J (1984) *Sisters and Brothers*, London: Fontana.

Elgar M and Head A (1997) *From Court Process to Care Plan: An empirical study of the placement of sexually abused children*, Oxford: The Centre for Socio-Legal Studies, Wolfson College, Oxford University.

Farmer E and Parker R (1991) *Trials and Tribulations: Returning children from local authority care to their families*, London: HMSO.

Farmer E and Pollock S (1998) *Sexually Abused and Abusing Children in Substitute Care*, Chichester: John Wiley & Sons.

Fratter J, Rowe J, Sapsford D and Thoburn J (1991) *Permanent Family Placement: A decade of experience*, London: BAAF.

Hindle D (1995) 'Thinking about siblings who are fostered', *Adoption & Fostering*, 19:1, pp 14–20.

Jones E and Parkinson P (1995) 'Child sexual abuse, access and the wishes of children', *International Journal of Law and the Family*, 9:1, pp 54–85.

Kosonen M (1994) 'Sibling relationships for children in the care system', *Adoption & Fostering*, 18:3, pp 30–35.

Macaskill C (1991) *Adopting or Fostering a Sexually Abused Child*, London: Batsford.

Martin G (1993) 'Foster care: the protection and training of carers' children', *Child Abuse Review*, 2:1, pp 15–22.

McFadden E J (1987) 'The sexually abused child in specialised foster care'. Paper presented at the First North American Conference on Treatment Foster Care, Minneapolis, Minnesota, USA.

McFadden E J and Ryan P (1986) 'Characteristics of the vulnerable child'. Paper presented at the Sixth International Conference on Child Abuse and Neglect, Sydney, Australia.

McFadden E J and Stovall B (1984) 'Child sexual abuse in family foster care', *Preventing Abuse in Foster Care*, Ypsilanti, MI: Eastern Michigan University.

McFadden E J, Ziefert M and Stovall B (1984) *Preventing Abuse in Family Foster Care, Instructor's Manual*, Institute for the Study of Children and Families, Ypsilanti, MI: Eastern Michigan University.

Monck E and New M (1996) *Report of a Study of Sexually Abused Children and Adolescents and of Young Perpetrators of Sexual Abuse who were Treated in Voluntary Agency Community Facilities*, London: HMSO.

National Children's Home (1992) *The Report of the Committee of Enquiry into Children and Young People who Sexually Abuse Other Children*, London: National Children's Home.

Nobbs K and Jones B (1989) 'Tread with care: fostering sexually abused children', in *After Abuse: Papers on caring and planning for a child who has been sexually abused*, London: BAAF.

Shaw I, Butler I, Crowley A and Patel G (1996) *Paying the Price? Young people and prostitution*, Cardiff School of Social and Administrative Studies, University of Wales.

Smith G (1995) *The Protector's Handbook: Reducing the risk of child sexual abuse and helping children recover*, London: The Women's Press.

Smith G (1995a) 'Do children have the right to leave their past behind them? Contact with children who have been abused', in Argent H (ed) *See You Soon: Contact with looked after children*, London: BAAF.

Smith G (1996) 'Brotherly love: ambiguities of peer abuse'. Paper presented to the Learning to Change Conference, Barnardo's, March.

Wedge P and Mantle G (1991) *Sibling Groups and Social Work: A study of children referred for permanent substitute family placement*, Aldershot: Avebury.

18 Sibling relationships in families adopting a child with Down's Syndrome

Peter Selman and *Kathy Mason*

Peter Selman is Senior Lecturer in Social Policy at the University of Newcastle upon Tyne. He has worked directly with adoptive parents in a local authority Children's Department and was for many years on the Case Committee of the Northern Counties Adoption Society. He is Chair of the Network for Intercountry Adoption and author of a number of articles and book chapters on various aspects of adoption.

Kathy Mason has worked on a number of research projects on adoption carried out by the Department of Social Policy at Newcastle University. She was responsible for all the interviews with the families adopting children with Down's Syndrome in the study represented here. She has recently been awarded an ESRC studentship for a doctoral study on families who have adopted from abroad.

The authors share teaching on a module entitled 'Adoption: a worldwide perspective', which is offered to honours students on the degree courses in Social Policy and Social Studies at the University of Newcastle upon Tyne.

Introduction

One of the most striking achievements of the permanency principle in child adoption has been the recognition that many children with "special needs" can be successfully placed in new families (Macaskill, 1988; Argent, 1998). Within this broad category there has been considerable success in the placement of children with learning difficulties and, in particular, those with Down's Syndrome.

We have reported elsewhere (Mason *et al*, 1998) on the third stage of a longitudinal study of children with Down's Syndrome placed for adoption by Barnardo's North East. In this chapter, we look in detail at the sibling relationships in these families in the context of the wider literature on children with Down's Syndrome (Gath, 1978; Carr, 1995).

The third stage of the research took place in 1997, when the children were aged 12 to 16, and consisted of intensive interviews with ten families. All had adopted a child with Down's Syndrome in the 1980s and, in each case, this was their first adopted child. Subsequently, six of the families had adopted at least one more Down's child, and a further two families had adopted or fostered other special needs children. This provided a unique opportunity to look at sibling interaction between children with Down's Syndrome since most studies of non-adopted Down's children have been able to consider only interaction with other non-disabled birth children, given the rarity of birth families with more than one child with Down's Syndrome.

Five of the families also had birth children, so that it was also possible to look at relationships with non-disabled birth children and, in one case, to examine relations in a family with two adopted children with Down's Syndrome and three (older) birth children. The family structure of the ten families is described in detail in the next section.

Family structure

When the children in the study sample (i.e. the first Down's child placed in each family) were placed for adoption, all the couples were married but, between the second and third stages of the research (in 1990 and 1997), two of the fathers had left the marital home and were no longer living with the family, although one maintained regular contact with the study child.

None of the children was being raised as an only child, i.e. all were in households with other children present. There were six families who, since adopting the study child, had adopted further children with Down's Syndrome and four families who had adopted or fostered other special needs children. Two of the families who had adopted additional children with Down's Syndrome had experienced the death of one of them.

Five of the ten families had birth children, either from the present marriage or from a previous marriage. Table 1 gives a summary of sibling relationships within each family.

Table 1

Family composition: number and kind of siblings in families with an adopted child with Down's Syndrome

Study child	Study family										Total sibs
	1	2	3	4	5	6	7	8	9	10	
Siblings											
Adopted Down's child (living)	1		1	2	1			1	1		7
Adopted Down's child (deceased)				1	1						2
Other adopted special needs children	1	2						1	1		5
Foster children	•					1			1		2
Birth children (present marriage)				3	3	3	1				10
Birth children (previous marriages)		7			2						9
Total siblings	2	9	1	3	5	5	4	2	2	2	35
Total children (inc. study child)	3	10	2	4	6	6	5	3	3	3	45

In summary, there were:

- two families with a single adopted child with Down's Syndrome, birth siblings and other non-birth children;
- one family with a single adopted child with Down's Syndrome and birth siblings from the current and previous marriage;
- one family with a single adopted child with Down's Syndrome and two other non-birth children;
- two families with two adopted children with Down's Syndrome and at least one birth child;
- two families with two adopted children with Down's Syndrome and another adopted special needs child;
- two families with two or more adopted children with Down's Syndrome but no birth children.

With this range of structures and the small numbers involved, it is impossible to generalise about the nature of relationships, but we have a unique opportunity to look at the complexity of sibling relationships created around the adoption of children with Down's Syndrome.

Sibling patterns in families adopting children with Down's Syndrome

The description of the family structures in Table 1 covers all siblings (including half-siblings) whether or not they were resident in the family home. The largest group of co-resident siblings, at the time of the study, was five.

In all the adoptive families we can identify a series of changing patterns of residency as birth children grow older, i.e. as they go to college, get jobs, get married, or as other children join the family, whether by adoption, fostering or birth. Therefore, the structure today is quite different from that when the child with Down's Syndrome first joined the family.

However, even if we focus on the present co-resident siblings, there are some very complex patterns. In all cases the study child was the youngest in the family at the time of the adoption, but in only two cases have they remained the youngest child. In one of these cases, a foster child joined the family but was two years older than the adopted child. In the other case, the family had two older boys, one of whom they had adopted and the other fostered (these are birth siblings). The elder of these two boys has never resided with the family since the adoption of the child with Down's Syndrome but the younger one continues to live with the family.

One family at the time of interview had three birth children of the present marriage living at home (all girls aged between 13 and 21 years), as well as the study child aged 14 years. However, there were also two birth children from a previous marriage (mother's), both of whom lived at home when K was first adopted. The youngest child of the present marriage was born after the adoption and was only 13 months younger than the adopted Down's child, the mother having become pregnant the very month K joined the family. Fortunately, the birth child was much quicker at learning and more able to care for herself, but nevertheless the mother commented that, 'It was like having twins! Because K didn't walk until she was two-and-a-half but L [the birth child] was walking at ten months'.

In one family, both the parents had children from previous marriages but no birth children from the present marriage. The adoptive father had two children from his first marriage and there was contact with these children. The adoptive mother had five children from her previous marriage, all of whom were raised by her and the step-father. However, only the mother's youngest daughter was living at home at the time of the research, although the others often visited. Along with the 16-year-old adopted child with Down's Syndrome, they had also adopted a brother and sister who both had special needs. At the time of the research, the boy was aged six and the girl nine. Both had originally been placed with foster carers because the severe learning disabilities of their birth parents meant they were unable to care adequately for the children. However, abuse by the foster carers was suspected and tests are presently being undertaken to assess whether the children's physical and mental disabilities were a result of this abuse or whether the problems are inherited. The girl's disabilities, both physical and mental, are quite severe but the younger boy has only mild learning disabilities.

Sibling relationships between adopted children with Down's Syndrome

Six of the ten families included more than one child with Down's Syndrome. Two of these had adopted another Down's child who had subsequently died.

Differences between siblings with Down's Syndrome

Several of the families commented on differences between siblings with Down's Syndrome, with one emphasising that each of their children seemed very different and that having Down's Syndrome was only one part of their make-up. It was also noted by some of these families that the second child had greater health problems – two families had experienced the death of such a child – but the main comments made were in respect of differences in temperament.

The parents of S (a boy aged 13 years) commented that he was totally different from his younger adopted sister who also had Down's Syndrome. He was older and larger, very sociable, the one who always seemed to get caught doing anything wrong, whereas his sister was slim-built, generally more confident, and, in the words of the parents, 'crafty and cunning'. However, both showed similar caution about mixing with strangers.

A family with three children with Down's Syndrome commented that, while they got on very well together, each was very different. One was active and outgoing, another quiet and slower; one enjoyed going for walks, another did not; one would go off with anyone, another was more cautious and never wandered.

The parents of two adopted boys with Down's Syndrome noted that the brothers played well together because they seemed to have complementary skills; the youngest (in quite poor health) was an organiser, whereas his older brother was a 'big macho protector'.

As a final illustration of personality differences, one family gave a number of examples of ways in which their two adopted daughters differed: R would cry if told off but her sister would 'stare you out, storm out and always have the last word'; R 'is a slowcoach and needs chivvying along', where her sister would swear (a habit she had 'picked up at school' – something also noted by other families) and R would chastise her by saying 'That's naughty'. Their parents suggested that R "tolerates" her sister and has taken on the role of "moral police" in matters such as the above-mentioned swearing, or in the monitoring of punishments where she would remind her parents of what they had previously said they would do.

Relationships between adopted siblings with Down's Syndrome

In the six families who had adopted more than one child with Down's Syndrome, relationships were reported as being very good. In only one case was there any reported jealousy. A second adopted but older boy with Down's Syndrome was said to be very jealous of his sister but this had not caused any particular problems. However, their mother was a little concerned about the suggestion that the two be put in the same class at school because she felt that, 'in the same class [they] would definitely fight like mad', despite having no such problems at home.

One set of parents did comment that there was a degree of sibling rivalry between their two children, where the brother and sister 'fight like cat and dog'. However, the pair were left to sort things out for themselves, which they usually did without interference from their parents. Their mother also noted how both children were very protective towards each other, and that the younger sister had really missed her brother when he had been away on a school trip and was quite concerned about when he was going to be back.

Several other parents commented about degrees of protectiveness that the children displayed towards their siblings, or ways in which brothers and sisters helped and supported each other. One brother often interpreted for his younger sister because his speech was much clearer than hers.

Occasionally, relationships of mutual influence became worrying. One adoptive father referred to an occasion when their daughter had kissed a boy on the school bus. He had seen this as a 'natural part of growing up', but voiced concern when all three of their adopted Down's children 'got into huddles and started kissing', and both parents were very aware that they needed to keep an eye on the situation.

Overall, there seemed to be no evidence of major problems between the adopted children with Down's Syndrome, and most parents who had adopted a second or third Down's child felt very positive about this (Glidden, 1990). Certainly, there was no evidence that multiple placements made the families mini-institutions (Sinclair, 1985), and much to suggest that the presence of a sibling with similar appearance and difficulties could be reassuring.

Families with children with other special needs

Five families had either adopted or fostered children with other special needs. This presented rather different problems which involved practical issues such as transport. For example, one family commented that they looked like 'homecare on wheels' whenever they went out anywhere because one of their daughters was in a wheelchair and another needed breathing equipment to be available at all times.

A further problem can be balancing the very different needs of each of the children. One family was concerned when M's younger sister (with special needs) was going to start attending the same youth group he went to because they felt it would be intruding on his 'special time'. They were concerned to maintain this special time because there were several children in the family and the parents were therefore trying to organise a regular night out for him by himself. This was being done in conjunction with an agency that organised befriending services. M was very protective towards his adopted sister, aged nine, but clashed with his adopted brother who was ten years younger than himself and shared a bedroom with him, although he was always protective towards him against other people.

There was only one family that experienced serious problems when the child with Down's Syndrome joined them. This family already had living with them two biologically related brothers, the elder of whom they fostered and the younger whom they had adopted. In this case the older, fostered child, "flipped" and threatened to kill the child with Down's Syndrome. This brother was, at the time, living in a home for children with mental health problems but his visits home were stopped. However, over time, his curiosity got the better of him and he now has a good relationship with G. Although he never returned home on a permanent basis he visits regularly and now brings with him his own new baby. The younger adopted brother was fine and has always got along well with the child with Down's. The two birth siblings always got on well together – the elder being very protective toward the younger.

Relationships of Down's children with their own birth families

Most of the research children had been adopted at a young age from foster families where they had been placed shortly after birth. They had, therefore, had little or no contact with any other children of their birth mother. After the adoption there had been no further contact with their birth parents or any siblings born at a later stage. Only five of the adoptive parents had told the children they were adopted (Mason et al, 1999) but in one of the families where the adopted Down's child did not know he was adopted, the issue of awareness of adoption was raised when a brother and sister with special needs were adopted at a later stage. These two children were aware they had another mother and father and had photographs of them, but they referred to them by their Christian names rather than as "Mummy" and "Daddy" . The child with Down's Syndrome had never questioned where his younger brother and sister came from when they joined the family and the situation did not seem to have caused any confusion for the children, but it did highlight the problem of a lack of awareness of origins and the absence of potential contact with (or even knowledge of) any birth siblings.

Sibling relationships between birth and adopted children

Five of the parents had birth children (two from previous marriages) as well as their adopted child(ren) with Down's Syndrome. In most cases, the birth children were older and had been in the family when the adoption took place in the 1980s. Some of these older siblings had left home but, in all cases, there was still at least one birth child living at home and, in two of the families, the children had been born after the adoption and so were younger than the study child.

Interaction with birth siblings

Although there has been little specific research on siblings of children with Down's (Nadel and Rosenthal, 1995), most studies have found harmonious relations (Byrne *et al*, 1988; Carr, 1995). Fewer concerns have been raised than about the impact of birth siblings on adopted children in general (Beckett, 1998; Howe, 1998).

In one of the families with a younger biological child, there was a ten-year age difference, but this did not seem to have caused any problems for either child. The elder child with Down's Syndrome liked to be helpful and would make toast and get drinks for his younger sibling, while the young brother liked to sit on J's knee if there was no adult around. In the other family with a younger birth sibling, the situation was different because the age difference was small and the roles were reversed, with the birth sibling taking on the supporting/protective role towards her older sister with Down's Syndrome.

Where there were older birth children, they had often provided a role model for the younger adopted sibling with Down's Syndrome. One boy was determined to follow in his sisters' footsteps by changing schools at the same age as they did. The family was finding it difficult to convince him that he had to stay at the school he presently attended until he was at least 16 and preferably until he was 18.

Another family noted how their child with Down's Syndrome 'sees how her older siblings help and react to things and she tries to do that with younger children'. This was offered as an explanation for their daughter's leadership qualities at school and for her receiving a certificate for being 'the most considerate child' in her class. This certificate is proudly displayed on the living room wall.

In our sample, no families reported any jealousy being directed from the birth children towards the siblings with Down's Syndrome, nor had they been resentful of extra attention they might possibly have had. However, most parents stressed that they had not felt a need to treat the Down's child(ren) differently: 'I just thought, "well, they are children". I haven't brought M up any different from the way I brought the girls up.'

Having older birth daughters had both negative and positive aspects. In two families, older birth children had married and given birth which had helped the child with Down's Syndrome understand certain aspects of sex education. One boy loved to hold, feed and wind his sister's baby. However, one family noted that there had been occasion for concern when their son with Down's Syndrome used to walk into his sisters' bedroom. It had taken about four months for them to get him to knock before entering. This has since become a source of amusement for the family because he now demands that everyone knock before entering his bedroom – a request they all respect and honour.

It was suggested by one family that the chronological position of their adopted son in the family (youngest) meant he got on better with bigger/older people. This child had a good relationship will all the birth children and with his foster sister; sometimes he was the only one who did get on with her because he ignored her attention-seeking behaviour. These feelings were mutual with the foster sister being very fond of J – she was described as a 'parental child' and the mother thought that J filled a (caring) gap in his sister's life where she tried to "mother" him.

Support from older birth children

As the birth siblings grew older – and, often, even after they had left home – the chronological gap became more evident, their relationships changed, and they became more of a source of support.

Two families illustrate this transition very well. One mother noted how all five siblings, birth and adoptive, would play together when they were young but, as the birth daughters were getting older, she was finding they were not as supportive as they had been in the past because they 'have their lives to live'. She was quite happy with this because, if there was an appointment, for example, they could still be relied on to be there and would 'drop everything' in an emergency.

The second family had found that, despite all but one of their birth children leaving home, they had continued to be supportive. For example, one of their sons often took all three adopted children to his home for the weekend. In fact, the parents thought that, if there were to be a problem in the future, it would be deciding which one of them got to care for the adopted child with Down's Syndrome and the two adopted special needs children.

Another family recently felt confident enough about their teenage children's ability to care for their adopted son to go away for a weekend, leaving all the children behind at home. These same siblings have always cared for J after school until their mother gets home from work and she commented that, 'Sometimes I wonder if J thinks he has grown up with two sets of parents'.

L (a 13-year-old birth child) now acted as an interpreter for K, who was a year older, and has always been able to understand her. One of the two older birth siblings used to take K to a drama group but when she went to college this stopped. In the past, all four siblings had gone to the same church summer camp, where the older daughters had been able to keep an eye on K. This year, only the youngest one was going but the family was confident that she and K would both cope. All the families were confident there would be long-term support from their older birth children in the future.

Summary

There was little evidence of resentment of the adopted child by birth siblings and, in most cases, the older siblings had obvious affection for the child with Down's Syndrome, saw them as part of the family, and offered active support (Nadel and Rosenthal, 1995). The Down's children, in turn, related well to the birth children of their families and clearly benefited from their friendship and support. Parents with mixed families pointed out the advantages in this for both birth and adopted children, and especially in the availability of a "normal" role model for the Down's child as he or she grew up.

Conclusions

Families adopting children with Down's Syndrome afford the opportunity to explore two unique types of sibling relationships – those *between* children with Down's Syndrome (who are usually the only one in a birth family but may be placed together in an adoptive family) and those between adopted Down's children and birth siblings in the family. Both situations arose in the families we studied, and five also included at least one adopted or fostered child with other special needs.

Where parents had chosen to adopt more than one child with Down's Syndrome, there was no evidence of any additional problems and many reported advantages for the children in growing up with a sibling with similar appearance and difficulties. Birth children had good relationships with the adopted child(ren) and were often important as a source of support and in providing role models.

The recognised success of the adoption of children with Down's Syndrome was not diminished by multiple placements or by the presence of birth children, but the nature of sibling relationships was constantly changing as children grew up. The next stage of this study will afford an opportunity to explore how these relationships survive into early adulthood, when the children are likely to continue to live in their adoptive families, but birth siblings may gradually be leaving home. We also hope to explore more about the personal qualities of the families or other factors which affect the success of these placements, including the parents' ability to cope with the complex sibling relationships which we have been describing.

References

Argent H (1998) *Whatever Happened to Adam? Stories of disabled people who were adopted or fostered,* London: BAAF.

Beckett C, Groothues C and O'Connor T G (1998) 'Adopting from Romania: the role of siblings in adjustment', *Adoption & Fostering,* 22:2, pp 25–34.

Byrne E, Cunningham C and Sloper P (1988) *Families and their Children with Down's Syndrome,* London: Routledge.

Carr J (1995) *Down's Syndrome: Children growing up,* Cambridge: Cambridge University Press.

Gath A (1978) *Down's Syndrome and the Family: The early years,* New York: Academic Press.

Glidden L M (1985) 'Adopting mentally handicapped children: family characteristics', *Adoption & Fostering,* 9:3, pp 53–56.

Glidden L M (1990) *The Wanted Ones: Families adopting children with mental retardation,* Binghampton, New York: Haworth Press.

Howe D (1998) *Patterns of Adoption,* Oxford: Blackwell.

Macaskill C (1988) ' "It's a bonus" – families' experiences of adopting children with disabilities', *Adoption & Fostering,* 12:2, pp 24–28.

Mason K, Hughes M and Selman P (1998) *Adopting a Child with Down's Syndrome: Stage three of a longitudinal study,* Barkingside: Barnardo's Policy, Planning and Research Unit.

Mason K, Selman P and Hughes M (1999) 'Permanency planning for children with Down's Syndrome: the adolescent years', *Adoption & Fostering,* 23:1, pp 31–39.

Nadel L and Rosenthal D (eds) (1995) *Down's Syndrome: Living and learning in the community,* New York: Wiley-Liss.

Sinclair L (1985) 'Multiple placements of mentally handicapped children', *Adoption & Fostering,* 9:4, pp 37–40.

19 Single adopters and sibling groups

Morag Owen

Morag Owen is a Research Fellow in the School of Cultural and Community Studies at the University of Sussex. During the last ten years she has worked on several research studies concerned with child care and child protection. Her most recent work is 'Novices, Old Hands and Professionals: A study of adoption by single people', published by BAAF in January 1999.

To many people who have witnessed the moral and political maelstrom surrounding single parenthood in the last ten years, it may seem strange that single people are allowed to become adoptive parents. It is true that single adopters, unlike most other single parents, are carefully selected for the task, and this may help to deflect some criticisms; but single people risk even more opprobrium if they adopt more than once. To some traditionally minded people, the adoption of more than one damaged or disabled child by a single person might seem like folly or an excess of virtue.

Not surprisingly, in view of their prevalence, these views have been held at various times and with varying degrees of conviction by single adopters themselves. The research which underpins this chapter was a study of single-person adoption undertaken between 1993 and 1995 with funding from the Department of Health (Owen, 1999). The sample consisted of 30 adopters (28 women and two men) who had been approved by one of three voluntary adoption agencies during the last ten years. File studies were conducted, and interviews were held with all the adopters and with 21 children over the age of six. Since many of the single people had made further applications to the agencies because they wanted their adopted children to have brothers and sisters, the total number of children adopted or placed for adoption was 48.

The research showed that all the placements were surviving and some were highly successful, but a surprising number of people – more than half the adult sample – had been attracted to the notion of adopting one or more children for some time without realising that it was an option which was available to them. Alternatively they had not had enough courage to pursue it. (This applied particularly to black adoptive parents, of whom there were 11 in the study.) One adoptive parent of African-Caribbean origin said that she had been thinking about re-applying on and off for ten years. Another white woman who adopted three children in succession said that when she first heard of single-person adoption she thought it was 'a daft idea'. Similarly, one of the two male adopters had been interested enough to 'cut something out of a newspaper' some years previously, but he felt that he could not apply because 'it was not the done thing'.

Official policy in the UK, as in the rest of Europe, tends to support the notion that, in the approval of adoptive parents, married couples are to be preferred. In spite of some positive North American research on single-person adoption (Feigelman and Silverman, 1977; Shireman and Johnson, 1985; Groze and Rosenthal, 1991), the government White Paper *Adoption: The future* (Department of Health and Welsh Office, 1993) suggested that 'particularly careful matching' would be necessary when children were linked with a single adopter. However, single carers in the UK have not always had such a bad press.

Far from being a radical or modern innovation, the provision for single people to adopt has existed since the first legislation in 1926. In the wake of the First World War, "spinster adopters" were seen to be doing a valuable job in caring for bereaved, abandoned or seriously neglected children. Between the Wars, too, the English upper classes were still heavily dependent on the child care skills of single women employed as nannies and governesses, and the assumption was that such women would be able to care for more than one child at a time. Adopters with a sense of history can explore the many images thrown up by the past (Anderson, 1990; Parker, 1990; Ungerson, 1990) and draw strength as well as understanding from them.

The single adopters and their children

Although widely scattered geographically and heterogeneous in background and experience, single adopters might be considered to be a small, select group. The study showed that even in agencies which were sympathetic to applications by single people, they accounted for little more than ten per cent of those approved for adoption, and recent figures suggest that the approval rate in local authorities may be even less than this (Dance, 1997). This says a great deal about the social and professional context in which "careful matching" has taken place.

The single people in the research study wanted to be mothers or fathers, but, for various reasons which included divorce, desertion and deliberate choice, they had no partner. (Single adopters who were cohabiting were excluded from the research, since they might be considered to have a *de facto* marriage.) Because of the caring roles traditionally attributed to mothers, it is hardly surprising to find that most of them were women. A high proportion (slightly more than half the sample) also had professional backgrounds in health, education or social care. In spite of the fact that all the women had good family and friendship networks, they felt that they had often been seen as disadvantaged because they had no male partner. Male adopters, on the other hand, were made to feel equally disadvantaged when their caring skills were denied because of stereotypical views about gender roles.

All of the single applicants chose to adopt one child in the first instance. They were invariably linked with a child who was classified as having special needs. Forty-six per cent of the children in the study had been placed as older children, their average age at placement being eight years, and many of these children had experienced an unusual degree of pre-placement adversity which included abuse and neglect. Another 21 per cent had a learning or physical disability, and the other 33 per cent were black children or children of mixed parentage who were placed mainly for cultural reasons.

Extending the family by further adoptions

The single adopters had enormous commitment, and once the first children had settled, there was a tendency for further applications to be submitted. Out of the 30 adopters in the study, there were 12 who had adopted more than one child, and another seven who expressed a wish to adopt again when their present child was older. Some of those who had already adopted twice also said they would like to adopt again for a third or fourth time.

The result was that, in addition to living with their single adoptive parents, 65 per cent of the children in the study lived in households where there was at least one other adopted child. When resident non-adopted siblings are added, this proportion rises to 70 per cent, but the relationships with adopted siblings clearly had a special importance because the children in these households could feel that there was someone else in the same position as themselves. Most adoptions were consecutive and only two parents received sibling pairs; but the people who were contemplating further applications did not rule out existing sibling groups and in some cases said that they would actively welcome them.

In contemplating further adoptions, the single carers were concerned to meet their own and their adoptive children's needs by creating what they considered to be a normal family. The idea of joint sibling place-ments had an immediate appeal, not simply because of the natural link between the children but because it enabled the adopters to reach their targeted family size as quickly as possible. The approval process had often been experienced as harrowing and long drawn-out – especially by women who were already over the age of 40 and felt that their biological clock was ticking at an accelerating rate.

Financial support is clearly needed, not simply for single parents but for all adopters of special-needs children (Hill *et al*, 1989), and economic factors could play a part in decisions. For three single women, withdrawal from work became financially feasible when a decision was made to adopt for the third time, because it was at this point that the cumulative supply of adoption allowances and other benefits began to replace existing salary. A more important factor, however, was the value placed on sibling relationships both by the children and by the adopters. The children had often left behind siblings in the birth family and, being conscious of their absence, they sometimes asked to have a younger adopted brother or sister. For most of the adoptive parents, positive relationships with brothers and sisters were part of their childhood experience and therefore part of the emotional heritage they were bringing to the adoption – in addition to which, the continuing support of these relatives in an aunt/uncle role was important both for the new parents and for the adopted children. For all these reasons it was seen as important that the adopted children should have siblings as well.

Surprisingly, there were hardly any parents who suggested that they would not adopt again because the one-to-one relationship between themselves and their child was too fragile or important to be put at risk. The people who came nearest to it were three who said that further adoption would be against the interests of the present child who was very demanding of their attention. Most parents regarded the presence of another child as an unmitigated benefit, as long as they had the personal resources to cope with the extra work involved.

This throws a new light on the notion of "one-to-one relationship" which was often used on official forms as a justification for single-person adoption. The adopters valued the relationship with their child but they did not regard it as being in any way exclusive, and it was certainly not compromised by the arrival of another child, although most people felt that it would be compromised by the arrival of a partner.

Sibling relationships in the adoptive family

Only nine out of the 30 adopters had had their own children. These children were usually grown-up and independent or on the point of leaving home. The age gap is probably significant because there was a notable absence of conflict between them and the adoptees and, in the accounts which were given by parents and children, these older non-adopted siblings served variously as adult role models, protectors, advocates and companions for the adopted child. Where all the children in the household had adoptive status they were closer in age, but, either by accident or design, the structure of the adoptive households confirmed the research-based principle that the placed child should be younger than any new step-sibling by at least three years (Wedge and Mantle, 1991).

Relationships between adoptees were aided by the fact that adolescent and pre-adolescent children were regularly given a "voice" when it came to choosing a second child, and, in at least one case, the child was given the right to veto the proposal. The adoptive parent said:

In some ways it sounds as though I was placing a lot of emphasis on Gina not liking her [the proposed second child]. But it was important, because you have to make them gel.

Intensity of relationship has been noted as one of the features of single-person adoption. It was not unusual to find a strong alliance between the parent and the first child at the time when a second placement was undertaken, and it took time for the second child or children to be integrated. Naturally enough, the children placed together in sibling pairs formed a unit and they clung together for support. (They had usually been placed together for that very reason.) This meant that the first child tended to ally himself or herself even more clearly with the adoptive parent. However, as the adoptions progressed these tensions decreased. The occasional negotiation of conflict was treated as part of the normal experience of living in a family, and it provided valuable training in social skills.

The value of good preparation is illustrated by one nine-year-old girl, Joanna, whose adoptive mother decided to adopt a second child who was developmentally delayed. Joanna looked forward to her new brother's arrival, but he responded to her advances by pinching and biting. The single adopter in this case had nursery school experience, and the child's account of her mother's explanation was as follows:

She told me that he was very young. He's three, but in his brain he's younger. He doesn't know it hurts, and he's trying to show us how he feels 'cos he can't talk.

As well as explanations, she had been given some advice from her mother about how to deal with the incidents of pinching and biting. Her account continues:

When he's calm you give him hugs and play with him, but when he's excited you don't really give him lots of hugs. You can cuddle him a bit later, when he's stopped being excited.

257

The adopters often worried that children who had suffered sexual or physical abuse would show signs of disturbance when there was a second placement, because the new children's arrival was likely to remind them of unpleasant experiences. On the whole these worries were unjustified. The children who had been placed first were of course upset by revelations of abuse which resembled what they had suffered; but they were usually sympathetic when they recognised in another child the trauma of experiences similar to their own.

Contact with siblings in the birth family

For most of the adopters, the term "sibling group" referred first and foremost to the constellation of children in the adoptive family. However, links with the birth family were also seen as important and considerable efforts were made to sustain the contact arrangements which had been set up at the time of the placement.

Sixteen children in the study (one-third of the sample) had face-to-face contact with one or more members of the birth family. In 13 of these 16 cases, there was interaction with at least one birth sibling. Usually the child saw more than one – for example, two brothers, or a brother and a sister. There was some contact with other relatives in addition; but, in most of the cases in the study, children and young people carried the main brunt of the liaison between the different families. The reverberations of this notion are quite considerable.

There seemed to be two main situations in which face-to-face contact with siblings and other relatives took place. Firstly, there were six cases where the adopted child saw one or more relatives in the presence of the birth parent. In these cases the contact with other relatives was secondary to the contact with the natural parent, and it sometimes had a lower priority. In eight other cases contact with a sibling or grandparent was arranged in its own right.

Meetings with birth siblings as an adjunct to parental contact

Where the adoption was very "open", it was not unusual to find that family access meetings were attended by a number of relatives. The families in these cases were very supportive of the adoption.

One adopter who had regular meetings with the birth family gave this account of the contact visits which were arranged at a local access centre.

There are usually about 12 people there. Family, friends, neigh-bours . . . You never know what to expect, because they bring all sorts of people along to see him [the adopted child]. It's a big family day out for them, bless them.

When commenting on the relationships in the above case, the adopter said that the child preferred to spend the access time playing with his brother and his older sister. This same pattern was reported by other adopters. For example, a woman with two teenage daughters said of one of them: 'She goes back to see Andy and Maureen [her brother and sister], not to see her Mum.'

In some but not all of these cases it does seem as though the sibling contact was of more value to the child than the adult contact. Allowance must be made for the feelings of the adoptive parents, who may have preferred this interpretation of events because they felt threatened by the presence of the birth parents. However, there is also support for the same viewpoint in the children's interviews. Ten-year-old Jerry, for example, said that he would like to see his brothers more often and that he was especially pleased to discover that his sister was expecting a baby, as he looked forward to becoming an uncle. It was frustrating for him to be limited to twice-yearly visits to his siblings. He knew that his birth family was not allowed to come to his present address, but he did not really understand why.

Contact with birth siblings in their own right

There were eight cases of face-to-face contact which did not include visits to or by the natural parents. Five involved access to siblings only, and in one other case the child had access only to a grandparent. In the remaining two cases, both siblings and grandparents were included in access arrangements.

Apart from the single adopters' willingness to participate, there seem to have been a number of reasons why these particular family members were encouraged to stay in touch or resume contact with the adopted child, when contact with the birth parents had been discontinued.

Firstly, there were issues of attachment which were readily recognised by the adopters. Some relatives – and particularly older birth siblings – had fulfilled a parental role in relation to the child. In addition, some children and their siblings had been accommodated together in foster care or residential homes and they had clung together for support. As a result, they had a close bond and a continuing need to see each other, if only to verify that the other brothers and sisters were all right.

Secondly, there were child protection issues. In some cases where it was felt that face-to-face contact with the birth parent or parents was too dangerous to be allowed, sibling contact was seen as beneficial and the single adopters supported it. They were usually willing to keep contact with birth siblings even though, for some single women, the risk of physical violence from other members of the birth family was an ever-present worry.

There were, additionally, a few unusual cases in which family contact had been lost and sibling contact was seen as a way of recovering it. For example, in one case of sexual abuse to a young girl, the child had not only been separated from her father who was responsible for the incidents but from her mother and siblings as well. Both the social worker and the adoptive mother (who was herself a social worker) were keen to extend the girl's contact with the birth family, and reunion with one of the child's brothers was seen as a necessary and feasible first step.

For all these reasons, contact with siblings and sometimes grand-parents was encouraged. There were only a few situations which posed problems for the adopters. The first was where the siblings had not only been sexually abused by others but were suspected of having abused each other (see also Chapters 16 and 17, this volume). The second was where siblings had privileged access to other family members, which tempted them to seek power by spreading gossip and also made them feel superior to the adopted child. The third was where different contact arrangements were seen to be needed for two or more children who lived in the same adoptive family.

Whether or not the adopters had anxieties about face-to-face contact, the children who were interviewed usually valued this movement across the boundary between the adoptive family and the birth family and they wanted it to continue.

Another way of maintaining contact between birth siblings, in single-person adoption

In the requests which had been made to the voluntary family-finding agencies by local authorities to locate the placements, single adopters had rarely been sought directly. The file study revealed only one referral which had actively invited the names of single applicants to be brought forward as a first priority. This request represented a change of plan, since the original intention had been to place the members of a particular sibling group together in a two-parent family. The letter of referral says:

> When their Form Es were first completed in [date given] it was pre-sumed we would be seeking a family to take all three children together as a sibling group. However, after a further review held on [date six months later] we have decided to place the children individually with single parents.

The 'Form E' designed by BAAF (British Agencies for Adoption and Fostering) is of course the document which gives details of a child to be placed and makes recommendations for the type of placement. In the above case several parts of the form had been scored out, bearing witness to recent changes in direction. Under "family structure" the original entry read as follows:

> Two parents are necessary for this sibling group, and ideally they will be a mature couple who have already had parenting experience. Frank, Matt and Josie will require a great deal of energy, patience and nurturing.

It is interesting that this was deleted. What brought about the change in direction, so that one parent was eventually sought for each child rather than two for all? The recommendations appear to have been shaped, at least in part, by a sensitive assessment from the resource centre in which the children were living at the time. This report focused in detail on the individual needs of the children, and its author had clearly envisaged that their needs might be met by single adopters. In particular it was suggested that the girl, Josie, should be placed separately from her siblings, since she had an extreme need to form 'a deep and meaningful attachment to one person, perhaps with additional professional input'. At the same time, it was seen as important that she should keep in contact with her brothers when she was placed. The report concluded:

These very special needs could most suitably be met by a single, mature woman who has no other children, but who has a strong support system of her own to cope with the rejections she may face. I feel that the carer will need to have a central maternalistic drive, without traditional illusions about motherhood, in order to appreciate Josie's considerable strengths and potential.

It is a tribute to the success of the family-finding process that a single woman with exactly these qualities was found to parent Josie, and that one of the girl's siblings was adopted by another single parent in the study. (The eldest child lingered for a while in the residential home; but he too has now been moved to an adoptive placement.) Previously, in the birth family, these children had clung together for survival. They were seen as an undifferentiated group by their parents and by some of the people who had looked after them subsequently. Through separate placements with single people their individual needs have had a chance of being met, and, because of the adopters' sensitivity to the underlying family situation, an appropriate level of contact between the siblings has been maintained.

This is a fascinating case with a great many reverberations, many of which are concerned with the relationship between adoption and family structure. Apart from the single parent issue, it raises questions about how local authorities may best respond to the spirit of the law, when considering the requirement to place siblings together 'so far as is reasonably practical and consistent with their welfare' (Children Act 1989, section 23.7b). Fifteen years ago, Triseliotis commented on the need to keep sibling groups together and not to allow them to be divided on placement 'for sheer administrative convenience'; but he saw the preservation of the group as being more necessary in residential care than in adoption, because of the quality of nurturing available to the children, and he also maintained that the ill-effects of division could be alleviated if attempts were made to maintain the links between the siblings (Triseliotis and Russell, 1984). More recent research has explored the relationships between brothers and sisters in the care system in greater detail, and in general it supports the joint placement of siblings wherever possible; but suggestions have also been made that 'proactive ways of working with siblings should be developed by social work practitioners and carers', and that the focus of this work could be the children's separate experiences as well as those which are shared (Kosonen, 1994).

It is interesting to note that, in spite of the networking abilities of single people, single person adoption was not a first choice of the referring agency in the above case. In fact it was assumed that these children's needs would best be met by joint placement in a conventional family structure. It was only when the children's needs were disaggregated, without actually losing sight of the wider perspective, that the viability of single person adoption was understood.

The shift of view represented here is thought provoking; but, given what we know about the energy and commitment of single adopters, is it right that single people should have been automatically excluded when one family was being sought for the group?

Conclusions

Single people are a flexible resource, and the research described here uncovered a great variety of sibling or sibling-type relationships in the adoptive families. First, there were relationships between the original adoptees and younger children adopted either singly or in sibling pairs. These children were brothers and sisters in every respect except birth. Secondly, there were the relationships between adoptees and very much older children who were the natural children of the adoptive parents. These young adults formed part of the extended family network, especially in African–Caribbean families with strong community ties, and they maintained close links with the adoptive household. Thirdly, for roughly one-quarter of the children, there was contact with siblings in the birth family, maintaining significant links with the past. Fourthly, there was some planned contact with birth siblings in other adoptive households, uniting these families in a social network which in, an ideal situation, would be supportive to single parents and children alike.

Good outcomes were generally recorded for the children in the study. However, single adopters are not a particularly powerful group. We need to remember that most of them are women, and many of them are black. In our white and largely male-dominated society, it is not within these groups that the main power lies so recognition may be hard to win.

Historically, single women who wish to care for groups of children have done so by the professional route, seeking medical or educational qualifications which will give them status as well as expertise in order to parent the children of others. Single adopters are no exception to this pattern. It is not coincidental that so many of the women in the study had backgrounds in health, education or social care, or that they tried so hard to fulfil the demands of the professional agencies.

In recent years the priority given to psychological forms of assessment, and particularly to the development of attachment theory (Howe, 1995), has lent support to the applications of single people by diminishing the importance of family structure and shifting attention from the marital relationship to the relationship between parent and child. This can only be beneficial. Nevertheless, the single adopters in this study were happy to be assessed on their family structure in addition to personal factors. Women who lacked specifically professional skills showed that they were capable of parenting even quite difficult children with affection and sensitivity, and if access were given to less severely damaged children, it is possible that more single people could be approved for both singletons and sibling groups. However, this will not happen until the focus of assessment is firmly on caring skills and social supports, and single people are assessed and approved on the same basis as everyone else.

References

Anderson M (1990) 'The social implications of demographic change', Thompson F M L (ed) *The Cambridge Social History of Britain, Volume 2*, Cambridge: Cambridge University Press.

Dance C (1997) *Focus on Adoption: A snapshot of adoption patterns in England – 1995*, London: BAAF.

Department of Health and Welsh Office (1993) *Adoption: The future* (White Paper), London: HMSO.

Feigelman W and Silverman A R (1997) 'Single parent adoptions', *Social Casework*, 58, pp 418–25.

Groze V K and Rosenthal J A (1991) 'Single parents and their adopted children: a psychosocial analysis', *Families in Society: The Journal of Contemporary Human Services*, February, pp 67–77.

Hill M, Lambert L and Triseliotis J (1989) *Achieving Adoption with Love and Money*, London: National Children's Bureau.

Howe D (1995) *Attachment Theory for Social Work Practice*, Basingstoke: Macmillan.

Kosonen M (1994) 'Sibling relationships for children in the care system', *Adoption & Fostering*, 18:3, pp 30–35.

Owen M (1999) *Novices, Old Hands and Professionals: Adoption by single people*, London: BAAF.

Parker R (1990) *Away from Home: A history of child care*, London: Barnardo's.

Shireman J F and Johnson P R (1985) 'Single-parent adoptions: a longitudinal study', *The Children and Youth Services Review*, 7, pp 321–34.

Triseliotis J and Russell J (1984) *Hard to Place: The outcome of adoption and residential care*, London: Heinemann.

Ungerson C (ed) (1990) *Gender and Caring*, Hemel Hempstead: Harvester Wheatsheaf.

20 The residential home as serial step-family
Acknowledging quasi-sibling relationships in local authority residential care

Christine Horrocks and *Judith Milner*

Christine Horrocks has for the past two years been lecturing in psychology at the University of Huddersfield. She is currently writing up her PhD thesis on young people leaving care and life course trajectories. Her main research interests are social exclusion and self-belief and the use of biographical research methods.

Judith Milner is an occasional Lecturer in Social Work at the University of Huddersfield and a freelance solution-focused counsellor with the Northorpe Hall Trust project for young people who have experienced violence and adults who have suffered abuse in children's homes. She has recently completed work as a mentor for a children's home which lost staff following investigations into institutional abuse.

Residential child care has had its share of attention and serious criticism both in the past and the present and it would be naive to imagine that concerns raised will ever completely disappear. Nevertheless, residential child care is a key element serving an important function as part of a range of services for children and young people (Wagner, 1988; Department of Health, 1991a, 1991b). In this chapter, we intend to explore a topic which has been given very little consideration: the personal relationships which exist between young people living in the same residential community home. Our interest in this topic originates from two sources: a qualitative research project into the life course experiences of young people who had been "looked after" by the local authority and the practice experience of one of us working as a mentor to a reception unit and, later, a counsellor for young people who were experiencing difficulties which were grounded in current or recent experiences of being looked after. The existence of close relationships analogous to sibling relationships was an emergent sub-theme to the main body of work in both projects. The extent of these relationships only assumed significance when we brought our findings together. We will illustrate our contention that "quasi-sibling" relationships are a central, if neglected, issue in child care planning with examples from young people who participated in the research project or were resident in the reception unit. All names have been changed. The data from the counselling project were also found to support the thesis but we will not use these young people's words because of the impossibility of obtaining genuinely informed consent due to the nature of the power imbalance in the counsellor–client relationship.

Personal relations between staff and young people have been viewed as vital in terms of the well-being of the young person but Frones (1996) challenges the received notion that adults are the significant others as far as children are concerned, describing how peers are significant in the development of the capacity for friendship and socio-emotional relationships as well as serving as a correction to the self-image a child brings from its family. Similarly, friendship groups have the capacity to act as important sources of support and security at times of emotional need (Measor and Woods, 1984), becoming a sort of surrogate family (Brown, 1987), particularly where positive family relationships are absent (Sletta et al, 1996). There also exists considerable research evidence that an overdue emphasis on adult–child relationships, allied to a tendency in social work to view children's individual needs in relation to adults as the most important, has led to biological sibling separation with emotionally damaging results (Cousins, 1989; Rushton, 1989; McClean, 1991; Bilson and Barker, 1992; Hindle, 1995; Dobson, 1996). Kosonen (1994, 1996) found that these effects were long lasting as few of the separated children were found to have plans which included reunification with their siblings. Yet maintaining contact with siblings was considered more important than being reunited with parents by young people in the Sinclair study (1998). He found that young people leaving the care system would look for accommodation near enough to the parental home to promote contact with siblings but far enough away to maintain distance from parents. Therefore, the view that the adult–child relationship transcends all others is highly questionable and relationships with siblings and peers should be given serious recognition.

In this chapter, we aim to make more visible both the relationships that may exist between young people who are looked after and the potential outcomes of these relationships. Young people who are looked after often experience a range of placements but those who enter care in their mid-teens will frequently find themselves, at some point in their "care career", living in a residential community home. Therefore, it would seem logical to explore the dynamics within the residential home. Initially, we will consider the way in which conditions there might replicate the more conventional family unit, before moving on to examine in more detail the relationships which develop between young people and their implications for practice.

Does living in a residential community home mean being part of a family?

The Utting report (1991) emphasised the move from providing children simply with residence, to offering a place where children and young people could be cared for in much the same way as they would be in a loving family environment. Nevertheless, in the report there was the distinct recognition that the ideal of endless parental love and affection would be outside the capabilities of the corporate parent, though young people had a right to experience warmth and personal concern extending beyond the traditional expectations of institutions. What seems evident is a willingness to move towards some kind of compensatory family environment. Yet the term "family" is imbued with ambiguity and emotion. Families are represented as loving, caring and desirable for children, but the reality for young people who are looked after in residential care is that their experience of family life has often been very different. The Department of Health (1992) report, *Choosing with Care,* estimated that almost a third of young people in local authority residential homes had been sexually abused. This was felt to be probably a low estimate, with actual numbers being difficult to quantify. This disturbing revelation makes two important points: the first being that the idealist notion of family can be extremely misleading; the second point, and possibly a more relevant one in relation to this chapter, is the idea that the residential home provides a possible alternative/additional family – a "serial step-family". For a young person whose experience of family life has been a traumatic one, placement with another family may be highly undesirable. The following comments tell of this kind of dilemma and show residential care as a positive alternative:

> *I used to have trouble living with another family, after everything, so at that time community homes were better. I couldn't cope at the foster placement, they tried to make me one of their family.* (Jenny)

> *I don't want to be fostered. I don't think I can live with a family yet . . . not after what my family did to me. It [a foster placement] wouldn't be right for me yet.* (Rachel)

After disappointment, loss and separation, being placed within a conventional foster family may be the last thing needed or wanted. For some children and young people, an alternative approach to the notion of family, where the relationships they develop in the residential home are given serious thought, should be considered. The residential home may provide some space where young people can build relationships with others in similar positions which are beneficial and supportive, not only at the present time but possibly in the future.

However, "family" has conventionally referred to those we are related to through birth or marriage (Harris, 1990). Hill and Tisdall (1997) question the commonly made assumption about "nuclear family", which consists of parents and children and the "extended family" which usually includes grandparents, cousins and so on. They argue that this is an 'oversimplified picture', especially in the light of changes in social practices and household patterns, drawing attention to the changing social landscape where family relationships may be established through cohabitation, or children may be adopted, or their parents may have been involved in assisted reproduction, and thus one or both of their legal parents is/are not the biological parent. Family networks may be reconstituted through divorce and/or remarriage. For Hill and Tisdall, 'the idea of family is to some degree a fluid one, with a mix of concepts at its core–direct biological relatedness, the parental caring role, long-term cohabitation, permanent belonging' (p 66).

It is obvious that the concept of biological relatedness is not present for young people living in residential care – they are unrelated in that sense. However, this is the case too for many reconstituted families – as a consequence of divorce and remarriage for both partners there is the coming together of biologically unrelated individuals with the un-questioned acceptance that they are a family. If this is the case, maybe we should consider more carefully the coming together of young people in residential settings and whether there exists a sense of family for them also. Other core concepts of family referred to by Hill and Tisdall are arguably to be found in a residential community home. Residential workers take on a parental caring role. Indeed, the report, *Setting Quality Standards for Residential Child Care* (Central Council for Education and Training in Social Work, 1992, p 30), states that residential child care skills should include: undertaking the broadly educative functions of parenting, for example, helping children learn about their social world, about themselves in relation to others, and helping children to feel loved and genuinely cared for. It would be difficult to deny that, if a residential worker fulfils such laudable aims, they are taking on a parental caring role.

In relation to long-term cohabitation with other young people, it is well documented that those who are looked after experience considerable movement and disruption. However, for many young people, their arrival at the residential home may be the consequence of there being no other available placement. They arrive at the residential home in their mid- to late teens and often stay there until they leave to live independently (Sinclair, 1998). Their stay may be measured in months or years but, for those who have experienced one move after another, their stay at the residential home may indeed constitute, for them, long-term cohabita-tion.

The core concept of family which seems to provide the strongest argument for considering the dynamics within a residential community home as a kind of serial step-family is that of permanent belonging. What is it that enables us to gain an awareness of permanent belonging? Is belonging associated with biological relatedness, or care, or long-term close proximity, or might it be that all these core concepts of family are important ingredients but that, at the heart of permanent belonging, it is often a whole range of shared experiences which bind people together and foster a deep sense of belonging? Within families there is no need continually to describe, explain and justify past events. The past will always impinge on and construct the present but it is a shared past, and the knowledge of a shared past is something that, we would argue, also creates a sense of family belonging for young people in a residential home. Already referred to is the often shared experience of sexual abuse; in addition, many young people will have serious conflicts within and with their families and some young people will be experiencing serious difficulties at school. We are not suggesting that each young person will share the same biography; merely that the acceptance and understanding of adversity is akin to the shared past experienced within the more conventionally recognised family. John and Hayley's accounts, below, present not only the positive side of residential care which is often subsumed beneath publicised scandals, but the comfort which can be drawn from knowing that others share similar experiences. Is not this notion of shared experience, and, most significantly, the feeling of acceptance, part and parcel of belonging in a family sense?

It was the best because they always seemed to be there for me and, like, when I didn't go to school, they didn't bawl at me, they just sat me down and talked about it. It were like a group of us going through the same thing – made it feel a lot better knowing it weren't just me. (Hayley)

We were together, like, we all knew what it were like – I felt better at the kids home, there was no need to pretend. Foster places were good in having a family around you but it weren't your mum and dad. (John)

Developing the notion of quasi-sibling relationships

Hopefully, we have by this point convinced the reader of the merits of acknowledging the close relationships that might develop between young people living as part of a household in residential care. If so, then the concept of a serial step-family should indeed be considered. We are not suggesting that this family formation could or would usurp the young person's natural family; rather, we seek to highlight the potential benefits and additional pressures that such an acknowledgement might bring. If we then subscribe to the view that what some young people experience can be likened to a family sense of belonging, then there is a need to respect the relationship which may develop between young people as a "quasi-sibling" relationship. We say "quasi" in order to mark a difference – to concede that these relationships may not have the same level of parental involvement, historical significance or biological linkage as do others. However, there may be a bond that would need to be taken account of, both in terms of how it might benefit the young people involved and the consequences of separation.

Much of the research on sibling relationships is to be found within developmental psychology and concentrates attention on younger children or those in middle childhood (Dunn and Kendrick, 1982; Bryant, 1992; Jenkins, 1992). The young people discussed here are in early to late adolescence; however, possibly similar criteria are applicable. Cirirelli (1976) observed that sibling and familial relations are thought to be distinguished from other peer relations in the following ways: frequency and amount of interaction, durability of relations, accessibility, and degree of common experience. The case for frequency, amount of interaction and accessibility has been made previously, as has the value of shared/common experience. However, can relationships between residential quasi-siblings be durable? We are taking the meaning of durable to be two-fold; that is, relationships that last over time and that survive life's misunderstandings and disagreements. Here, it might be useful to present an abridged excerpt from Shannon's life course biography:

> Shannon entered care when she was in her mid-teens. Initially, she was placed with foster parents but this didn't work out and a place was found for her at the local residential community home. Jenny was also living at the residential home – Shannon and Jenny went to the same school but hadn't previously been close friends. They developed a close relationship at the home which may not always have been seen in a positive light by residential staff. Jenny was felt to encourage Shannon into situations where she might become involved with the police. Ultimately, Jenny was found alternative accommodation and

residential workers breathed a sigh of relief. However, Shannon and Jenny continue their relationship today, almost three years after leaving care. They have had serious disagreements, often relating to choice of partners and friends. Nevertheless, both now have children and, although they live quite a distance from each other, in times of crisis they pull together.

A relationship started in middle childhood has been durable, not only over time but has persevered through separation, a level of condemnation, and serious conflicts. Their story is not an isolated one; much in evidence as young people's biographies unfolded was the value placed on the relationships developed with young people individuals had met while in residential care. A typical example is Charmain's comment after meeting up again with a friend recently "released" from a secure unit:

We just fell on each other. Whatever happens, we'll always be friends. When we were in the same bedroom [in a previous placement] we told each other everything. I've never told anyone the things she told me about what happened to her at home. We're more like sisters.

Thus far, we have painted a very favourable picture in support of acknowledging quasi-sibling relationships among young people in residential care. We do not in any way mean to diminish that view; however, there are, according to Pfouts (1976), two sides of the sibling coin. Like most other human relationships, those between siblings are rooted in ambivalence. On the one side, there is psychological close-ness and supportive caretaking and, on the other, sibling rivalry which might relate to garnering parental approval and recognition, frustrated dependency needs and/or emotional struggles (Bryant, 1982; Kosonen, 1994). With biological siblings, Kosonen (1994) introduces the notion of "high access" sibling relationships to describe those which have the most capacity for emotional intensity – for nurturing *and* conflict. These occur where siblings are closely spaced, of the same gender, and share the same physical space – the conditions most likely to occur among looked after children in the same residential home. The accounts of three young people clearly express frustration regarding a level of sibling rivalry:

The staff were always rushing about after other people. Only certain kids would be rushed about for. The staff were choosy who they were close with. (Suzanne)

They used to have one rule for one and it would be different for another. It depended upon who you were, what problems you had. I used to get grounded for nowt, another used to get pocket money stopped – 'cos they knew they couldn't keep them in. It was one rule for one, different for another. (James)

Since Rachel came, she [his key worker] hasn't had any time for me. 'Cos she's the only lass, they're all over her. They don't know her like I do. I know Rachel, what she's like. They'll soon find out. (Carl)

In terms of dependency needs and emotional struggles, young people in residential care may, and probably do, have a range of serious problems which may relate to their past and be manifest in their present lives. The strain this must place on the residential serial step-family should not be underestimated.

Power between quasi-siblings should also be taken into account in terms of age and gender. Bigner (1974) found that the older sibling in a family was consistently assigned high-power attributions and the younger siblings low-power attributions. Also, older brothers were experienced as more powerful than older sisters. In a residential home, the worst features of a step-family are inevitably present – being supplanted from one's sibling position with each new admission. Thus, young people found their precariously won position in the residential family constantly undermined. This manifested itself in a wide range of ways: from not being the youngest any longer (with expectations that the young person's behaviour would suddenly become more "mature"), to close pairings being threatened by the admission of another young person of the same gender and similar age, or loss of "top dog" status. This latter was particularly acute in the reception unit among the male residents. Relationships were invariably severely disrupted by the admission of a 15- or 16-year-old male. Some of the ensuing disruption was due to staff concentrating on settling the new resident into the routines with the resultant loss of attention for the other young people but, in addition, the boys fought hard to maintain their pecking order. This expressed itself in a range of undesirably macho behaviour, from jumping down the stairs in one go, increased sexual harassment of girls, increased verbal abuse of staff and fighting, to more stubborn forms of resistance which undermined the young people's progress to date. For example, Johnny's non-school attendance had its origins in the threat to his position by the admission of a boy a few months older than himself:

No. NO. I'm not going to school until I've sorted that bastard out.

Johnny also gave up his eagerly anticipated first date in order to attend to his power struggle with the new resident. Later, he was to lose the power struggle totally, along with his relationship with an existing male resident. He lost out in every dimension of his life, and his distress affected others: staff were increasingly sworn at and had furniture thrown at them and he withdrew his "protection" from the girls:

Johnny was right good when I was being bullied by the girls but he turned out to be the worst bully of them all. He did it all upstairs.
(Rachel)

Residential staff are continually confronted with the difficulties of being serial step-parents and with the social dimension of the care experience. However, there is a necessity to recognise the possible outcomes and effects for young people too. Carefully constructed plans may be over-turned by a shift in the relationships between and among young people. For example, one young woman suddenly demanded a foster placement she had previously been rejecting in order to escape same-sex bullying which followed a quasi-sibling relationship breakdown, while another refused a desired foster placement to remain with a quasi-sibling. Both residential and field social workers tend to focus on the conflictual elements of quasi-sibling relationships and attempt to resolve them by separating the young people concerned. Removing one young person from the social situation has serious emotional consequences for the remaining young people. It adds to their sense of insecurity and realistic fears of seemingly summary rejection, and it prevents them from learning how to handle conflict in their personal relationships. This leaves young people in residential homes with no other relationships than the ones severed – the shared experiences ultimately becoming more important than the conflict. For example, despite their complaints about each other and subsequent separations, Johnny, Carl and Rachel make strenuous efforts to keep in touch with each other through attendance at a young person's rights group. These three young people were typical in their sustained interest in other young people's current activities and progress to independence; their commitment and loyalty to their quasi-sibs persisting despite regular and severe conflicts. By neglecting fully to allow for this social dimension of young people's lives, a fundamental and possibly intrinsic aspect of their experience could be underestimated or even overlooked in making decisions about their lives.

Implications for practice

We mentioned at the beginning of this chapter the way in which the adult–child relationship takes precedence in judging young people's need for a significant other. We have challenged such a complacent assumption since it does not translate so easily into the actual lives of young people. Those with past adult–child relationships which have been problematic may find a significant other among other young people with a shared type of experience. The value placed on such relationships and the potential positive outcomes in terms of closeness, supportive caretaking and enduring affiliations should not be underestimated. Furthermore, to miscalculate the potential effect of separation and loss would be to compound the emotional suffering with which young people may previously have been burdened.

Nevertheless, accepting residential community homes and the relationships within them as a serial step-family is not without its problems. Such a view would have wide-ranging implications for practice. Residential staff already try to maintain a balance between professional objectivity and the parental caring role engendered by their unique position; adding the responsibility of serial step-parenting might seem to be asking too much. However, we would argue that this is exactly what their role entails at present and that failing to acknowledge this makes their position even more difficult and ambiguous.

By recognising the residential home as a serial step-family, a more measured and planned approach to managing relationships within the home could be achieved, drawing on contemporary knowledge regarding family relationships. Furthermore, when placing young people, consideration would need to be made regarding existing quasi-sibling relationships in the residential home and their possible subsequent effects. We have highlighted the nature of close sibling relationships and the way in which gender, age and position within the family can have resounding effects on the experiences of young people. Failing to recognise the complexity and hazardous characteristics of such relationships seems naive and perhaps harmful to young people.

Finally, despite fostering the notion of serial step-family and quasi-sibling relationships in residential care, we would once again emphasise that there is no intention to displace or diminish the importance of more conventional family relationships. Rather, our aim has been to raise an awareness of an alternative set of relationships which should be given due regard and accommodation within child care services.

References

Bilson A and Barker R (1992/3) 'Siblings of children in care or accommodation: a neglected area of practice', *Practice*, 6:4, pp 307–18.

Brown P (1987) *Schooling Ordinary Kids*, London: Tavistock.

Bryant B K (1982) 'Sibling relationships in middle childhood', in Lamb M E and Sutton-Smith B (eds), *Sibling Relationships: Their nature and significance across the lifespan*, London: Lawrence Erlbaum Associates.

Bryant B K (1992) 'Sibling caretaking: providing emotional support during middle childhood', in Boer F and Dunn J (eds), *Children's Sibling Relationships: Developmental and clinical issues*, London: Lawrence Erlbaum Associates.

Central Council for Education and Training in Social Work (1992) *Setting Quality Standards for Residential Child Care*, London: CCETSW.

Cirirelli V G (1976) 'Mother–child and sibling–sibling interactions on a problem-solving task', *Child Development*, 47, pp 588–96.

Cousins J (1989) 'Keeping siblings together', *Social Work Today*, 6 April, pp 34–5.

Department of Health (1991a) *Children Act 1989, Guidance and Regulations: Volume 4, Residential care*, London: HMSO.

Department of Health (1991b) *Patterns and Outcomes in Child Care: Messages from current research and their implications*, London: HMSO.

Dobson R (1996) 'Separate lives', *Community Care*, 5–11 September, p 25.

Dunn J and Kendrick C (1982) *Siblings: Love, envy and understanding*, Cambridge, MA: Harvard University Press.

Frones I (1996) *Among Peers – On the meaning of peers in the process of socialization*, Oslo: Scandinavian University Press.

Harris C C (1990) *Kinship*, Buckingham: Open University Press.

Hill M and Tisdall K (1997) *Children and Society*, Harlow: Longman.

Hindle D (1995) 'Thinking about siblings who are fostered together', *Adoption & Fostering*, 19:1, pp 15–20.

Jenkins J (1992) 'Sibling relationships in disharmonious homes: potential difficulties and protective effects', in Boer F and Dunn J (eds.) *Children's Sibling Relationships: Developmental and clinical issues*, Hillsdale, NJ: Lawrence Erlbaum.

Kosonen M (1994) 'Sibling relationships for children in the care system', *Adoption & Fostering*, 18:3, pp 30–5.

Kosonen M (1996) 'Maintaining sibling relationships – neglected dimension in child care practice', *British Journal of Social Work*, 26, pp 809–22.

Maclean K (1991) 'Meeting the needs of sibling groups in care', *Adoption & Fostering*, 15:1, pp 33–7.

Measor L and Woods P (1984) *Changing Schools: Pupils' perspectives on transfer to a comprehensive*, Milton Keynes: Open University Press.

Pfouts J H (1976) 'The sibling relationship: a forgotten dimension', *Social Work*, 21, pp 200–204.

Rushton A, Treseder J and Quinton D (1989) 'Sibling groups in permanent placements', *Adoption & Fostering*, 13:4, pp 5–11.

Sinclair I (1998) 'Evaluating children's homes: how to keep the lid on and produce results'. Seminar held in the Department of Applied Social Studies, Bradford University, February.

Sletta O, Vlas H and Skaalvik E (1996) 'Peer relations, loneliness and self-perceptions in school-aged children', *British Journal of Educational Psychology*, 66:4, pp 431–46

Utting W (1991) *Children in the Public Care: A review of residential child care*, London: HMSO.

Wagner G (1988) *Residential Care: A positive choice*, London: HMSO.

21 **Adult birth siblings**
Who are they and why do they search?

Anita Pavlovic and *Audrey Mullender*

*Anita Pavlovic is Senior Lecturer in Sociology at University College,
Northampton. Formerly at the University of Warwick, she conducted
research over a number of years into the criminal justice system and
into law and social policy, including in the areas of adoption and social
work practice with looked after children. Her current research interest is
in foundlings and the circumstances of the women who abandon them.*

*Audrey Mullender is Professor of Social Work at the University of
Warwick. She is Editor of the 'British Journal of Social Work' and has
herself produced over ninety publications in the social work field,
including ten books. Two of these were published by BAAF: an edited
collection in 1991, 'Open Adoption: The philosophy and the practice',
and, in 1997, ' "I'm Here Waiting": Birth relatives' views on Part II of
the Adoption Contact Register for England and Wales', written jointly
with Sarah Kearn.*

Introduction

This research grew out of a larger study which examined birth relatives'
use of Part II of the Adoption Contact Register for England and Wales
(Mullender and Kearn, 1997). The earlier study revealed that, after birth
mothers, siblings formed the next largest group of relatives putting their
names on the Register, yet there were no available studies of their
particular experiences.

Consequently, this follow-up project aimed to explore:
- the distinct reasons birth siblings had for searching;
- what the loss of a sibling and the desire to search for him or her can
  tell us about what it means to be a sibling;
- the implications for policy and practice of understanding this better.

Methodology

In order to try and capture the range of experiences among those on the Register, the sample drawn from the 347 siblings in the original study was stratified according to three factors:

- age (divided into three bands because the age range covered more than half a century and the social context of adoption has altered considerably over that time);
- sibling status (full and "half" or, as we preferred to say, maternal/paternal; no one in the study was searching for a step-sibling);
- gender (reflecting the roughly 2:1 ratio of women to men among the siblings in the original study and in post-adoption work more generally).

The sample selected consisted of 30 women and 15 men. The method chosen was to conduct telephone interviews, with the interviewee making the call to the reseacher at a pre-arranged time. This was the only way to preserve the confidentiality required by the Office of National Statistics whose staff maintain the Adoption Contact Register and who kindly provided the channel for all correspondence with the respondents. In the event, interviews were completed with 15 women and nine men. Not everyone who had originally been approached and who had agreed to take part actually made the call and, after issuing one re-arranged appointment, it was considered that some might have changed their minds and their privacy was respected. A small number of additional people were then added in order to retain the planned stratification (e.g. there would have been too few men) but with the research scaled down to 24 interviews overall.

The interviews were semi-structured and covered a consistent range of topics that included the personal circumstances of participants, their discovery or memory of the adopted person, and the broader meanings of being a sibling and of adoption.

Findings

Family or care background and range of sibling relationships

Among the sample, it was possible to identify a diversity of family and care backgrounds, with a resulting multiplicity of sibling relationships. Respondents had experienced a variety of family forms and of settings within the public care system. "Families" ranged from the ideologically dominant family form of two birth parents and children, through its socially constructed "deviations" of lone mothers and step-families and its broader variants of extended family care, to the legally-constructed counterparts of stranger adoptions and step-parent adoptions. "Care" extended right across the public care system and included foster care, children's homes, "orphanages", convents and cottage homes.

Reflecting the very wide age range of respondents, experience of these care alternatives was rooted within a broader historical and political context of parenting and parental responsibilities. Thus, whilst the fact of diverse child care arrangements remains all too familiar today, the details can look different over time. Two participants (both now over 40 years of age) had entered the public care system following the death of their mother, even though their father was still alive, for example. Another participant (aged over 50) had been placed in care following her father's death because her mother had been 'unable to cope' in that context at that time. Extended family care was the dominant category for respondents but might not be so today; it spanned all ages. Lone parent and step-parent upbringings, on the other hand, were concentrated in the younger, 30 to 40 year age group, perhaps reflecting the increasing prevalence of divorce. Step-parent adoptions were similarly most common among the rather younger participants, as one might expect. Stranger adoption applied to the personal experiences of only two participants in the study, both over 50 at the time of interview (though, by definition of course, all respondents had had a sibling adopted by strangers).

Since respondents' introduction to these alternative forms of care had typically come about in the context of family upheaval or trauma, the arrangements did not necessarily remain fixed throughout childhood. Rather, it was not uncommon for participants to have experienced a shifting pattern of care which, in turn, gave rise to a multiplicity of sibling relationships.

I was raised by my grandmother until I was four or five, then my mother got married and they adopted me, then they had my two younger brothers. But my mother had had another child before me. (Maternal sister, 30–49 age group)

I was with my mother in a mother and baby home at first. Then my grandmother brought me up for the first few years and then, when my mother got married, my step-father adopted me. But then they divorced and I went to live with [my adoptive] dad and his new wife – I went from being an only child to going into a family of six. Then, once I was 18, I came back to my grandmother. (Maternal sister 30–49 age group)

Sibling status and relationships need to be understood within this broader familial complexity, with participants talking about full, maternal, paternal, adoptive and step-siblings, as well as non-siblings whom they described as siblings or valued in a similar way. Relationships with these siblings ranged, at the time of interview, from enduring to non-existent or lost, and complex family histories also meant that the adoption was not always the respondent's first experience of sibling separation or of severance of sibling contact. The difference was that the typical, closed adoption made later searching for adopted siblings extremely difficult, often impossible, whereas siblings scattered through other alternatives could more easily be found again.

For some people, there had been multiple losses of siblings, not all of whom were necessarily even known about until searching began in earnest. One man who participated in the study was the third of five full siblings who had been placed in care following the death of their father during the 1940s. He later discovered that he had a further ten paternal siblings from his father's first marriage, all of whom had also spent periods of separation in care following the death of their mother. Another participant had grown up in care believing that he was orphaned and an only child, only to discover later in life that neither status was accurate.

Not all change resulted in loss. As well as being separated from their own birth siblings, some respondents found that the moves occasioned by family vicissitudes brought new children into their lives. Some moved in with cousins or step-siblings or, through adoption, into households where they were not the only child. One man, now in his 70s, looked back on an upbringing in which he had become quite attached to other children in an "orphanage", and he had managed to trace some of them in later life (see also Horrocks and Milner, this volume). Whilst having other peer relationships in their lives did not dictate how strongly respondents would feel about the loss of a brother or sister to adoption (for many, it was no kind of compensation), being brought up alone could compound the loss:

Being an only child, it would be nice to have a sibling – I know I wanted to find her for a long time. (Maternal sister aged 50 plus)

Adoption, then, was located within this broader context of separations and continuities, and some participants in the study had more than one sibling who had been adopted. A total of 24 respondents were seeking 26 adopted people.

We might expect most of the adopted people being sought by respondents to be their elder siblings because the popular image of them is of first-born children, born to mothers outside marriage. Whilst a majority of adopted people named on respondents' entries in the Register were indeed their older siblings, the division between older and younger was not particularly marked; of 26 adopted people being looked for, 15 were older and 11 younger than their siblings.

What was more striking from the sample was the way in which family position correlated with sibling status. Here the stereotype *was* fulfilled. The majority of adopted people being sought who were older than the sibling seeking them had the same mother but not the same father. (A small sample such as this cannot reveal the surprising number of birth mothers who went on to marry the birth father and to have subsequent children with him, though the earlier study had been large enough to demonstrate this and it is a familiar feature of post-adoption practice.) Most of the siblings sought had indeed been the first-born children of unwed mothers, including two examples of birth mothers who were unable to keep their babies because they were the second unmarried mother in the family and, in that context, extended family support had been exhausted. The majority of those placed for adoption who were younger than their siblings on the Register, on the other hand, were full siblings, i.e. sharing both a mother and a father. Their adoptions had occurred in contexts of hardship, large families and bereavement: typically the death of a mother as primary carer or of a father as primary provider. Regarding the baby of the family as most easily placed for adoption is by no means a recent phenomenon.

Losing a sibling: why is it significant?

Sibling status

Precise sibling status (whether maternal, paternal or full) did not explain the sense of loss or the depth of feeling associated with it. Thus the loss of a maternal or paternal sibling was no less significant to those who had experienced it than the loss of someone with both parents in common. It was the authorities who tended to ask about precise sibling status, rather than this being an issue rooted in respondents' own feelings.

She's my half-sister – it doesn't matter. But for clarity in terms of trying to trace her, I've had to define my relationship to this person. (Maternal sister aged 50 plus)

The status of full sibling was, however, important to those who possessed it, as something additional. In interview, this group described their adopted siblings as 'real', 'true', 'proper' siblings or, as another put it:

We are full blood relations, not just half or bits. (Full sister aged 20–29)

Thus it was not that "half"-siblings suffered any less loss but that "full" siblings saw themselves as something more, a cut above. In relation to the authorities, again, full siblings sometimes used their status as a lever with which to assert their claim to "rights". This was a level of refinement that the in-depth study was able to add to the earlier one. Though the talk about rights had come through from siblings' original questionnaires

(Mullender and Kearn, 1997), this "pulling of rank" by full siblings had not:

> *I'm a full sister – not a half-sister or a distant relative or anything –*
> *it seems wrong to me that I don't have rights.* (Full sister in the 30–49
> age group)

What it means to be a sibling

Other than awarding siblings a definitional place in families, we know very little about, or perhaps are unable to articulate, what being a sibling actually means to people. Although this was explored in some depth with respondents, no single definition was forthcoming that adequately defines the role or describes the relationships involved. Instead, the researchers arrived at a range of meanings based on the ideals and experiences of participants in the study.

The blood tie

In the narrowest sense, siblings were described in terms of a blood tie, as "your flesh and blood". Biological explanations like this, however, held broader meanings within them; used, for example, to convey the particular significance of being maternal siblings:

> *In your mind you think, 'Oh well, you came from the same mother as*
> *I did'. You know, you share the same mother, therefore you must share*
> *something in common. It's the womb thing, you know, definitely. It's*
> *the fact that we were both born of the same woman, come from the*
> *same place – yeah, that's it.* (Maternal sister aged 20–29)

A lifelong relationship

Like the blood tie, the lifelong aspect of being a sibling may seem obvious. What was interesting, however, was the meaning respondents attached to it, in that it tended to exacerbate and deepen the sense of loss. As one woman put it:

> *It's a very deep and meaningful relationship . . . one, you know, is the*
> *longest you will ever have in your life with anybody. And one of the*
> *most changing relationships as well – the rivalry tends to go and*
> *something deeper comes in.* (Maternal sister aged 20 –29)

This gives considerable food for thought to those who may be involved in trying to keep siblings together or in seeing them parted in current practice.

A special relationship and a shared history

Most commonly, being a sibling was described as a 'special' relationship. Siblings were people who were 'always there for you' and who represented a 'special friendship' or 'closeness'.

This "bond" emanated from, and was consolidated by, a shared history – though it need not have been positive to be important. Negative events, too, could highlight the supportive role of siblings who had had a life together before being parted by adoption:

Through our childhood we've had a lot of negative experiences that we've shared – so although we don't see much of each other [now] we are very close in that we've been through all the bad experiences together. (Full sister aged 30–49)

And, even when participants had been raised as lone children, this equation of being a sibling with sharing was still mentioned by many, often as a key part of what had been lost and sometimes to the point of interfering with the sense of being a sibling at all. Paradoxically, perhaps, this only added to the feeling of loss, rather than assuaging it:

I imagine [if we are reunited] it will be different because there's a great deal of our past that neither of us know about. (Maternal sister aged 30–49)

I'm not sure if I actually see her as a sister – [the rest of] our family were quite close. I think because she's been away all that time it's different. I was out with my two [reunited] sisters one time and some- one we know said 'Who's that?', and I said 'It's my sister'. It just didn't feel right somehow. (Maternal brother aged 20–29)

But the majority of participants did see the adopted person as a sibling who was lost. In this context, the concept of being a sibling resided in a sense of shared history, closeness, support or responsibility which was not only retained but could take on an added significance over time.

Childhood memories

Loss itself was expressed and experienced in a range of ways. For those who had had a period of shared life with the adopted person, feelings of grief, anger, resentment and even betrayal were associated with their memories of that time and of being parted. This loss, that was rooted in one period of their lives, both spanned and (as we shall see in the next section) became multidimensional with the passing of years. Such complexity in many ways mirrors the adoption experience itself in being not a single event, but a lifelong process.

Some of the participants in the study who had lost younger siblings to adoption, for example, had retained vivid childhood memories from many years before. Some had a single, fixed image only, perhaps because they were themselves quite young at the time or because the baby was not in the house for very long.

I remember this baby as if it were yesterday. I remember this baby in a basket – I was coming up for six at the time. (Full sister, now aged at least 50)

For others, there had been the beginning of an emotional bond with another human being, with a real or imagined reciprocity:

I can remember the day she was actually born – she was born at home and we were all in the house. I have memories of pushing her in the pram, going in before I went to school to look at her in the carry-cot. She was at the stage where, soon as she saw me, she knew who I was. There was recognition there, even though she was only a small baby. (Full sister aged 30–49)

Unexpected discovery of the existence of a sibling

But it is people who have no memory of the adopted person, especially those who had already lost an older sibling before they were even born, whose motivation to search represents the biggest mystery. There is simply nothing resembling their experience in the literature. Whereas the above accounts of unresolved separations feel familiar to us from their resonances with the literature on birth mothers, though the detail of their childhood context is clearly different, understanding what it is like to experience the revelation of a lost sibling whose very existence has been an unknown up to that point must pose a whole new series of questions. What emotions does this evoke and what impact does it have? How much difference do context and personal circumstances make?

For some respondents, the discovery of the existence of an adopted brother or sister they had never met, or even heard of, coincided with a period of personal trauma or with a key event in their own lives and thereafter became part of the need to resolve that personal phase or issue, either at an emotional or a practical level. One woman explained how her mother had disclosed having relinquished a baby at a point when she herself was 'about 17 and having a pretty rough patch' (maternal sister aged 20–29). Another discovered she had a sister in the process of another revelation, her own adoption; she was approaching retirement at the time and described the discoveries as 'a double shock' (full sister aged 50 plus). A third participant was told that she was adopted when she tried to recruit family members to donate blood for her sick child; learning of the existence of a blood-related, adopted sibling gave hope in this context, but also created a sense of anxiety and urgency in finding him.

The circumstances of the discovery varied as much as those of the person to whom it happened. Several respondents who were adopted themselves had come across siblings lost to separate adoptions while attempting to trace their own origins. Others had been told by their birth mothers – one of whom, for example, had tentatively embarked upon a search but had given up before the participant in our study took up the task – or had had to wait until the death of a parent for the revelation to come from sorting through family papers, "chance conversations", or official indiscretion in relation to family records.

Not all respondents who lacked actual memories of the adopted person, though, had experienced the sense of "devastation" or "disbelief" that making the discovery unexpectedly and in the midst of other grief could occasion. For some, it was as if there had been a shadowy presence of the adopted person throughout their childhood, in the form either of events half remembered or of a family secret whose existence was sensed but whose actual nature had remained unknown. In these circumstances, the affirmation of a vague sense of knowing there was "something" could come as a relief:

289

I reached a point where I wondered if [this memory] was a figment of my imagination. (Full sister aged 50 plus)

[The disclosure] confirmed something I had come across when I was younger and not been able to understand – a letter that Mum had had from somewhere or another. (Maternal sister aged 20–29)

Even so, not everyone who had a memory of there having been a lost sibling was immune from painful revelations about them in later years. These discoveries, once again, only make sense in the context of the life-cycle, however much they may stand out as stark, one-off events:

When Mum came home without the baby we were told that the baby had died. We were only children ourselves then and we didn't think much of it. But when we were old enough to have children ourselves, we started to wonder what the baby had died of. It turned out that she hadn't died, she had been adopted. I was really angry. I had only been eight but I had grieved for that baby I never saw. I remember being really upset about it. (Full sister aged 20–29)

Taking this group overall, whatever the range of their experiences, what they have in common is an intense interest in finding someone they have never met and yet to whom they are related by blood. Explanations of the motivation to search ranged through: a notion of the sibling as part of the self and/or of the family, curiosity about them (expressed as a need to know), wanting to pass on or obtain medical or genetic information, and the sheer sense of loss and grief. Different stages of life could bring different motivations to the fore.

For me, I think it was just basic curiosity and the desire to find her. (Maternal sister aged 20–29)

I can't grieve for her because she's not dead – she's out there and that makes me feel sad. (Maternal sister aged 30–49)

With genetics now, you've got to know who your relatives are. On my side of the family we've got a history of thyroid cancer, which is genetic. (Paternal brother aged 50 plus)

Well, she's my sister – she's part of me, part of the family. I feel I need

to find her. I just need to know – I can't put it into any other words.
(Full sister, aged 50 plus, who discovered her own adoption and the
existence of another birth family at retirement age)

Motivations were often very complex and were expressed in the context
of the respondent's upbringing, their need to establish a sense of self,
and the meaning of the loss of their identity:

*A lot of people don't appreciate your feeling of a lack of sense of
identity – I have no knowledge of, no relatives at all on my mother's
side. There are absolutely no links.* (Full sister aged 50 plus)

These motivations were often associated with feelings or an interest in
the sibling strong enough to conjure up an image of them which might
be based upon information obtained from a shared birth mother about
the baby and sometimes about the adopters, assumed family resemb-
lances or other manifestations of the blood tie. From these, the adopted
person was constructed in physical, familial, social and life history terms
as a real person, albeit never seen in the flesh:

*I'm sure she would be something like me because we have the same
parents.* (Maternal sister aged 50 plus)

*I reckon she's probably short, has curly dark hair and wears glasses –
because all the women in my family seem to. She went to a couple who
couldn't have children and had already adopted a boy, so I know she
had at least one brother. I reckon she's probably married with a few
children by now – I wonder if she's ever tried to search, if at some
point she just reached a dead end.* (Maternal sister aged 50 plus)

Parental aspects of the sibling role

The last person quoted above spoke about the new layers of understanding and meaning that come with being a parent. For those who
have lost a sibling to adoption, this is one among many aspects of parental
feeling, beginning with those that may have been felt for the baby
directly.

A familiar image from the social work literature of the past is that of
the eldest daughter as "little mother". The sample in the sibling study

certainly included some who had taken on responsibilities in the house-hold in this kind of way:

From the age of nine I could cook a roast meal, clean the house from top to bottom, feed a young baby, bath it, change its nappy – every-thing. (Maternal sister aged 30–49)

This has been equated by professionals with the loss of a childhood – a lack of freedom to play and so on – but those siblings in the study who had themselves taken on a parental role sometimes spoke of it very warmly indeed, as part of a bonding process and as a key element of why the loss had been so keenly felt (see also the account of 'Our Mavis' in Hodgkins, this volume).

I used to look after him – feed him, change his nappies, things like that. I was about 12, I think, and I came home from school one day and he had gone. That's all I can remember. (Full brother aged 50 plus)

Rather as with birth mothers, then (see, for example, Winkler and van Keppel, 1984; Ward, 1991; Howe *et al*, 1992; Wells, 1993), there could be a strong sense of unresolved grief – or, at least, a lack of resolution – that prompted some respondents to search.

Years went by and then I said to my own daughter – 'I've often wondered what happened to her'. I mean, this is the thing, I keep seeing this baby in a basket. (Full sister aged 50 plus).

There are other ways in which the experiences of birth mothers and those of siblings who search can be seen as intertwined. The connections are multi-layered, complex, and almost always gendered. Discovery or disclosure of an adopted sibling could occur in the context of respond-ents' attempts to trace their birth mother, or of birth mothers' own attempts to trace. Hence sibling searches sometimes came about either on behalf of the birth mother or as a means to finding her.

In other instances, it was the respondent's own childbirth experience that was the key to the revelation:

When I was pregnant with my first child, and when he was born, my grandmother got extremely upset. She made a comment that I wasn't sure that I was even meant to overhear, about a baby that was given away. I asked her what she meant and it just sort of all came out. (Maternal sister aged 30–49)

So the pregnancy of the past and that of the present come together. For many women participants in the study, becoming a mother themselves had both forged a commonality with their own mother and elicited an associated awareness of her grief at relinquishing an infant.

Obviously I can't possibly feel what mum felt. Except, now that I've got my own daughter – if I thought that, when I'd given birth to her that I was going to have to hand her over, I don't think I could have lived. I said to Mum, 'I don't know how you survived having to do that'. (Maternal sister aged 20–29)

Responses like these may well have been associated at several levels with sisters' motivation to trace. Some were encouraged to search by their mothers, who felt too anxious or disempowered to conduct searches themselves. Others found feelings engendered within themselves that we could equally imagine ourselves reading in accounts written by birth mothers:

I worry – I want to know how she's got on. My whole interest is in her welfare. (Full sister aged 30–49)

If he knows he's been adopted, he may always wonder why he was given away. I would like to try and explain to him that he wasn't just abandoned – he was wanted. It was just the circumstances. It just wasn't possible to keep him at the time. (Full sister aged 30–49)

A sense of injustice

Finally, birth siblings' personal sense of loss and need to search was, for many, accentuated by a feeling of injustice. The earlier study (Mullender and Kearn, 1997) had already noted this indignation as characteristic of many siblings and as very different from the tone in which birth mothers speak (which is often tempered by the guilt and shame of the past, and by not wanting to intrude into the adopted person's life in the present). It was emphatically heard again in the telephone interviews.

*We've grown up apart and we shouldn't have done. We shouldn't have
been parted. We could have been friends and we've missed out on all
that.* (Full sister aged 30–49)

It's a childhood you never had. (Paternal brother aged 50 plus)

But this should not be regarded as a selfish reaction. Separation – the
denial of a shared history – has, by definition, a two-way impact and
many participants referred to the loss to the adopted person as well as to
themselves that this severance brought about.

*She has got a sister out there [yet] she may have been brought up as
an only child, wishing she had a brother or sister.* (Full sister aged 50
plus)

Implications for policy and practice

From the above findings, a number of conclusions can be drawn. This
study, like a number of others in this book, found that birth siblings are
not a homogeneous group. The many different models of care they
experience between them, and sometimes even over one childhood, mean
that there are not only degrees of sibling relatedness but also of importance among other children in a child's life (who may take on some of the
significance normally reserved for siblings). Searching can be for any or
all of these siblings or other children and can consequently become an
enormously complicated process, sometimes involving a whole string of
revelations along the way. The only means of protecting people from
these traumatic discoveries in later life, and particularly from encounter-
ing brick walls when they try and trace, is to provide them with, at the
very least, regularly updated information about their relatives, and, better
still, with shared placements or continuing contact.

This study has also shown us that adoption can never be fully understood if it is seen as occurring in isolation from the rest of the birth
family, with all its continuing complexities. It is certainly not only birth
parents who are affected by adoption in the birth family, although they
are the only ones the law requires to be consulted. Rather, the loss of a
child to adoption has a deep-seated and wide-ranging impact both within
and across generations. For birth siblings, it is frequently experienced as

a major loss – even when they never knew the adoptee – and having only one parent in common does not lessen the feelings involved (though more people search for maternal than for paternal siblings). The impact, both of loss and reunion, also continues to be felt by siblings' own children.

Why siblings experience such a deep sense of loss relates to a broader perception of what it means to be a sibling than has hitherto been acknowledged by policy or practice. Being a sibling resides not only in a blood tie and in a potentially lifelong relationship, but also in what should be a shared history, a sense of the self continually renewed in relation to and as reflected back by the other, and a mutual feeling of responsibility and concern. Even siblings who have no memory of the person lost to adoption feel strongly about many of these things. Indeed, the sense of loss which, for other separated siblings, is sharpened by vivid childhood memories and still unanswered questions, for siblings who never knew the adopted person may be exacerbated by the distressing circumstances of an unexpected revelation, often at a time of personal trauma or of difficult family circumstances.

There are many parallels between the elements of the loss experienced by siblings and that which birth mothers go through, for example, in the responsibility felt towards the sibling then and now, and the concern about their welfare; sometimes even in having physically cared for them as babies. Furthermore, as for adopted people, full and maternal siblings' own later experience of parenthood (and perhaps especially motherhood) frequently makes them feel more in tune with what their mothers went through and may also be tied up with searching.

At the same time, the issue of parenthood clearly points up the key difference between birth mothers and birth siblings. Whereas birth mothers have to face up to the relinquishment of their child for adoption, for birth siblings this separation is typically unexplained and comes as something they experience as imposed on their lives without their volition or involvement. It can engender a deep sense of injustice and anger which may be characteristic of siblings and which leads them to talk about their "right" to have contact with the brother or sister lost to adoption – a perception with which current legislation and policy is almost entirely out of step. Though there has not been the space to outline it in this account, a further finding of the study was the length to which siblings will go to search for lost brothers and sisters and the constant frustration of attempting to trace when closed adoption has concealed the new name of the adopted person from their family of origin. For some siblings, the process of searching not only costs them large sums of money but also appears to take over their lives. Is it really the state's intention that so much distress should continue to be caused to so many people such long years after the event? Where the experience of searching is so negative, it can further accentuate the isolation of the persisting separation and of having lost a relative to what was perceived in siblings' younger days as the stigma of adoption.

Siblings' experiences of the enduring nature of their loss, as conveyed by this long-term, retrospective view of their lives, holds lessons for the immediate policy and practice dilemmas faced by social workers and other child care professionals. These relate not only to the nature of adoption itself, and to the forms it takes and the roles it plays in contemporary society, but also to the continuing separation of siblings in and by the care system. The study furnishes further evidence of the need to value sibling and peer relationships and to continue to work at understanding them more fully. Legally and socially constructed decisions about children's present needs do not wipe out the past or make an irrelevance of its continuation into the future (in the form of still living birth relatives). They merely add further layers of complexity. This study did not look at the adoption experience and so can have nothing to say about whether or not adoption is a good thing or under what circumstances. It can emphatically state, however, that closed adoption has caused untold pain in the lives of many people, including whole groups who have never been thought about before. It is not too late to think about them now.

References

Howe D, Sawbridge P and Hinings D (1992) *Half a Million Women: Mothers who lose their children by adoption*, Harmondsworth: Penguin.

Mullender A and Kearn S (1997) *"I'm Here Waiting": Birth relatives' views on*

Part II of the Adoption Contact Register for England and Wales, London: BAAF.

Ward D (1991) 'Closed adoption – a lifetime loss', in Mullender A, *Open Adoption: The philosophy and the practice*, London: BAAF.

Wells S (1993) 'Post-traumatic stress disorder in birth mothers', *Adoption & Fostering*, 17:2, pp 30–32.

Winkler R C and van Keppel (1984) *Relinquishing Mothers in Adoption: Their long-term adjustment*, Melbourne: Institute of Family Studies Monograph.

22 The search for lost siblings

Pam Hodgkins

Pam Hodgkins is an adopted person. In 1982, having traced her own birth family, she founded NORCAP (National Organisation for Counselling Adoptees and Parents) and she remains a Trustee of the charity. Following professional social work training she became a Regional Consultant with BAAF and was appointed Manager of the West Midlands Post Adoption Service when it opened in 1994.

Background: who are siblings seeking?

Ever since NORCAP was established in 1982, there have been a number of enquiries each year from people who need assistance in making contact with a brother or sister from whom they have been separated by adoption. The nature of these enquiries is quite diverse:

1. People who were adopted who have searched for their birth parent and discovered (s)he has died, or is infirm, who want to consider initiating contact with a sibling subsequently born to their parent and raised by her/him.
2. People who have their own memories of a baby born to their mother who left their family by adoption.
3. People who have been told by their parent that (s)he had a baby who was placed for adoption either before they themselves were born or unbeknown to them. Likewise, people who discover this information from other family members or family papers, often after the death of the parent.
4. People who know they were adopted by one family and their sibling(s) by another, and where contact was never arranged or ceased during their childhood. This includes twins.
5. Adopted people who, in gaining access to their own birth records, learn that their mother/father had other children who were adopted. This too may include twins.
6. Adopted people who learn through access to birth records that their

mother/father had other children – sometimes older, sometimes younger than themselves, who it seemed they were raising themselves but whose birth certificates when purchased are endorsed "adopted".

Most enquiries are about a mother's other children, with only occasionally a father's other children being identified. It seems that the protracted nature of pregnancy and the drama of birth are seen as more tangible than the significant, but brief, role of the father at conception. People anticipate that even a pre-school child is likely to have some recollection of their mother being pregnant or the birth of the baby – or mother's absence – while it is assumed to be much less likely that they would be aware of their father having fathered another child. In general, people are unsure of the wisdom of revealing information which was previously unknown but are more confident in reminding others of details of which they may already have hazy memories.

The help available under current law and policy

There has been little practical assistance that NORCAP, or more recently the independent regional post-adoption services, have been able to offer most of our sibling enquirers. While adopted people are entitled to access to birth records (under section 51 of the 1976 Adoption Act) this provides for information from their own birth records only and not from those of any other individual.

Nor does the law give siblings of adopted people any right to information about their brother or sister. It is even debatable whether they have the general right to support and assistance required by section 1 of the Adoption Act 1976. The establishment of the Adoption Contact Register by the insertion of section 51A into the 1976 Act during the passage of the Children Act 1989 marked the first recognition by government of the needs of birth relatives, including siblings, who are separated from a relative by adoption. They have also always been able to use the Contact Register and searching services provided by NORCAP, although the latter have been of little practical application if the sibling is devoid of the basic post-adoption identity of the brother or sister.

Some adoption agencies have shown themselves sympathetic to the wish of our enquirers to contact their adult siblings, and have been willing to work with us to facilitate any mutually desired contact. Work of this nature is discretionary and so there are wide inconsistencies in its application across the country, and it can never meet the needs of those who do not know which agency was involved (or where there was no such involvement). The most frequent enquiries at the West Midlands Post Adoption Service over the past four years have been about siblings who were "lost" in the 1930s and 1940s before the establishment of local authority children's departments. This means that, even in areas where a service would be offered under existing policy, this is often not possible because there are no locally held records for that period available for anyone to access. Paradoxically, these are also the individuals in the greatest need as they are already in their 50s or older, as are the missing siblings. They are people for whom the sands of time are already running out and we are committed to do all we can to assist them.

Testing the law: section 50(5)

During the late 1980s and early 90s, as NORCAP developed its service provision to supplement the self- and mutual-help initiatives originally offered, it sought ways of providing more effective practice services to siblings. Some of us studied section 50 of the Adoption Act 1976 to try to find any possible opening. It was concluded that it might be useful to test the law by making an application under section 50(5) when a suitably strong case became available.

The case of P arose. P was a British woman settled in Australia from 1947 and now in poor health as a result of a lung disease with genetic implications. She wanted to contact her brother, J, born to her mother in 1946. All efforts to locate an adoption agency or local authority holding records had failed. I contacted the office of the High Court and asked how one set about making an application under section 50(5). Did one have to engage a solicitor/barrister? – 'No'. Did one have to set out the application on an official form? – 'No'. Did one have to supply specific documentary evidence? – 'No'. So I really did only need to turn up at the Law Court at 10am, head for the Applications Court and tell the usher what I was seeking? – 'Yes'. In great trepidation, I travelled to the court with a NORCAP colleague, armed with every imaginable piece of paper and the text of what I hoped to say to the judge. To us, the whole place appeared overwhelming; everyone except us seemed to know what they were doing, where they were going, and why. The usher, while friendly and encouraging, seemed uncertain of the procedure we were invoking but, eventually, we were led into the court of the (then) Mr Justice Thorpe.

He simply asked what I wanted! I asked permission to read what I had written down and, the judge having checked it was only one page long, told me to proceed. Mr Justice Thorpe interrupted me for clarification about NORCAP and the specifics of the case but, before I had completed my submission, he had referred to his reference books and his clerk and pronounced that he would grant the order. We were dumbstruck and uncertain what to do next. Does one express thanks? (We did.) Bow? (I think we did.) Leave? (We gathered up our papers and exited like school girls escaping chastisement from a head teacher's study.)

We later collected the order and took it to the General Register Office. The order instructed the Registrar General to provide me with the information which would link the birth entry of J with his adoption entry. No one knew how to process such paperwork, so it was agreed it would be sent to the Adoption Section in Southport. We waited a week before daring to enquire how long it would be before we received the adoption certificate. The response came from the solicitor for the Registrar General. I was chastised by the solicitor for having done what the High Court Office had instructed me to do! I was told I should have 'joined the Registrar General as Party to the application'; I should have 'submitted the case for the application to both the court and the Registrar General, and an appointment for the hearing should have been made in advance'. I was told that the Registrar General – in the public interest – would wish to appeal against Mr Justice Thorpe's decision. The only good news was that the Registrar General would fund the cost of my having legal representation – in the public interest – regardless of the outcome. Two weeks later, along with my solicitor, Sally Ashmore of Varley, Hibbs & Co, and our barrister, Andrew McFarlane, we returned to the High Court. After hearing submissions from both sides, Mr Justice

Thorpe confirmed the order and his judgement is reported in *Re H 1995* FLR 236.

To hear that an application under section 50(5) should succeed if the applicant could present a case of sufficient weight and justification to persuade the judge of the reasonableness of the application was wonderful. Surely it is unquestionably reasonable for a brother or sister to want the opportunity to know their sibling?

However, when we eventually received the adoption certificate of J, the challenge of establishing his present whereabouts was immense. Faced with very common first and surnames of both J and his adopters, the trawl through public records was extensive and time consuming. The up-to-date information was nevertheless achieved in three weeks, together with confirmation that his adoptive parents had died many years earlier. A letter was sent asking if my colleague and I could visit to discuss a 'sensitive family matter'. After a difficult telephone call when I maintained I would not disclose the nature of our business over the telephone, we arranged an evening meeting. J was at home with his wife and his sister. We explained the work of NORCAP and our roles within the organisation. Neither J nor his sister M appeared to recognise that they had any link to adoption, although M told us that their parents had adopted a little boy in the early 1950s who had drowned when aged four.

They appeared to make no connection that they too might have been adopted so we had to gently tell J that he had been adopted, show him his adoption certificate and explain our purpose. J did not appear shocked by this revelation and was intrigued by news of P and her long quest to find him. He was quite clear that he would wish to communicate with her. It seemed that the potential for contact with a sister more than compensated for any shock or distress caused by the late disclosure of his adoptive status. Sadly, our disclosure to J caused his sister, M, to immediately question whether she too was adopted. We had discovered this in the process of locating J and had to confirm this for her. She was very distressed; she had considered herself very close to her adoptive parents, especially her mother whom she nursed through her terminal illness. M could not understand why her mother had not told her, even in the last days of her life, and this hurt her considerably. The factor most obvious to myself and my colleague was that, while the shock for J had been eased by the revelation of a caring sister, the shock to M had no counterbalance. Her only option was to begin a long and painful journey through her own section 51 application which, having in due course acted as her intermediary, I am aware ended in rejection for M.

This experience reinforced for us the knock-on effects of such work and flagged up the need to keep an open mind. We, like Mr Justice Thorpe himself, had thought it 'intensely unlikely that J is unaware he is adopted', but he was. Even the knowledge that J had joined the family when M was already eight years old, or that the little boy who drowned was adopted when J was five, had not caused either M or J to question their own status within the family. These events further reinforced our view that, if it is only as an adult that an individual learns of their adoption, the pain of that late disclosure will be eased if the cause of the disclosure is a caring and sensitive enquiry from a birth relative.

Case studies

The sibling around the corner
After the reporting of another high profile test case, the West Midlands Post Adoption Service (WMPAS) was given information by a court which enabled us to assist three other siblings. All information was given on a non-disclosure basis, with WMPAS giving an undertaking to the court that the new identity of the adopted sibling would only be given to our enquirer if the adopted sibling, once located, agreed to this. This resulted in WMPAS having to do all the researching of public records to locate these "lost" siblings with the work funded by our enquirers.

With the synchronicity which no longer surprises those of us working in post adoption, we located two siblings in the same week. John and his sister had been boarded out together in the early days of the war. When John was three he was adopted by one family and his 18-month-old sister by another. The adoption applications had been heard in the same court on the same day and John's adoptive mother had tried to arrange to keep in touch with the adoptive family of his sister, but the other family had rejected her suggestion. Fifty years on, John had only one photograph of himself and his sister, taken on the last day at the foster home, as a reminder of her. Yet we found that in all that time they had never lived more than three miles apart.

The case of the unexpected sibling

We found Barry and John's second brother rather further away: 3,000 miles away, in fact, in Canada. Barry had been brought up by his birth mother; in 1990 he had been contacted by John who had been adopted as an infant and who, having traced his birth family, wanted Barry's assistance in contacting his octogenarian mother who was also Barry's mother, A. A's response to John was warm but confusing – was he John or K or G? Searching the birth records revealed that, in addition to John, A had given up two other sons for adoption in the pre-war years. John and Barry wanted help in locating both, but the court only found records of K, who became Roger and who had emigrated to Canada 20 years before. Both these siblings' reunions were positively received and all the people involved have confirmed that, two-and-a-half years later, they are very pleased we contacted them and gave them the option of knowing their siblings.

Roger is now supporting Barry and John in the search for G. He recently wrote to me:

> *I knew my birth name was K W. I had not made any effort to find my birth family due to the risk of upsetting my mother and the life she may have. Another factor was the fear of rejection . . .* [after letter from WMPAS] *I was delighted to learn that I had brothers and would be happy to contact them . . .*

> [Following a visit to the UK] *My life has been changed for the better. . . being offered the opportunity to contact my original family has brought a new and wonderfully happy dimension into my life. I feel very strongly that Barry, John and I would be failing in our family duty if we did not try to locate G and offer him the opportunity of joining the family if he wishes.*

'Never mention her again': the case of D and S

All our enquirers have strong feelings about their siblings and their wish to renew contact with them. For us, as post-adoption workers, their stories are possibly even more poignant when they have their own memories of the siblings who has been lost. D, the third case the court was able to assist with, recalled coming home from school one day in 1935 when she was six and being ordered by an aunt to stay outside until bedtime. On going upstairs and climbing into the bed she shared with her mother, she recalls her surprise at being warned to be careful as she climbed in, else she would 'squash the baby' – her first indication of and introduction to her baby sister S.

D recalls that her mother soon returned to work and that baby S was boarded out during the week but returned home each weekend. D told us of her happiness and of S's gurgles of delight when she played peek-a-boo round the hood of the pram. After several months, one weekend S was not brought home. D questioned her mother and was told, 'I can't afford the boarding fees so she has been adopted. You must never mention her again'. And D never did, for 60 years, until after the death of her mother, her aunt and her aunt's husband when she finally dared to approach WMPAS. D and S were reunited in November 1997.

'That was my Mavis'

Although the difficulties of long-term searches are frustrating, especially when one is so aware that these are elderly people we are seeking, for whom time is running out, this difficulty pales into insignificance compared to the utter frustration of being powerless to offer any practical assistance to enquirers when we are unable to establish the post-adoption identity of the person sought. Besides G, the missing brother of Barry, John and Roger, WMPAS is particularly concerned for KB and for John. KB's story is not untypical but its inherent sadness is made all the more poignant by our present inability to do anything to bring about resolution.

KB was 13 when, in the closing days of the War, his mother gave birth at home, unassisted, to a baby girl. She handed the apparently lifeless baby to K and instructed him to get rid of it. K sought the assistance of an elderly neighbour and, together, they stimulated the baby into life. K called her Mavis. He fed her, cuddled her, changed her, sang to her and, guided only by advice from the neighbour, nurtured her for four weeks or more.

It then seems that, in late August 1945, K's mother received news that her husband, who had been in the Far East offensive, would soon be demobbed. She instructed K to get "Mavis" dressed and they went to the municipal offices in Birmingham. K was left sitting on a bench while his mother took the baby into a room; a short while later his mother returned and said they were going – but without "Mavis". K recalls protesting loudly and being sharply slapped. His mother ordered him – just as D had been instructed – never to mention the baby again. K told me:

> *I followed my mother out the side door of that building in disbelief. I hung about and made her cross because she clearly wanted to get away as quickly as possible but, as we walked round to the front of the offices, a posh young couple were just coming down the steps of the Council House carrying a baby who was crying. Mrs Hodgkins, I can tell you that was my Mavis – I knew her cry, even if she was in a big new shawl. That was my Mavis – I recognised her cry. I would recognise her cry even now.*

K followed his mother's instruction and did not mention the baby, except to his wife, until he approached WMPAS for help in 1994. All the staff team share his distress and frustration that we have not been able to identify his "Mavis" because we know that, if "Mavis" as a thirty-something had applied for access to her birth records when first able to do so in 1977, she would have been warned of the risks of approaching her birth mother. If she gained access to any court-held records or reports, she would have learned that, as an extra-marital child, her mother was anxious to complete her adoption before her husband returned home. She would expect her mother to be long dead; the papers may even contain reference to her mother's apparent indifference to her daughter. It is most unlikely that there would be any reference to a brother who loved her, nurtured her and remembers her cry, having cared for her single-handedly throughout a summer school holiday; a brother who, over 50 years later, is desperate to see his "Mavis" once again.

John's story
John only learned he was a twin when he applied for birth records 15 years ago. His wife, a midwife, understood the significance of the time

of birth being quoted on his English original birth certificate. At first he assumed his twin must have died in infancy because the court records of his adoption make no mention of his having been a twin and his adoptive family had no information that he was not a singleton. However, his twin's original birth certificate is endorsed "adopted" so his twin brother, who may be an identical twin, must have survived several months at least and probably into adulthood. Maybe, like John, he does not know he is a twin; he may not even know he is adopted.

Conclusion

Why did we not apply for section 50(5) orders in these latter cases? The breakthrough achieved in *Re H* was short-lived. In December 1996, the case of *D v Registrar General* was heard on appeal and the comments of the appeal court judges, reported in 1997 FLR, effectively reverse the helpful views expressed by Mr Justice Thorp in *Re H*. The more stringent hurdle, now seeking "exceptional" grounds for deviation from the norm of not allowing birth relatives to have linking information, has left the initiative for renewing contact between adopted people and their birth relatives firmly in the hands of adopted people alone.

Yet we feel strongly, as post-adoption workers, that the wish of KB to find his Mavis is not exceptional, but more likely the norm for a brother in circumstances such as his. Likewise, with John, it is hard to imagine that any individual learning in middle age that he was one of twins would not want the opportunity to contact that missing twin. Two futile years have passed, but recently a firm of solicitors and a leading barrister have agreed to work on a *pro bono* basis on these two cases. They will bring the plight of lost elderly siblings before the court again and hopefully convince them that such sadness and frustration constitute exceptional circumstances in today's society. We hope the case they present will be sufficient to convince the judge to make section 50(5) orders which will enable WMPAS actively to help our waiting enquirers.

Better still would be new adoption legislation which gives siblings (and other birth relatives) the right to information, or a statutory service which would ensure that they all had the opportunity for contact with their lost brother or sister. Meanwhile, as Roger wrote, we would be failing in our duty if we did not try to offer that opportunity.

Note

Names have not been used, except where the individuals involved have requested that I name them because they are seeking all possible publicity in the hope that it may assist their search.

23 Looking back
Childhood separations revisited

Barbara Prynn

Barbara Prynn counsels adults who were adopted or who grew up in the care of the local authority for which she works. She is a director of the Centre for Adoption and Identity Studies at the University of East London and a part-time lecturer at the Tavistock Centre. Her MPhil (1990) was on the subject of supervision of parental contact with looked after children. She is completing a PhD thesis entitled 'Family Building in Adoption'.

This chapter is based on the preliminary data from a qualitative research project which is ongoing, and on the pilot study for the project. The purpose of the study is to investigate the life stories of adults who were adopted or fostered, and to consider various aspects of the respondents' childhoods which may be seen to be relevant to their later life experience and feelings about identity. Their views on family life – their relationships with parents and siblings if any – form part of the enquiry.

All the interviewees had experienced the loss of one or both parents in infancy or early childhood and, for most of them, this loss was compounded by separation from siblings and removal from the family home. There may be a link between such disruptions in childhood and issues in adult relationships: 'The implication is that early disruption of parenting may be particularly damaging to the development of those aspects of personality concerned with social relationships' (Rutter, 1988, p 343). On the other hand, the work of Main *et al* (1985) suggests that relationships in adulthood are not exclusively dependent upon the attachment experiences of early childhood. For at least some adults, they are mediated by other and later attachment relationships. It will be seen from the examples which follow that some of the respondents to the study demonstrated great resilience (Fonagy *et al*, 1994) following difficult periods in childhood.

The research study

The purpose of the small pilot study was to test the method to be used in the main part of the study, so the number interviewed was small. Eight people were seen. They included both men and women, and they were from 30 to 65 years old. The five "foster people" were found with the help of the National Foster Care Association, as all of them were in touch with members of the organisation. The three adoptees were found from the membership of Parent to Parent Information on Adoption Services (now called Adoption UK). They were both adoptees and adopters.

The plan for the main study was to interview people who were adopted or fostered and who were born before the Second World War. Twenty-four people have been interviewed, aged between 60 and 90. One person volunteered to be interviewed when he heard about the study, because he is both a Governor of the Thomas Coram Foundation and was himself a Scholar of the Foundling Hospital. Otherwise the first group of inter-viewees was found by visiting day centres for the elderly in the local authority areas surrounding the University of East London, and asking whether any user of the day centre had been adopted or fostered and would be prepared to be interviewed.

The second and larger group of interviewees came via the writer's membership of the South-East Post Adoption Network. A number of interviewees were asked by their post-adoption counsellors if they would like to take part in the study. A letter asking for volunteers was published in *The Barnardo Guild Messenger*. A very large number of people responded to this letter, unfortunately far more than the size and scope of this project could accommodate.

The plan was that the interviews would take place in people's own homes, on a day and at a time of their choice. This has been the case except for two women who chose to be seen at their day centres. Each interview was tape recorded. Before the beginning of each, there was a discussion about the ownership of the material and the eventual disposal of the tapes. (They will be lodged with the University of Essex Archival Resource Centre, and each potential interviewee was invited to agree or not with this plan.)

The interviews were unstructured, apart from initial confirmation of the interviewee's name and age. Thereafter, respondents were encouraged to speak about the events of their life from infancy to adulthood. Some were keen to talk about their adult lives as well. At the end of the interview they were asked, firstly, how they would sum up the childhood experiences recounted, and, secondly, how they thought those experiences had affected their adult life in terms, for example, of their careers as marital partners, parents and grandparents. Finally, each respondent was asked if a question should have been asked by the interviewer but had not been. While most felt that the ground had been covered to their satisfaction, some used this final question as an opportunity to talk about an issue about which they felt strongly. One instance of this is the matter of why they were separated from their birth family in the first place.

Each tape was transcribed in full and examined for common themes. It is intended that a discussion and analysis of these themes will eventually form the basis for a full presentation of the findings of the project.

The choice of respondents who were born before the Second World War was made not least because their testimony will be lost forever if not gathered soon. They grew up at a time when family policy and attitudes to children and families more generally were different from those of today. Their childhood memories and retrospective reflections on their childhood shed light on the way in which decisions about children were made, and the way in which children were thought about, in the 1920s and 1930s. In spite of the structural differences in terms of social policy and legal context between then and now, the respondents' perspectives on sibling relationships are relevant today. They are in a unique position in being able to demonstrate the very long-term influence of their childhood experience through their behaviour and attitudes. They have also had a lifetime to think about the ways in which the circumstances of their childhoods may have affected their adult lives and relationships, so their perceptions and understandings are important.

The majority of the people interviewed were fostered rather than adopted. Although the total number is small, it is possible to discern common themes from the narratives, in which powerful emotions are displayed about sibling relationships. Most of the respondents were in the care of one of the large charitable child care institutions during at least part of their childhoods. The others were cared for in the homes either of extended family or of strangers. Only one of the people interviewed so far, who had left her birth parents' home in infancy, was returned home. Ten of the respondents have clear memories of having lived with siblings when they were at home with their parents, and of being separated from them following family tragedies. Nine either discovered in later life that they had full or half-siblings, or rediscovered the siblings with whom they had lived in infancy.

There must be many factors which influence the ways in which children who have been separated from siblings with whom they have previously lived, think about them following separation. They, like children who grow up with no close age mates, may have powerful fantasies about the nature of imagined relationships with absent brothers or sisters. When, in adulthood, they rediscover or are acquainted for the first time with biological siblings, their approach to the new relationship will be determined by their childhood remembrances or imaginings, as well as their later experiences of other relationships.

The findings: varying experiences of separation and reunion

It was a feature of the interviews that a number of the respondents had searched for their birth families very late in life – in their 60s or 70s. For some this was an outcome of the Children Act 1975, which allowed adopted people to obtain a copy of their original birth certificate and possibly thereafter to try and find birth family members. For others, it was the result of the opening of records by some local authorities and voluntary agencies following the Access to Personal Files Act 1997 and the Access to Personal Files (Social Services) Regulations 1989. For most of those who had grown up in the care of Barnardo's, the impetus to obtain access to their records was the showing of the series of television programmes entitled *Barnardo's Children* during 1995.

All the respondents who had had the experience of separation regretted very much that the years they should have spent with their siblings had been taken from them. Sadly, for some it was already too late. In Bert's case for example, his much-loved older sister, from whom he had been separated at the age of six, had died before there could be a reunion. Bert has invested much in the ideal and the memory of his sister. His childhood was one of constant losses, rejections and separations. He has been a somewhat solitary adult and he regrets that he has never married. However, meeting his sister's children and grandchildren has been a joy to him in his old age, even though implicit in his affection for them is the still painful loss of his sister.

Andrew, who was 38 when interviewed for the pilot study, described a separation which occurred many years later than Bert's. Andrew was three years old when he entered the care system. His mother left him with his father when she took his two younger brothers away with her. His father could not manage a young child and put Andrew into care. As he grew up, he knew that he had two younger brothers but he did not know where they were. He says he found this 'frustrating'. It was not until he was in his late 20s that he rediscovered them, and also learned that his mother had had a second family. By then, he says, it was too late for them to have a real relationship.

Not everyone has needed to search. Patricia is 69. She lived until she was six with her parents and her sister who was seven years older than she. Then their mother died and she was fostered by strangers. She saw her sister occasionally as they grew up and, when Patricia was an adult, they lived together for a time. Patricia describes herself as a fiercely independent child. She always knew where her sister was – they lived in the same small town – and had contact with her from time to time, so that their relationship was not broken despite their living in separate households. Hence, perhaps, there was not the same need to reforge a contact in later life as is experienced by many who were kept apart.

What siblings mean to one another

Where siblings grow up together they are able to share information and feelings and to see themselves as part of a group. When they are separated they lose a part of themselves and their children are deprived of extended family relationships. They are unable to pool knowledge of their parents. They miss the pleasure of acknowledging someone who is physically similar to themselves who is of the same generation.

Molly is 70. She has a non-identical twin sister, and a half brother and sister. When her mother died, when she and her sister were in their infancy, they lived with their father who remarried. Molly believed that her stepmother was her mother, and that her children were Molly's full siblings. Her stepmother died when Molly was in junior school, and she and her sister continued to live with their father who died when they were ten. They were then fostered by a paternal aunt and the other children went to their maternal grandparents.

Molly describes her childhood with her aunt as being rather like a "Cinderella" experience, with her cousin in the role of an Ugly Sister. Having her twin sister with her meant that Molly was not alone. They are still emotionally very close – Molly describes how she felt in her own body a bereavement which her sister suffered. Molly's sister lives in Australia. It was only recently, with the impetus of her sister's need to do so, that Molly has found out about their family history which had always been a mystery to them. They have retrieved photographs and certificates of their mother and her parents, a side of the family which was closed off to them when they were growing up.

When their father died, Molly and her sister 'never saw ever again' their half-siblings. She discovered later that the two children were 'put in a home'. She and her sister tried to find them when they were teenagers but without success. 'We went up to London and all over the place, places where we *thought*, you know, he [their brother] might come under. And he didn't, so we gave up.' Then when they were both married:

He found us . . . and then we lost touch again because he was a stranger and we was strangers you see, brought up in a home, and I haven't been able to find him since. I mean I couldn't find him. [She spoke here with more emotion than in the whole of the rest of the interview, and cried.] I'll have to find him.

She found that her half-sister had died.

She might have died of a broken heart. I think it's possible. Little girl shoved into a home from her grandparents and 'what's happening to me?' We was that little bit older; that, you know, could have rubbed off on us a little bit.

She very much regrets that she has not kept in touch with her half-siblings: 'It would have made a heck of a lot of difference.'

Damaged relationships

Amy was 30 when interviewed. She knew that she had been received into care with her sister and brother when she was about 18 months old. She remembers being taken to meet her brother once when they were children but has seen him only on rare occasions since then. She and her sister Bonnie spent part of their childhood together in children's homes. Both were fostered at different times and in different places. In contrast to Amy, who now has a partner, a child and a job, Bonnie has been in prison and has lost two children to the care system. Amy's relationship with her is based on her attempts to support Bonnie. When Amy thinks about her siblings and the way they relate to each other now, she is acutely aware of the influence of their separations in childhood, and says when describing their present relationship: 'There is no foundation – there is no bond.'

Enid, who is 70, was a "residual evacuee", that is, she was a child who was not returned to her family at the end of the Second World War. She had two younger brothers. Their early childhoods were fraught by separation from their parents and each other during their mother's long illness, and by the inability of their father to care for them adequately after she died. The youngest of the family, Keith, was particularly badly affected by the changes and losses and, unlike Enid, who formed a close and loving relationship with her quasi-foster parents, her brother was ejected from more than one foster home before he was sent back to his father and a 'wicked stepmother'. In adulthood, Enid tried to maintain a relationship with both her brothers. This was not successful with Keith. He was unable to settle after his disrupted childhood and resented the comfortable home life Enid had achieved with her husband and three children.

Arthur, who was 33 at the time of interview, lost contact with his

315

siblings partly because, in the aftermath of their mother's death, it was of essential importance to him that he continued to live in the area where he had lived with his family and to attend the same school. He was the oldest of five siblings. He insisted on continuity. Therefore, the original plan to place the five children in a foster home in another area was abandoned. The four younger children were placed together and away from him. Since they have all grown up, Arthur has met three of his younger siblings again. He learned that they had been told that he did not want contact with them when they were all children. He had also been told that they did not wish to have contact with him, and this has poisoned their relationship now. He said:

> *My family's split apart . . . we can't be together. When I first met my brother – a few years back – I actually said 'I haven't got a brother' because I felt that anger about being told they didn't want to hear from me . . . It's like being with somebody else from primary school . . . we just have nothing in common.*

Arthur spoke eloquently about the hurt he continues to feel as a result of the events of his childhood. His distress about the discontinued relationship with his siblings is a part of his total unhappiness about the legacy of his early years.

More than 50 years before Arthur was born, Irene was separated from her siblings by her mother's death. Irene is 87. She was the eighth child of ten. When her mother died, all the children were parcelled out among relatives. She was the only one who was not taken back by her father when he remarried. She had been fostered by his much older sister, and Irene believes that her aunt would not let her go back to her father. She saw her father and the rest of the family a lot while they were growing up and used to stay with them. But she really missed being part of a family – she was brought up as the only child in a house full of adults – and she used to like to visit school friends who had big families.

When the Second World War came and her two sons had to be evacuated, Irene insisted that they be kept together. When their first billet failed she was dissuaded with difficulty from bringing them home – their house had been bombed. Although her younger son was really too young she demanded – and succeeded in her request – that the two boys be evacuated with the older one's school so that they could be together. She was quite clear when she spoke about her War experience, that it was her own childhood separation from her siblings which had made her so insistent on her sons being together.

Some happier accounts

Rosemary, who is now 78, was fostered from the age of three until she was 13, when she was recalled from her much-loved foster home to Barnardo's Village to be educated and taught a trade. She had not known anything about her family background until she was in her teens, when her mother (and grandmother and an aunt) came to see her once at the Village. When she was 17 and working, Rosemary sought out her mother and found that she had a full sister and a half-brother. She also discovered that her mother had put her sister into care when she was a small child (which was her own experience) but that her brother (who had a different father) had been kept at home. She and her sister are in touch. Rosemary believes that her sister had a bad time in care and 'knowing what we both sort of been through, I think that brought us together'.

Jean was placed for adoption at the age of nine. She believed that she was her mother's only child. When she was about 11, a remark from her adoptive mother informed her that her mother had had another child who was placed for adoption as a baby. When she was in her early 60s, Jean determined to discover her origins and was able to contact a maternal aunt. She plucked up courage to write to her asking about her brother. She has since met him. All her life she had felt different because she had no family. She never felt part of her adoptive family. When she met her brother and as they have got to know each other, Jean's feeling of "difference" has gradually dissipated. She says that it has taken her four years to be able to say that she has a brother without bursting into tears. Now she feels connected to him and her previous – and lifelong – feeling of isolation, has gone.

"Siblings" in foster care and children's homes

People who grow up in children's homes may regard their age mates as family in some way and may also be important to one another. In fact

May, who is 80 and who did not form a close relationship either with the unrelated children with whom she was fostered or with a brother found in adulthood, now describes all the other people who grew up in the care of the same organisation as her "family". Andrew, too, said he and the other children in his children's homes were like siblings in that they would protect one another. He keeps in touch with people he knew in children's homes but 'now I don't look on them as family'. He mentioned someone he grew up with who has mental health problems and who 'still thinks I'm her brother'.

It was a slightly different story for Gaynor and Glenys who are both 80. They each lived until their teens with much loved foster mothers. They both define their foster sisters as 'real' sisters, not the biological sisters whom they discovered in their 70s.

Our language is deficient in the appropriate terms to refer to these kinds of relationships. Is the "true" or "real" sibling the one with whom one shares one or both biological parents, or the one with whom one grew up? Gwenneth, who is 70, illustrates this dilemma. Like Gaynor, she was fostered by a much loved couple until she was 14, when her birth mother reclaimed her. She had been the eighth of ten children, and the youngest of them to be put into the care of a charitable institution after her father's death when she was three years old. For her, now, the people she thinks of as her siblings are one biological sister, two biological brothers, and the "sister" with whom she grew up in her foster home, with all of whom she has maintained relationships throughout her life.

Conclusion

The loss of a sibling in childhood is a traumatic event which continues to be felt in adulthood with pain and feelings of isolation. For those who stay with their siblings after separation from their parents, the relationship may act as a protective factor in terms of their feelings of identity, security and self-worth. Those who grow up in substitute families where there are other children who are regarded as siblings, may also find that this relationship – and a good relationship with their foster carers – can help a good deal. The respondents in the present study for whom neither of these conditions applied, however, grew up in a situation of enforced independence and sometimes yearned for a close relationship with lost siblings.

The examples outlined here suggest that the damage inflicted by sibling separation in childhood may manifest itself, not only in the sadness of being kept apart, but also in difficulties which, for some, may be experienced in developing feelings of warmth towards one another, even should a reunion take place in later life. This is a further reason for caution in placing siblings apart. It may leave them not only searching for one another but searching, too, for a way to relate when they pursue what, for a proportion at least, does emerge as a deep-seated need to reclaim the past.

References

Ainsworth M D (1985) 'Attachments across the lifespan', *Bulletin of the New York Academy of Medicine*, 61:9, pp 789–812.

Bank S and Kahn M D (1982) *The Sibling Bond*, New York: Basic Books.

Department of Health and Social Security (1986) *Social Work Decisions in Childcare*, London: HMSO.

Dunn J (1984) *Sisters and Brothers*, London: Fontana Paperbacks.

Dunn J and Kendrick C (1982) *Siblings*, London: Grant McIntyre.

Fonagy P, Steele M, Steele H, Higgit A and Mayer L (1994) 'The theory and practice of resilience', *Journal of Child Psychology & Psychiatry*, 35:2, pp 231–58.

Kosonen M (1994) 'Sibling relationships for children in the care system', *Adoption & Fostering*, 18:3, pp 30–5.

Kosonen M (1996) 'Siblings as providers of support and care during middle childhood: children's perceptions', *Children & Society*, 10, pp 267–79.

Kosonen M (1996) 'Maintaining sibling relationships: neglected dimension in child care practice', *British Journal of Social Work*, 26:6, pp 809–22.

Hindle D (1995) 'Thinking about siblings placed together in foster care', *Adoption & Fostering*, 19:1, pp 14–20.

Main M, Kaplan N and Cassidy J (1985) 'Security in infancy, childhood and adulthood: a move to the level of representation', in Bretherton I and Waters E (eds), 'Growing points of attachment theory and research', *Monographs of the Society for Research in Child Development*, 50:1–2, Serial No. 209, pp 66–104.

Millham S, Bullock R, Hosie K and Little M (1989) *Lost in Care*, Aldershot: Gower.

Mann P (1984) *Children in Care Revisited*, London: Batsford.

Mavinga McKenzie I and Perkins T (1991) *In Search of Mr McKenzie*, London: The Women's Press.

Nalden C (1989) *Half and Half: The memoirs of a charity brat*, Wellington, NZ: Moana Press.

Packman J, Randall J and Jaques N (1986) *Who Needs Care? Social work decisions about children*, Oxford: Blackwell.

Prynn B (1997) *Growing up in Substitute Family Care*, Working Paper 3, Centre for Adoption and Identity Studies, Barking: University of East London.

Rushton A, Treseder J and Quinton D (1989) 'Sibling groups in permanent placement', *Adoption & Fostering*, 13:4, pp 5–11.

Rutter M (1988) 'Functions and consequences of relationships: some psychopathological considerations', in Hinde R A and Stevenson-Hinde J (eds) *Relationships within Families: Mutual influences*, Oxford: Oxford University Press.

24 **Drawing out the messages for policy and practice**

Audrey Mullender

An overview can now be attempted of what the new research and the personal and professional insights reported in this edited collection have told us and where they leave us in terms of policy and practice. This will involve gathering together material on exactly who and where siblings are in relation to one another, exploring issues of separation, contact and loss, summarising new findings on outcomes while challenging certain areas of received wisdom, and suggesting implications for practitioners and their managers.

Who are siblings?

A neat formulation is the one Prevatt Goldstein offers: that siblings are children who have 'one or more parent in common, or residing or having resided together and being or having been "parented" together' (this volume). Elgar teases out the complexities of this in relation to common genes, a common history, family values and culture, and a common legal status, any or all of which may be shared by siblings or by those who grow up together. In addition, as Prevatt Goldstein and also Shobha remind us, the terms "sister" and "brother" have deeply rooted cultural, religious and political resonances which extend far beyond nuclear families and shared households. Perhaps this is why one common theme throughout this book has been that social workers do seem to be largely aware of the enormity of the decision-making they and their agencies undertake in relation to siblings, even if the realities of practice lag far behind this consciousness.

But even families and households are complicated matters in social work. Kosonen's important work on foster children has shown that they have more complex families than other children in the community. This is not new for families in difficulties, as Barry's discovery of multiple siblings in Hodgkins' chapter amply demonstrates, though it has taken on contemporary variations. Children probably go less routinely to live with grandparents or aunts nowadays, marriages are more likely to break down and remarriage is common, care involves multiple moves. Neil found children being placed for adoption from complex home backgrounds, with various types of siblings known, in more than one branch of the family, living in different locations, and sometimes also having had several moves where other children might have become important to them. Social workers had not been able to keep track of the children's family constellations, especially among birth relatives. There was a particular lack of contact with paternal siblings. Wilkings describes the combined effect of all this diversity and uncertainty within one family of four adopted children.

Additional issues come into play when we consider individual needs alongside those of the group as a whole. Shelagh Beckett found that around one in five of the children in sibling groups in her study had special educational needs and one in ten was of mixed parentage. Prevatt Goldstein reminds us that black and white siblings will have different experiences in the world, notably in relation to racism, as will brothers and sisters in the face of sexism.

Thus practitioners who want to take sibling issues seriously face a challenge of comprehension and comprehensiveness even before they begin.

Where are the siblings – together or separate?

If we do not know who siblings are, we will clearly have a hard time keeping track of where they all are. Separation remains a very real issue for siblings who have had social work involvement in their lives.

In long-term fostering, over time, all of the children in Kosonen's study experienced premature separations from siblings. No child in her study had all their siblings of all kinds continuously living with them throughout the study. Younger children had longer separations as a proportion of their lifetimes. Comparison children, not in the care system, also experienced separations but these tended to be of a type that did not threaten the continuity of sibling relationships in the same way as do placements and moves in care. Ellison also found foster children very likely to be separated. Where the current plan in the cases she surveyed was long-term foster care, in 11 out of 13 cases children were separated from all of their siblings.

In adoption planning, Ellison found that virtually two-thirds of the children in her study who were to be adopted were separated from some or all of their looked after siblings, and almost half of these were placed apart from all of their siblings. Again, in Neil's adoption study, two-thirds of those with siblings were placed without any of them and, where they *were* with at least one of their siblings, this was typically because they had come into placement together rather than because of active planning. A sequential entry to care meant separation (see 'Is there scope for innovation?', below). The number who were living apart from at least one sibling rises to 95 per cent of all those with siblings in Neil's sample and, even among those living with one or more of their siblings, 85 per cent had others elsewhere (with the birth family, in the care system, adopted), often with more than one legal status.

In Neil's study, social workers were not necessarily keeping track of all the other siblings, especially those still at home, so there will be no information about them on the agency file in future years should the adopted person choose to ask. There may well also be other children who are born after the adopted child has been adopted and consequently after professional involvement has ceased in their life. Unless there is an element of openness (at least through a regular exchange of information) built into the placement, the adopted person will have no knowledge of these siblings' existence. Perhaps there should be an after-adoption updating service or perhaps, rather, we need to recognise more fully that it is wrong for adoption to cut people off from their roots.

Four out of five children in permanent placements in Dance and Rushton's research had siblings living elsewhere, and for one-third of the total this included others in the care system. In half of these latter cases, there had been separations while in care – typically planned – though one wonders whether these children's needs might have been met in some other way. In placement and reunion planning, social workers were influenced by closeness of age and by whether or not children were "full" siblings (Kosonen also found more emphasis in practice on "core" than on "kin" siblings), though none of the research or personal feedback contained in this volume justifies making this distinction. It might have made more sense to have made particular attempts at effecting reunion or contact where only accidents of placement timing or placement availability had kept siblings apart – but this was not happening, according to Dance and Rushton. Shelagh Beckett also found that permanence was more likely than not to involve separation. Yet one odd point she picked up in her study was that two groups of five were being kept together, while those who were to live apart included several with just one sibling. Separation clearly cannot be explained by the challenges of placement finding alone.

Ellison found accommodated children just as likely as children subject to care orders to be separated from all of their siblings (around 30 per cent of each, though contact did differ – see below). Placement availability at entry to the care system can lead to siblings being separated against social workers' better judgements according to Shelagh Beckett's study.

An inconclusive picture emerges about children being considered for a return home. Ellison found they were more likely to be with all of their siblings, particularly where this was a short-term intention (three-quarters of those for whom a return home was planned within six months), but Shelagh Beckett found seven children likely to be placed individually while their siblings went home and no child going home permanently with all of his or her siblings. These are small-scale studies – the numbers are too low to establish cause and effect – and there could also be differences in agency practice operating.

Overall, Ellison found sibling planning to be service led rather than needs led. Social workers in her British sample reported a lack of placements for larger sibling groups and for those where one or more of the children had special needs. As in Selwyn's study (see below), social workers tended simply to state that their plan to separate children was 'in the best interests' of at least one of the siblings which can be a suspiciously "catch-all" phrase, implying an inability to spell out what the children's needs actually are. Furthermore, there appears to be no needs-led explanation for the different decisions Dance and Rushton found being made for children with similar problems.

Both placement finding and the making of sibling group placements need urgent attention if children are to be less routinely separated. There is evidence that many separations happen without intent or on the basis of practice assumptions that are not borne out by research.

Attachment to, and separation from other peers

There are further complications beyond this. Children's peers in the care system, in foster and adoptive homes and in residential care, can become significant others to them. In Wilkings' family of four children, the two who were related by blood did not look most alike or even have the closest relationship. Selman and Mason describe how good it can be for children with Down's Syndrome, for example, to find support, warmth and positive role models among their adoptive parents' birth children, and sometimes to be given their only opportunity to grow up with someone else like themselves when another Down's child is adopted into the same family.

We may find it more difficult to admit that the same kind of peer support and bonding goes on in residential settings, especially as these have become associated in the public mind with bullying and abuse. Yet Horrocks and Milner give us a clear picture of a residential home as a "serial step-family". Children who have come through comparable experiences of sexual abuse and family difficulties understand one another at a level which means that mutual support and friendship may extend into lasting relationships: 'more like sisters', as one of their respondents remarked. Vying for staff attention and struggles in the pecking order with each new admission resemble sibling rivalry but, as with sibling disagreements in families, do not automatically indicate a lack of important interaction and support. Both for positive and for negative reasons, children and young people in establishments are very conscious of each other but, writ large in residential practice, is the tendency only to consider how children relate to the adults, the staff, and not how they relate to one another.

We need to think more carefully about which other children matter in the lives of the children and young people for whom social workers have responsibility.

Contact between separated siblings

There is general agreement that, where placement together is not possible, contact assumes particular importance. Yet Harrison tells us loud and clear (see also Kosonen for a literature review) that looked after children lose contact with their birth families, including their siblings, and that there are rarely plans to reunite them.

In the permanence study reported on in this volume by Dance and Rushton, only half the children with siblings elsewhere had contact plans with at least one of them, in two cases for postal contact only. Nearly half the placements lacked a definite contact plan, for no good reason, and it was rare to include all siblings. Many children had other siblings with whom there was no contact at all and, in 11 cases, social workers thought this lack of contact plans might cause difficulty. In Neil's study of young children placed for adoption, two-thirds of those who were separated lacked the potential for contact with any of their siblings. Paternal siblings were particularly neglected. So, initially through separation and then through lack of contact, adoption is still meaning that many siblings are lost to one another, with other kinds of permanent placement frequently implying this too.

Where there *was* contact, according to Dance and Rushton, it was not necessarily at the most desirable frequency; indeed, five social workers in their study thought it insufficient. Shelagh Beckett, too, draws attention to the need to think about frequency of contact and about what makes contact "real", for example when it can last for more than an hour or so at a time. Prevatt Goldstein cites Kosonen as thinking through what contact means in terms of child–child interaction not mediated through adults and positive joint activities.

Dance and Rushton report that arrangements were more frequent between siblings each placed separately in the care system; lack of contact with birth parents was a significant complication for those with siblings at home. Indeed, a complete lack of contact most often signified that all the other siblings had stayed at home. Face-to-face contact in Neil's study, too, was more likely with other siblings who were looked after or adopted than with those still in the birth family. Although there are complications with birth family contact, Neil does regard it as at least a route for siblings to stay in touch, now or in the future, yet child–child contact is rarely considered in its own right in these situations. Loss of siblings is still happening by default, she concludes. Birth family disruptions and changes in Kosonen's study tended to lead to loss of contact with siblings for the fostered children, not to the arrival of new or reunited siblings into the placement. At the same time, the loss of relationships with the wider birth family (notably grandparents), smaller friendship groups (especially for boys), and the fragmentation of everything else in life made siblings even more important to the foster children than to other children, both as people and as one of the few constants when the rest of life was shifting and changing.

Social workers in the Dance and Rushton study thought contact mattered more for those placed singly, but it is unclear on what they based this view since there is nothing to suggest that children share it, either in childhood or in later adulthood. Moves in care had been associated in this study with attrition in the numbers of siblings children were in touch with. A few more lost contact when plans were not carried through. Contact was most likely where children knew each other well and were close in age (overlapping with the factors that worked in favour of keeping children together in placement), again for no reason that appears to be rooted in research or children's expressed preferences. Worryingly, Shelagh Beckett found social workers taking a fatalistic rather than a proactive approach to contact and leaving matters to whether the new carers were keen, especially if they were going to be hard to find or long distances were likely to be involved. She, like Jones in her chapter, teases out some of the practicalities involved in promoting contact: venue, transport (including special provision for children), supervision where needed, availability of support staff, the role and attitude of foster carers.

Caregivers may require support both in understanding the importance of contact and in practical forms wherever possible. We need to be thinking about recruiting and training carers (adopters, foster carers, residential workers) on the basis of their understanding of the importance of contact with birth relatives, including siblings. Prevatt Goldstein suggests that black families may have a better record here. Contact arrangements can be enormously complex (see examples in the chapters by Jones and Tomlinson) and hence expensive of time and money. It is also relatively easy to scupper complicated arrangements which may be demanding, boring, or expensive for the adults to sustain. Alternatively, contact may simply fade away over time unless practitioners, managers, carers, policy and practice guidelines all promote it. One of Shelagh Beckett's respondents suggested that foster carers could be paid an enhancement to promote links and she herself sees the need for some practical recognition of the extra costs and tasks involved. It was good to read that carers of Dance and Rushton's study children were positive about contact, and actually reported that difficulties with it declined over the study year. Some of the other siblings' carers (including birth parents), on the other hand, were resistant.

Occasionally, in Dance and Rushton's study, contact did bring other problems, for example, in exposing a child to difficult behaviour or relationship issues, or in evoking negative feelings such as fear of the sibling. Of course there are particular issues involved in placing children who have exhibited inappropriate or abusive sexual behaviour towards their siblings or other children (see chapters by Elgar and Head and by Farmer and Pollock). Here, the wishes of all the siblings need to be taken into account, as well as their experiences and needs. Safety needs must be predominant. But present practice is such that caregivers are frequently not being told what has happened or given the full picture; hence, we cannot claim to be meeting the needs currently of either the young perpetrators or of those they may go on to abuse. Separating them from their birth families, including siblings, is not a substitute for a policy. It simply imposes a fresh form of damage on top of that which is inflicted if caregivers are not adequately informed of the dangers or supported in providing close supervision and avoiding recreating the circumstances of earlier abuse. And contact may not be ruled out in every case, if sufficient care can be exercised.

Ideally, where it works well, contact can become something the siblings themselves can organise. Tomlinson, as well s pointing this out, also gives a good example of sustained contact making possible a later reunion in the form of a sequential placement in the same family.

Contact is always invoked as the next best thing to a shared placement. Clearly, it remains a very hit and miss affair at present.

Children's perceptions

Children's wishes, as expressed in Kosonen's research, are often not reflected in their current placement circumstances. She found that children do understand their widely varying family structures, with their range of full, half- and step-siblings, and that they define their family in terms of roles and relationships rather than biological relatedness. If we place the emphasis on what children themselves perceive and value, we find that different children in the same family will not necessarily list the same siblings (especially those on the periphery of the family) or the same degrees of emotional closeness. Their social workers see things differently again.

Regarding contact, the children Kosonen interviewed value being placed with their siblings and like the continuity; they also worry about separation. Even if there are particular siblings with whom they do not want to be placed, they want to be nearby and they want to be able to stay in the vicinity and do things together in adulthood. Even those siblings with whom there is a less good relationship are wanted nearby, but not too close.

Unfortunately, there is evidence from Selwyn that the voice of the child is often not being heard. Despite the requirement of UK adoption and wider child care legislation and of the UN Convention on the Rights of the Child that a child should have a voice in proceedings concerning him or her, Selwyn's study of adoption case records and forms submitted to court, covering the period 1990 to 1996, found that this was often not happening in practice. The Schedule 2 forms contained very few direct quotations from children (guardians *ad litem* were more likely to include these than social workers). There was a tendency to treat a sibling group as a unit, melding together what they had said into one combined comment and also blurring it with what adults thought and with what had happened to the children. Child–child relationships were not commented upon. Nor was there any sense of the differences in personality and perception between different children in the same family or of treating them as individuals. At one and the same time, siblings are viewed as a combined unit when they are together, but are not commented on in terms of contact when they are apart. This is because the unit of siblings is treated as a homogeneous item, not as more than one child with distinct needs.

We need to start listening to children (Thomas and Beckford, 1999) and incorporating their views into assessments, decisions and plans. The one limitation perhaps to place on children expressing their views about siblings might be that they cannot possibly know what they are going to feel in the future so that making them responsible for any decision that would lead to an irrevocable separation would arguably be unfair. Keeping the door to reunion information at least open is, according to the retrospective accounts in this book and to Harrison's chapter on lost siblings, a crucially important matter.

Why it matters – issues of loss

These chapters written from or about an adult perspective – those by Shobha and Marylin, Pavlovic and Mullender, Hodgkins, and Prynn – all indicate the persistent feelings of loss among those whose siblings were lost to them through adoption or the care system. This is as true of "half-" (maternal, paternal) siblings as it is of "full" siblings. The feelings of loss leave no doubt that the separation of siblings can inflict pain and sadness which may remain throughout life and that adoption legislation as it stands in England and Wales leaves many people with no opportunity ever to find their adopted siblings again, no matter how hard they try. Where renions are reported in these chapters they are largely positive. Prynn also has some examples of reunions which, though much desired, were less joyful than they might have been because of the separation experience. In other words, most if not all of these people would have been enormously helped if the separation, or at least the loss of contact, had never taken place.

The damage inflicted by sibling separation is not a minor issue. As the chapter by Pavlovic and Mullender shows, it can involve the loss of: a lifetime's close and loving relationship; support in adversity; a some-times parental degree of personal care; a shared history; a sense of kinship; of "flesh and blood"; for full and maternal siblings of a "bond" (coming from the same womb) which is understood by all the peoples of the world; of continuity and rootedness; a source of knowledge about the family; and a resource for the individual's own development of identity. For those with a memory of the sibling, the unresolved grief can be akin to that we now acknowledge to be felt by birth mothers (Howe *et al*, 1992). For those who unexpectedly discover that they had a sibling, their foremost feeling may be more of a devastation, a disbelief, followed by a sense of injustice and of loss of all the things the relationship would have meant to both parties and to the wider family.

There are lifecycle issues with which, again, we are familiar from work on adult adopted people seeking knowledge of their origins. Searching for siblings may be prompted by looking for a mother or by a reunion with her; it may be triggered by becoming a parent; it has aspects of transgenerational loss in that the lost sibling is a lost aunt or uncle to the searcher's own children. Severing a bond between two young children may thus have repercussions in their lives for seven or eight decades.

Where children are also cut off from any possibility of finding one another again in later life, as UK adoption law still inflicts on the siblings of those placed into closed adoption (or, at least, leaves to the whim of the placing agency to determine in future years), this may mean a lifetime of anguished (and costly) searching. Are our assessment methods and skills as social workers really good enough that we can ever unreservedly say this is the right thing to do?

Findings on policy and practice

Several contributors (Beckett, Ellison, Tomlinson) found a lack of consistent policy and practice guidelines on sibling placements and contact in the agencies they studied. Consequently, Jones and Tomlinson are both clear, from their practice perspectives, that children frequently become separated for adult reasons that have little or nothing to do with their current or future needs, even when expressed in terms of the latter (*cf*. Selwyn on the blurring of these perspectives in reports).

We also need to start gathering the relevant data about siblings who are accommodated, looked after or for whom adoption is planned. Tomlinson suggests that this would include information about numbers of children with siblings elsewhere in the care system or with the birth family (and we could add "or adopted"), numbers of referrals of sibling groups, and categories of reasons for separation – which would allow targeting of resources at prevention. At present, as Tomlinson remarks, resource decisions are being made in an information vacuum. Managers told Shelagh Beckett that they lacked an information system that could handle sibling groups as anything other than a succession of singletons. She found that only five out of 16 authorities that responded to her survey said they monitored siblings, and often then in an incomplete or unanalysed way. Only two could give information on the number of siblings within their care together with their placement patterns (and they may not have known about other siblings outside the care system). Action on gathering this information could begin at once. As Tomlinson also points out, although social workers and their managers already profess a commitment to sibling placements, without the necessary data we do not know how often this priority is pushed aside by other, competing factors in the situation. Nor can we record the long-term effects in terms of eventual loss of contact. Harrison's research suggests that these are very worrying.

Ellison concludes that more careful and proactive planning and a wider range of placements are needed across the board. She found sibling groups unable to go into long-term foster care or be adopted together, and also shortages of specialist placements for short-term and respite provision. There is no apparent practice reason for this. One group of five in Shelagh Beckett's study had had long-term foster carers successfully recruited through national advertising and, looking back to the Wedge and Mantle study that was revisited in Mullender's opening chapter of this volume, those authors found voluntary agencies well able to recruit families for sibling groups through a concerted approach.

Jones suggests that not the lack of suitable placements alone, but the need for placement teams to nurture those they do have (by not asking them to go above preferred numbers, for example) may mean that children are divided up to fit the places available. The tendency to work from an adult perspective also means that the viewpoints of caregivers, social workers or birth relatives may take precedence over those of the children as to what should happen to them. Thus, if contact with siblings is not valued or prioritised by any of these parties, it may falter and wither away. Conversely, social workers may sometimes be able to use their adult influence and the *ad hoc* policy context to insist that separation is avoided, either at placement or later, as in the examples in Tomlinson's chapter. Other practitioners and managers may want to achieve this but be simply unable to do so in the face of a policy vacuum or resource shortfall (Tomlinson, Jones).

There can be bureaucratic obstacles, too. Shelagh Beckett refers, for example, to the fact that a sibling group normally counts as one case in a caseload weighting system. This may not allow the social worker to devote the time and attention needed to assess and meet each child's needs including, for example, where there are complex contact arrangements. Shelagh Beckett further suggests that responsibility for key tasks in relation to siblings may fall between workers and Jones, too, refers to differing priorities and vested interests between teams. Yet again, this is compounded by the fact that managers are not guided by clear policies that might encourage them to take action to remove the blockages to best practice.

Carers need both practical help and improved support and training in respect of sibling groups. Tomlinson suggests that additional families might be enabled to take on sibling groups if they had help to purchase a larger vehicle, an extension to the house, help with ironing, or other such assistance. There are less tangible needs, too. At present, carers may influence whether a joint placement or a contact arrangement continues without having received any input on issues about siblings in general or about aspects of sibling support that may need working on in particular, including in families where one sibling may have abused another. Prevatt Goldstein writes about promoting a family climate in which black siblings, and black and white siblings, can value one another. Mutual support between them may, she argues, foster resilience both generally and in the care system, and the placement of choice will be one that can engender this within positive black traditions.

There are many obvious gaps in agency settings, at the most basic level of data collection, issuing of policy and setting support mechanisms in place.

Basing policy and practice on outcome research – new thoughts on closeness in age, sibling conflict and the carers' role

Shelagh Beckett found that social workers do want to know about research in order to improve their practice. They are already acting on earlier outcome findings, for example, they are not placing where there will be children with an age-gap of under three years (see Mullender's opening chapter), though Celia Beckett and her colleagues remind us that results on this point have not been consistent across all studies and, indeed, they themselves had a different and more complex finding.

Does separating siblings affect their well-being or development, their chance of rehabilitation, the survival of their placements? The call for contributions to this book has not revealed many studies currently looking at these issues. The only outcome study that is summarised here, in fact, is that by Celia Beckett and her colleagues on Romanian children (though Neil, in a longitudinal study being directed by June Thoburn, will have findings to report at a later date). Furthermore, the placements of the Romanian children are far from typical. Not only were the children born overseas, but the adopters, rather than social workers, located them, they sometimes adopted two, often unrelated children close in age, and they were themselves older and more likely to have children of their own than most adopters approved in the UK. Findings may consequently not be generalisable. Also, only a small proportion of the children were older than two at placement, and the oldest in the study were only three-and-a-half, which would not be the case with many looked after children being placed for adoption.

A key finding is that things change over time. Most notably, where there had been sibling conflict, it declined between the two points in time at which the younger cohort were studied. Close age spacing with a child born to the adopters did seem associated with sibling conflict and negative parental evaluation in these under two-year-olds at the first survey date, but the number of such negative evaluations had halved by two years later, a trend that was most marked in the placements with the close age spacing with a birth child. Two *adopted* young children close· in age, whether related or not, did not have the same problems at either point in time. Among the older cohort, dissatisfaction levels were generally higher and were not correlated with age spacing. Overall, then, it may not be as necessary to avoid closeness in age as had been thought although, it should be repeated, these were not typical placements.

There were also other factors at work. Perhaps the most important finding of all from this study is that something can be done about sibling conflict. Families *can* work on relationships. Echoing a strategy that Wilkings talks about in her chapter, the Celia Beckett *et al* study found that setting special time aside to spend with the adopted child was associated with far lower rates of sibling conflict, with the best results reported where this happened on three or more days a week. This, surely, is good advice that social workers can safely give to any adopting or fostering family – or, indeed, any family at all – and it need not cost money. The benefits were even more marked in those families offering "special time" to adopted children who had been older at placement, as against those who did not; in this older cohort generally there was the wider spread of problems and of satisfaction levels that might be expected among typical UK placements, making the lesson about this simple strategy even more likely to be useful. Follow-up has yet to show whether sibling conflict declines for those older at placement, as it did among the younger group, and only further experience will show whether parents and carers can repeat what appear to be the benefits of "special time" with other children in other circumstances.

Challenging received wisdom

Sibling conflict is one of those areas in which there is a danger that practice assumptions could be misleading. As we saw in the opening chapter, it is actually normal for sibling relationships to be marked by conflict right through to the mid-teens and this need not imply that the relationship is a negative one or that the children concerned can be parted without ill effect. An interesting personal insight comes from Wilkings who, having been an only child herself, had had no experience of siblings arguing and hence no yardstick by which to measure it but who came to see it as an important way of children expressing their fears and their allegiances in a family.

An apparently poor, even hostile, relationship at one point in childhood does not indicate that the children concerned do not care now and will never care about each other later on (see Jones' chapter). Nor does it mean that their relationship could not improve if each child's needs were to be fully met and the relationship itself to be worked on (see chapters by Tomlinson and by Dance and Rushton). As we have seen, Beckett *et al* offer some very important evidence that sibling conflict between an adopted child and a birth child may lessen over time, particularly if adopters spend "special time" with the adopted child. Jones suggests that conflict may actually be used as a *post hoc* rationalisation for a separation that was in fact prompted by a shortage of suitable placements or by other adults involved.

Just as conflict is a natural part of growing up, so is it perfectly normal for siblings to take on emotionally and practically caring roles towards one another, the more so in cultures where such mutual responsibility is an expected part of growing up (Prevatt Goldstein) and would never be taken as a sign that something was fundamentally wrong. This is not a new idea: 'Nor is there any support in the literature for choosing to separate siblings because one has a caretaking role towards the other. Like rivalry, that is a normal part of many sibling relationships' (Hegar, 1988, p 462). Of course, as the same author acknowledges, there may be damaging dynamics involved but, even then, there could be all manner of ways of working with these and supporting the individual children concerned before resorting to separating them. Yet social work has come to take a fairly fixed line that the "little mother" role is wrong because it is considered to deny a childhood to the child doing the caring.

In response to this, it is important to recognise that ideas on what constitutes a "normal" childhood are socially and culturally constructed. In this volume, for example, Jones and Hodgkins both give beautiful examples of such "mothering" roles being played, in one case by a sister in Romania and, in the other, by a brother in the England of the mid-1940s. Admittedly, these are both examples from turbulent times when parents were least able to offer care and attention to their offspring, but they do put into perspective the much greater chance that the older siblings in these examples would have been harmed by separation than by continuing to play a major caring role. And, if we take a historical overview of children's domestic responsibilities and of attitudes taken towards them (Newman, forthcoming), it becomes clear that a childhood detached from such roles is a recent Western invention. Social work would do well to question some of its more blanket assumptions about what does and does not harm children in favour of listening to children and recognising that, sometimes, the alternative imposed by intervention – for example, where this leads to painful separation – may be actively worse than the status quo.

Some other very specific findings in the chapters of this volume about apparent practice wisdom that is not evidence-based include social workers working hardest against separation and loss of contact for "full" siblings, those placed singly, those who have previously lived together and those close in age (Dance and Rushton), even though none of this is borne out by what children say about who matters to them (Kosonen) or by what adult siblings of adopted people tell us is important when they search for reunion. In practice, it might not occur to anyone to place together siblings who had never lived together or even known one another, yet Pavlovic and Mullender came across adults in this category who yearned to find their lost brothers and sisters. Similarly, Shobha and Marylin did not know of each other's existence until Shobha found Marylin's birth certificate and went to seek her out, yet their jointly written chapter testifies what they mean to one another now.

What research tells us is not always what our instincts would suggest. Also, the theories we grew up with, if they lacked a basis in research, may now be outmoded. Finally, to add to the need to keep updated, new research may round out a picture to the point where we have to relearn what we thought we knew. All of this points to the fact that the assessment frameworks several contributors call for will have to be very carefully constructed if they are not merely to legitimise the application of outworn ideas

Is there scope for innovation – what can be done in practice?

How can we move forward? It seems a daunting task when we do not even have a common understanding of which children are siblings or any national statistics on sibling relationships, either in the care system or in the wider society (Kosonen, Tomlinson).

One child-centred way forward would be to start from children's own understandings of who their siblings are and of which children (siblings and peers) are significant in their lives. Then we could, firstly, ensure that these are cross-checked against information held by social services and by current and former carers so that files are kept fully up to date, preferably with a family tree at the front of each. (Family trees are a national obsession – volunteers or hourly contract staff could certainly be found to help with this, under proper conditions of confidentiality. Post-adoption agencies also have special expertise in understanding and tracing families which they could be contracted to offer.) Secondly, children could be kept in touch with news of all their relations, however distant geographically or peripheral to their current nuclear birth family or care situation (the role traditionally played by the mother in an extended family and arguably one of the responsibilities of a corporate parent). Third, placement decisions and contact arrangements could be made with reference to children's expressed wishes and perceived needs in terms of child–child as well as adult–child relationships. Regarding any other siblings, it would generally be important to build in information and, in this way, generally to leave open at least the later option of contact.

A range of other imaginative ideas has emerged from the contributions to this book. First, the notion of moving siblings to the same placement but sequentially crops up several times (e.g. Tomlinson). The chapters by Neil, and by Dance and Rushton, both suggest leaving room in a placement in case another sibling follows at a later date. Second, the selection of two or more carers who ideally live near one another and who will network together to maintain good contact between siblings appears in various forms, including three single women adopters (Owen) and two branches of the same family (Prevatt Goldstein). These are options which can help prevent the disruption of a placement that suits one or two of the children by a sibling who is going to find it more difficult to trust and to settle.

Another emergent theme has been the missed opportunity to intervene and work on relationships rather than fatalistically waiting to see whether things improve. Examples include professional intervention with the birth family, including parents, where worries about them or their own reluctance may be blocking contact with siblings still at home, and then perhaps introducing telephone or postal contact if meetings still do not work out. (Dance and Rushton comment, incidentally, that the reactions of the siblings left at home to this situation of lost or continuing contact are relatively unexplored, and this is true as far as research on current placements is concerned, but this volume provides at least retrospective accounts of them in all those chapters offering adult accounts: Shobha and Marylin, Pavlovic and Mullender, Hodgkins, Prynn.) A still more graphic instance of the power of actively working at relationships is the good effect reported by Celia Beckett *et al* (and also by Wilkings) of adopters offering "special time" to their adopted children. Several contributors suggest, though no one really explores, the potential for working at the sibling relationships themselves, rather than leaving them to be negative or even harmful. It would be good to see research on this.

A very basic need is to work harder and more consistently at recruiting sibling group placements and then to support and deploy them effectively. Shelagh Beckett found four out of 16 authorities occasionally willing to pay a retainer to reserve foster carers for sibling groups. Other ways of accommodating groups include using a small residential home or, Prevatt Goldstein adds (drawing on the Black Perspectives Advisory Committee of BAAF), placement with siblings overseas. Some contributors found residential placements not available or not being used to keep siblings together. Shelagh Beckett did find one example of a small residential unit which was used to keep five children together for a time on entry to care, though they were subsequently split between foster homes when it closed. There is some evidence (see Prevatt Goldstein) that black carers may be particularly clued in to the importance of keeping children together or, failing that, of maintaining contact between them.

The wider agency can be important in establishing a planning framework (a common review structure, early decision-making), owning the decision-making about siblings, assisting more experienced staff to pass on wisdom to newer ones, offering relevant training including on research findings, and facilitating planning across teams (e.g. between case holding and family placement workers) (Tomlinson; see also Jones on this latter point). Resources can be important in paying an inter-agency or advertising fee to locate a group placement to keep children together, or in providing ancillary staffing for transport or supervision of contact visits. Overall, Shelagh Beckett sees sibling issues as needing to be on the agenda from the beginning, as well as the needs of each individual. She found individual social workers aware of the importance of the decisions they were having to make but relatively unsupported in doing so. She also found that those social workers who expressed the strongest views to her about sibling group placement were also those who had managed to keep siblings together or who were planning to reunite them. Thus individual commitment operated in place of agency policy or planning.

Conclusion

The key message from this book is that all decisions about siblings need to take into account sibling relationships over time and, in fact, over a lifetime (alongside many other factors) and to involve children as partners and as experts in their own lives. Despite the rhetoric and the raised awareness, at present most children are still being cut off from at least some of their siblings. Many will lack even the information to find one another in the future, should they wish to do so, and the evidence from retrospective accounts is that many are likely to want to. This leaves room for vast improvement in policy and practice. Though some very successful sibling group placements are achieved, there is a general lack of systematic policy, management information, detailed guidelines and best practice.

Catering for complex sibling or other family groups is never going to be easy but it can succeed as well as any other placement. The biggest challenge may be finding the commitment to make it happen.

Summary of practice pointers

Awareness

- Recognise the full and long-term impact of sibling separation.
- Start by recognising that sibling separation is a norm in child care and that, since it is happening by default (in the absence of policies, placement options and support for best practice), it is not acceptable that it should continue unquestioned.
- At the same time, recognise that family structures are complex (and for many families in difficulties have always been so) and that we do not even have agreed terms for all the types of siblings children may have, let alone other significant children in their lives, so solutions are not going to be easy to pursue.

Practice

- Become aware of, and validate, child–child relationships as much as adult–child ones.
- Give children a voice so that you can obtain their own understandings and perceptions of their child–child relationships, including where they have a range of different kinds of siblings.
- Learn from children about their family structures, which may be extremely complex and may not be fully recorded on file.
- Ensure that you record everything you know about the family structure over time, about children's understandings, perceptions and wishes regarding family contact, and about children's experiences and needs (including safety needs).
- Find out from the child who are the most significant other children in his or her life and try to retain the closest possible links between them.
- Within this, balance the needs and wishes of each child, including their safety needs, for example, if there has been abuse of one child by another (which may not need to involve loss of contact or maybe even separation if close supervision is available by carers who are apprised of all the details).
- Never close the door on contact between siblings of any degree of relatedness but, at the very least, give them the means to find one another in later years if they so choose.

- Consider innovative ways to place sibling groups, not necessarily all at once or all in one place, but in ways which are most likely to maintain close links over time. (This would be helpful even if there were enough placements for sibling groups, which there are not.)
- Work systematically on recruiting more placements for sibling groups and more innovative kinds of placements which can value and promote sibling (and other family) contact.
- Ensure (through training and support) that caregivers have all the necessary information, as well as the same understanding of the nature and importance of child–child relationships as you do and help them think about how to sustain and foster these at an appropriate level, including where there may have been difficulties or dangers between siblings.
- Never be satisfied with a "snapshot"-type assessment. Children's relationships with one another grow and change over time. Since sibling relationships are typically those of the longest duration in our lives, they are bound to go through many stages over that time. Carers can be helped to relate to children in ways which can lessen sibling conflict (notably offering "special time" to each child).
- Work with children on healing damaged relationships, rather than writing them off as unimportant.
- Understand that sibling rivalry and conflict are natural and do not indicate that siblings are not important to one another, either now or in the future.

Rapid reference

Sibling separation
- risks deeply felt and long-term loss
- is very common
- is happening by default (through lack of policies/placements/best practice)

Complexities
- complex family structures
- lack of a shared understanding of what degrees of sibling relatedness "count" in children's lives

- not asking who are children's significant others (may include peers in the care system)

Obstacles and challenges
- lack of policies and guidelines
- goodwill but confusion in practice
- rapid dissemination of new research findings required
- the need to channel resources

Good practice with children
- give children a voice (who is in their family; who is significant to them)
- value child–child relationships (siblings and peers)
- record family changes
- record children's perceptions and wishes
- be aware of the individual needs and wishes of each child (including safety)
- never close the door on contact (perhaps in later years)
- do not be satisfied with a "snapshot" assessment
- do not mistake sibling rivalry or conflict for not caring (now or later)
- work on problems in sibling relationships, do not write them off
- help peers ("quasi-siblings") keep in touch after care

Good placement practice
- recruit more families for sibling groups
- offer practical and/or respite support to help more families come forward for sibling groups or to sustain difficult placements
- innovate, e.g. sequential placements, single carers, exceeding approved number, cluster arrangements with close contact, small residential units
- work to reunite children within a single placement where resource shortfalls have meant that they have had to be split (blanket government policies on minimising moves may lose this kind of subtlety)
- give full information about children's experiences, family background, needs and wishes to carers
- ensure carers value child–child relationships, both existing and created

- support contact arrangements (including with cash where possible).

References

Hegar R L (1993) 'Assessing attachment, permanence, and kinship in choosing permanent homes', *Child Welfare*, LXXII(4), pp 367–78.

Howe D, Sawbridge P and Hinings D (1992) *Half a Million Women: Mothers who lose their children by adoption*, Harmondsworth: Penguin.

Newman T (forthcoming in 2000) 'Workers and helpers: perspectives on children's labour 1899–1999', *British Journal of Social Work*.

Thomas C and Beckford V with Lowe N and Murch M (1999) *Adopted Children Speaking*, London: BAAF.

United Nations (1989) *Convention on the Rights of the Child: Adopted by the General Assembly of the United Nations, 1989*, London: Stationery Office. (This edition published in 1996.)

Adopted Children Speaking ▬

*Caroline Thomas and Verna Beckford with Nigel Lowe
and Mervyn Murch*

If you really want to learn about children's wishes and
feelings about adoption and their experience of it, this unique
book is for you.

Adopted Children Speaking is part of a wider research project
published under the title *Supporting Adoption: Reframing the
Approach* (also published by BAAF) which throws light on
aspects of policy and practice concerning the support
available to older children and their adoptive families.
Adopted Children Speaking gives voice to the invaluable
perspective of the children themselves.

This book is full of moving and poignant testimonies and,
above all, revealing insights into what children and young
people themselves think and understand about adoption, the
support they received, their involvement in the process and
any unmet needs.

This is an essential read for anyone involved in the
formulation and implementation of policies for the care and
placement of children looked after by local authorities. There
are powerful messages here for social work practitioners and
those making decisions for children.

Published September 1999

176 PAGES   ISBN 1 873868 78 2   £9.95 + £2.00 P&P

Please contact **BAAF Publications,
Skyline House
200 Union Street
London SE1 0LX
Fax 0171 593 2001**

adoption &fostering

**NEW DEVELOPMENTS IN
CHILDCARE PRACTICE AND RESEARCH**
QUARTERLY JOURNAL

*To my knowledge, the
journal is the richest
source of articles on
adoption and fostering
anywhere.*

JOHN TRISELIOTIS
*PROFESSOR AND
SENIOR RESEARCH FELLOW,
UNIVERSITY OF STRATHCLYDE*

Published four times a year by British Agencies for Adoption and
Fostering – a membership organisation – **adoption & fostering** is
at the forefront of debate on child care issues relevant to social
workers, social work managers, carers, medical practitioners,
lawyers, researchers and students of social work.

What the journal offers:

- a multidisciplinary approach to current debates

- contributors renowned in their fields both in the UK and overseas

- an international peer review panel

- a readable and authoritative voice

- medical and legal notes

- book reviews

- a review of research in practice

Keep abreast of the latest practice issues! Become a subscriber to
the UK's most authoritative journal focusing on adoption,
fostering and child care and you will receive four issues a year and
an index, with your subscription beginning in April 1999.

A free sample copy and subscription details are available from the
Production Editor, **adoption & fostering**, British Agencies for
Adoption and Fostering, Skyline House, 200 Union Street, London
SE1 0LX, UK. Tel 0171 593 2040 Fax 0171 593 2001.

Individual rate: UK **£37.50** overseas **£45.00**
Institutional rate: UK **£52.00** overseas **£65.00**
Student rate: (UK only) **£22.00**

80 PAGES   ISSN: 0308–9759

British

Agencies

for **A**doption

and **F**ostering